GENDERING
CLASSICISM

GENDERING CLASSICISM

The Ancient World in Twentieth-Century Women's Historical Fiction

RUTH HOBERMAN

State University
of New York
Press

Selections from "Care in Calling" and "Back to the Mother Breast," from *The Poems of Laura Riding: A New Edition of the 1938 Collection*, by Laura (Riding) Jackson, copyright © by Laura (Riding) Jackson 1938, 1980. Reprinted by permission of Persea Books, Inc. In conformity with the late author's wish, her Board of Literary Management asks us to record that, in 1941, Laura (Riding) Jackson renounced, on grounds of linguistic principle, the writing of poetry: she had come to hold that "poetry obstructs general attainment to something better in our linguistic way-of-life than we have."

Published by
State University of New York Press, Albany

© 1997 State University of New York

Production by Susan Geraghty
Marketing by Dana Yanulavich

Printed in the United States of America

For information, address State University of New York
Press, State University Plaza, Albany, N.Y., 12246

Library of Congress Cataloging-in-Publication Data

Hoberman, Ruth.
    Gendering classicism : the ancient world in twentieth-century
women's historical fiction / Ruth Hoberman.
        p.   cm.
    Includes bibliographical references and index.
    ISBN 0-7914-3335-8 (alk. paper). — ISBN 0-7914-3336-6 (pb : alk.
paper)
    1. Historical fiction, English—History and criticism. 2. Women
and literature—Great Britain—History—20th century. 3. English
fiction—Women authors—History and criticism. 4. English
fiction—20th century—History and criticism. 5. Classicism—Great
Britain—History—20th century. 6. Civilization, Classical, in
literature. 7. English fiction—Classical influences.
8. Civilization, Ancient, in literature. 9. Greece—In literature.
10. Rome—In literature. I. Title.
PR888.H5H63 1997
823'.081099287—dc20   96-30584
                                                                  CIP

10 9 8 7 6 5 4 3 2 1

For my parents

CONTENTS

ACKNOWLEDGMENTS

This book, a long time in the making, owes a great deal to many different people and institutions. For financial support, I am grateful to Eastern Illinois University for a Summer Research Grant, and to the National Endowment for the Humanities, which funded the summer seminar in which I began the project and then awarded me a summer stipend to help me continue my work on it. For practical help I am grateful to the Interlibrary Loan and Circulation staff at Booth Library of Eastern Illinois University—Suellen Eggers, Leeila Ennis, Helen Gregg, Nancy Jones, Jane Lasky, Lon Miller, and Lucy Webb; for the last seven years they have tirelessly supplied me with the articles and books I needed. For allowing me access to Bryher's library, I would like to thank Perdita Schaffner.

The original impetus to write this book I owe to Dan Schwartz, director of the 1988 summer seminar "New Perspectives on the Modern British Novel." Without his encouragment I would never have had the courage to embark on so large a project; once I did begin work on it, his advice and support were invaluable. My colleagues and former colleagues at Eastern Illinois University have also provided advice, feedback, and moral support. Deb Clarke and David Raybin read and responded to early chapters; Susan Bazargan read and responded to nearly all of them. To Susan in particular I am grateful: for her intellectual lucidity, her collegiality, and her extraordinarily helpful readings of my work. The anonymous readers at *Contemporary Literature*, *Twentieth Century Literature*, and SUNY Press have also provided helpful suggestions; and my husband, Richard Sylvia, has not only read, critiqued, and encouraged my work, but has also virtually run the household so that I could complete it. For any infelicities of style and judgment these readers are of course not responsible; for pushing me toward ever greater clarity and coherence, I thank them. Finally, I'd like to thank my daughter, Madeline: for her indefatigable energy and love, her generosity in sharing me with this project, and for her help in dealing with the complexities of continuous-feed computer paper.

Two of the chapters in this book have appeared in somewhat different form as articles; I'd like to thank the University of Wisconsin Press for permission to reprint a revised version of "Multiplying the Past: Gender and Narrative in Bryher's *Gate to the Sea*," *Contemporary Literature*

31.3, © copyright 1990 by the Board of Regents of the University of Wisconsin System. And I thank *Twentieth Century Literature* for permission to use a version of "Masquing the Phallus: Genital Ambiguity in Mary Renault's Historical Fiction," due to appear in late 1996. For permission to quote from works by Mary Butts, I'd like to thank Camilla Bagg. For permission to quote from Laura Riding's poetry, I am grateful to Persea Books and the estate of Laura Riding, managed by the Board of Literary Management.

CHAPTER 1

Reading History / Resisting History

Children daydream. They make up stories about themselves in which they perform heroic deeds, earn admiration, receive love. Sigmund Freud divided these daydreams into two categories: the plots of ambition dreamed by young men, and the plots of romance dreamed by young women. The dichotomy is, of course, oversimple; what interests me the most about daydreams is that whether ambitious or romantic, daydreams derive from preexisting stories, often from history. Scraps of information about the past or present provide a bridge between fantasy and reality. When, in childhood, I imagined myself Annie Oakley, fearlessly facing the Wild West, or Francis Marion, outwitting the British during the Revolutionary War, the historical referents were a crucial way of making the dream real: what I used of actual history seemed to lend actuality to my own heroism.

Such daydreams become part of who a person is; how a child borrows from and shapes historical plots not only results from, but also shapes, her sense of self. History provides a repertoire of stories which collectively define the kinds of lives people live. Reading and responding to history is one of the ways in which young women figure out who they can be. History also often offers them their first exposure to the relation of gender to power, as these young readers notice that most of history's high achievers were male, as were most of its interpreters. Ambitious young girls, who yearn for power as much as love, may well identify with these heroes of history, the Great Men. Willa Cather, for example, admired Alexander the Great (O'Brien 82); Bryher, a historical novelist and H. D.'s lifelong companion, identified with Hannibal (*Coin* ix), and Radclyffe Hall's autobiographical Stephen Gordon imagined herself Admiral Nelson (Hall 13). One need not study history extensively to recognize the link it reveals between men and power. As Sharon O'Brien writes of Willa Cather, "to assume a powerful identity . . .—the female child must imagine herself as male" (26).

There is, however, a certain tension for young girls in identifying with a male figure, the tension of identifying with a male while knowing oneself categorized as female. Naomi Mitchison writes that reading Plato's *Republic*, she dreamed of becoming a Guardian, "But in my inside stories

I don't suppose I was ever a Greek woman" (*All* 40). And Bryher writes, in her autobiographical *Two Selves*, of the split between her obedient female self and her other identity, as "a boy, a brain, that planned adventure and sought wisdom" (5). Both Mary Renault and Naomi Mitchison write of feeling themselves "honorary boys," and Bryher writes of her "boy's heart" (*Development* 162).

The way in which historical discourse inscribed these interlocking issues of power, gender, and narrative authority provided a powerful motivation, between World Wars I and II, for women to write historical fiction. Born in the 1890s, reaching maturity during and after World War I, Naomi Mitchison, Mary Butts, Bryher (born Annie Winifred Ellerman), and Phyllis Bentley experienced childhood under the rule of Queen Victoria, then witnessed the feminist activism that immediately preceded World War I, the return to domesticity that followed it, and the political turmoil of the 1930s. All four women were raised emphatically as "girls"—to please, to serve, to look nice, to stay out of danger—and all felt themselves capable of more. Laura Riding (born Laura Reichenthal in the United States in 1901), and Mary Renault (born Mary Challans in 1905) escaped Queen Victoria, but dealt with similar pressures. Most of these six women read history, dreamed themselves grandiose dreams, then felt thwarted. Most struggled to get the education that would allow them to read Greek and Latin, finding their gender made that education more difficult. All grew up to write historical novels set in the ancient world.

In writing historical fiction about Greece and Rome, Mitchison, Butts, Bryher, Bentley, Riding, and Renault were working through the interrelationship of their gender, their desires, the possible roles with which reading history presented them, and the narrative power that the writing of history offered them. By *working through*, I mean that having read, they then, in their writing, synthesized, juxtaposed, and recapitulated their sources in such a way as to suggest the existence of a culturally repressed female past, a past both they and the culture as a whole needed to recognize as their own. Freud writes that resistance to unacceptable memories causes the patient to repeat the past rather than remember it (12: 150). In a therapeutic situation, the result of resistance and repetition is the "transference of the forgotten past not only on to the doctor, but also on to all the other aspects of the current situation" (12: 151). This transference can then serve to motivate remembering, though the patient, Freud insists, needs time to "become more conversant with this resistance with which he has now become acquainted"; this is the process of "working through" (12: 155).

Transference, as well as *working through*, is a useful term here in analyzing the interrelationship among these writers, their sources, and their novels. Dominick LaCapra has suggested that "transference" can also be detected in the "relation of the historian to the 'object' of study":

> Transference in this somewhat more indirect and attenuated sense refers to the manner in which the problems at issue in the object of study reappear (or are repeated with variations) in the work of the historian. (*Soundings* 37)

The process I see operating in these women's historical fiction is similar. For each writer, there is a complex interaction among the events and issues offered by ancient Greece and Rome, the novelist's experiences, and, most important, the novelist's own cultural discourses—out of which she constructs her sense of herself and the past.

In LaCapra's notion of *transference* I find a useful way of conceptualizing the intersection of the individual writer with cultural and historical discourses. My goal has been to combine the insights of psychoanalytic feminism and cultural criticism so as to explore the role of gender in these women's lives and work without decontextualizing either them or it.[1] Judith Butler argues that gender is not itself substantive but a "relative point of convergence among culturally and historically specific sets of relations" (10). My six subjects, while diverse in terms of sexual orientation and ethnicity, share race, cultural context, and historical moment: I have tried to emphasize the patterns formed by the role of gender in their work without overlooking their differences. But I have taken it for granted that Western culture is and has long been patriarchal and that among the discourses supporting patriarchy—however multiple and self-contesting it may also be—is history. The anonymous graffiti artist who asked at a women's history conference, "How come, if Clio's a woman, she's not on our side?" has not been alone in her observation (Gardiner, "Biography" 49).

My task, then, has been to examine these women's negotiations among the various texts defining them: the books they read that told them who they were. These books were often historical, read in preparation for their own historical fiction, but fiction, psychology, and anthropology also obviously influenced them. Their minds filled with other people's notions of women's identity and women's past, these writers wrote their versions of the ancient world. The books that emerged reflected their reading, their resistance, and their working through: their repetition of received versions, their hints of alternative versions, and above all the recurrence of gender and sexuality as issues linked to power. These writers thus *gender* classicism, exposing apparently gender-neutral accounts of the past as stories of male experience. And several—particularly those writing as nonheterosexists—question the notion of gender itself. "Intelligible" genders, Judith Butler writes, "maintain coherence and continuity among sex, gender, sexual practice, and desire" (17). By complicating gender as well as foregrounding it, Mitchison, Renault, and Bryher challenge that coherence.

In writing historical fiction, as I've suggested, these women were entering into a dialogue with their culture's sense of the past, a dialogue best understood by looking at how they alter and juxtapose the male-authored texts that often serve as their source material; how, when possible, they integrate the work of female scholars, undermine the authority of traditional scholarship, and walk a narrow line between the pressures of plausibility—which require that they reinforce their readers' assumptions about the past—and subversion.

Given the genre within which these writers were working, the pressure to recreate standard versions of the past—and thus reinscribe women's exclusion—was great indeed. The requirements of the historical novel as a genre would seem to conflict with the exploration of women's roles in history. Twentieth-century French historical novelist Marguerite Yourcenar sums up the problem neatly in *Memoirs of Hadrian*, where she explains why she could not write a historical novel from a female perspective:

> Women's lives are much too limited, or else too secret. If a woman does recount her own life she is promptly reproached for being no longer truly feminine. It is already hard enough to give some element of truth to the utterances of a man. (328)

Because women's lives are secret, the data essential to the historical novelist are lacking. Because they are limited, the portrayal of a woman's life is unlikely to capture the broad sweep of historical development essential—such theorists as Georg Lukacs and Avrom Fleishman claim—to the historical novel, and is less liable than a man's to typify a historical period's distinctiveness, at least as codified by traditional history. This process of typification is for Lukacs essential to the historical novel, the aim of which is "to portray the kind of individual destiny that can *directly* and at the same time typically express the problem of an epoch" (284).[2] This synecdochal relationship between characters and era requires central figures who are free to roam, meet people, hold power. Thus Yourcenar comments, referring to two of her historical novels, "it would have been impossible to convey the whole broad panorama of the sixteenth century through the Lady of Froso in her Swedish manor, just as it would have been impossible to convey the ancient world through Plotina" (*With Open Eyes* 226).

Theoreticians of the genre—Alessandro Manzoni, Lukacs, Fleishman, and Harry Shaw—agree that the historical novel's claim to generic identity rests on its treatment of a particular time period different from the writer's own.[3] Manzoni, for example, defines its purpose as the representation of "the human condition in a historical era through invented actions" (76). Shaw defines the historical novel as a novel in which "historical probability reaches a certain level of structural prominence" (22). Historical probability rests on the "realization that history is comprised of ages and societies that are significantly different from our own" (26). But if the past is, by definition, different, it is available to us primarily as encoded by narrative structures steeped, Hayden White points out, in ideology (*Content* 24). And integral to these narrative structures is historical periodization: the conceptualization of presumably coherent eras in terms of characteristic dress, behavior, social structure, and historical events. Traditional historical periodization, however, is itself based on the exclusion of women's experience, as Joan Kelly-Gadol has shown. Historians have divided up and categorized the past based on their understanding of men's lives alone. Those periods associated with "progress"— Athenian democracy, the Industrial Revolution—tend to be periods in which family life is divided from public life: periods, in other words, in which women's lives are most restricted (810). "Ages and societies that are significantly different from our own," then, are representable only through a system of synecdochal substitution that tends either to marginalize women or absorb them into categories determined by male rather than female status.

Avrom Fleishman articulates the strategy even as he shows how easy it is, employing such a strategy, to forget that women existed at all. "The typical man of an age," he writes, agreeing with and praising Lukacs, "is one whose life is shaped by world-historical figures and other influences in a way that epitomizes the processes of change going forward in the society as a whole" (11). As Fleishman's pervasive use of the term *man* to mean *person* indicates, scholars have tended to define history as precisely those activities—"war, wealth, laws, governments, art, and science"—from which women have been excluded (Kelly-Gadol 12). In the quest for a part that will represent the historical whole, the particularities of female experience are likely to get lost, with a resultant reinscription of women's absence from history.

Besides pressures of plausibility and genre, historical novelists submit to the pressures of reading. Because they are above all readers, historical novelists write out of a tangle of texts: those they have consulted about the past, nonhistorical texts that have shaped their asssumptions about human beings, the cultural ideologies they have absorbed—knowingly or unknowingly—since birth. As readers, they are particularly prone to "immasculation," the process Judith Fetterley describes in *The Resisting Reader*: "As readers and teachers and scholars, women are taught to think as men, to identify with a male point of view, and to accept as nor-

mal and legitimate a male system of values, one of whose central princi-
ples is misogyny" (26). Patrocinio Schweickart describes the process by
which the woman reader, identifying with the male protagonist's viewpoint, becomes alienated from herself:

> Androcentric literature is all the more efficient as an instrument of sex-
> ual politics because it does not allow the woman reader to seek refuge in
> her difference. Instead, it draws her into a process that uses her against
> herself. It solicits her complicity in the elevation of male difference into
> universality and, accordingly, the denigration of female difference into
> otherness without reciprocity. (Schweickart 27)

Bound by recorded history and their readers' notions of plausibility, historical novelists are particularly likely to produce novels in which women
are marginalized or powerless, novels that reinforce standard assumptions about women and women's role in history, novels that, to use
Dominick LaCapra's term, bear a "symptomatic" rather than "transformative" relation to their culture (*History* 5).

But even when reproducing female absence, the historical novels I am
examining are never without some "contestatory" element (LaCapra *History* 12). Along with immasculation, the women who wrote these books
experienced the social change wrought by late-nineteenth-century feminism and World War I. When forced by physical maturation into an
awareness of the female role they were expected to play, they found
available to them a range of oppositional stances, including feminism,
which allowed them to write as "resistant" as well as acquiescent readers.[4]

Perhaps it was the very explicitness of women's exclusion from history that made opposition possible. "History," Laura Riding wrote in
1933, "is the most discouraging word I know" (*Four* 68–69). Virginia
Woolf's Rachel Vinrace dozes over Gibbon in *The Voyage Out*; Kitty
Malone spills ink on her father's manuscript about the history of men at
Oxford in *The Pargiters*. All recognize that historical scholarship is not
gender-neutral but bent on the exclusion of women. Kitty's father
responds to her ink spill in terms of her gender: "You share the inability
of your sex, my dear, to grasp the importance of historical facts" (*Pargiters* 93). In doing so, he is echoing Woolf's own father's belief that a
"grasp of the facts" was intrinsically "masculine" (Annan 307). Gerda
Lerner writes of the "dialectic of women's history" as the "tension
between women's actual historical experience and their exclusion from
interpreting that experience" (5); certainly that tension was at its peak in
the late nineteenth century.

The tension, combined with the long-sought entry of women into
the universities, produced a consciously feminist alternative scholarship.
Although Oxford did not grant degrees to women until 1920 and Cam-

bridge not until 1947, women began entering Cambridge and Oxford in the late nineteenth century. As scholars entered fields like anthropology, archeology, medicine, history, and classical literature, they did so intensely aware of the barriers they had faced in getting an education and of the male-dominated scholarship in their disciplines. "I am not sure if the old universities believed that the Almighty had created [women] for the sole use of the male sex," Egyptologist Margaret Murray writes of Oxford and Cambridge, "but they certainly acted as if they did" (*My First* 155).

Women scholars in a wide range of disciplines, bringing a consciously female perspective to their work, took part in what Jane Tompkins calls "cultural work": a "monumental effort to reorganize culture from the woman's point of view" (83). Eileen Power's 1924 *Medieval People* used documents hitherto overlooked to recreate the daily lives of ordinary people. Paleobotanist Marie Stopes, in her 1918 *Married Love*, analyzed sexual intercourse from a specifically female perspective. Jane Harrison insisted that worship of a Mother Goddess preceded the worship of Zeus. Margaret Murray, Bryher's hieroglyphics teacher, saw European witchcraft as a survival of just such an early, matriarchal, nature-oriented religion.

British women novelists during the 1920s and 1930s were part of this ferment. Woolf eagerly read Power, Harrison, and anthropologist Ruth Benedict. Mary Butts devoured Jane Harrison's work, and Mitchison admired Marie Stopes and Eileen Power. Female scholars became role models; Bryher writes of Jessie Weston that she "became the shining flag of all my rebellions. Besides, she was a woman, and where she had gone, I could follow" (*Heart* 135). Many of these scholars were declared feminists, some were lesbians, and most participated in one way or another in a network of mutual support and inspiration. Bryher, who declared proudly in 1972, "I have always been a feminist if that word means fighting for women's rights, and I glory in it" (*Days* 35), was, during the 1920s and 1930s, part of the literary subculture Shari Benstock describes in *Women of the Left Bank*. She provided financial support to Mary Butts (Hanscombe and Smyers 112), among others, and her Contact Press (established with then-husband Robert McAlmon with her funds) published H. D., Mina Loy, Butts, Djuna Barnes, Dorothy Richardson, May Sinclair, and Gertrude Stein (Hanscombe and Smyers 41). Naomi Mitchison sent a copy of a Laura Riding book to Stevie Smith, and wrote for Virginia Woolf's Hogarth Press, which published some of Riding's work. Phyllis Bentley was befriended by Winifred Holtby, who wrote a book on Woolf. Mary Butts praised Mitchison's *The Corn King and Spring Queen* as a "book of the greatest importance" ("Story" 210). These women certainly did not all agree with or admire each other, but together they were fertile soil in which a feminist literary culture could take root.

Crucial to this feminist literary culture was the rethinking of history. Woolf herself constantly returned to the reading and writing of history, exploring the transformative impact of including women as its subjects and interpreters. Her "Mistress Joan Martyn," *Orlando,* and *Between the Acts* all suggest that history from a female perspective looks different than from a male one; that it is vital women write this history; and that when they do, not only its subject but its method will differ from male history. "A sudden light upon the legs of Dame Elizabeth Partridge," the historian Rosemund Merridew argues in Woolf's 1906 "Journal of Mistress Joan Martyn," "sends its beams over the whole state of England, to the King upon his throne" (Squier and DeSalvo 241). When women start writing history, Merridew assumes, they will focus on the roles of women, and as a result the entire course of history will look different.

How will it look different?

It will make use, first of all, of metonymy, as Woolf's "sudden light upon the legs of Dame Elizabeth Partridge" suggests. Metaphor, which substitutes one thing for another, implies a unifying vision, while metonymy, based on juxtaposition, suggests an unending chain of associations. Hayden White in *Metahistory* uses this contrast to distinguish between two kinds of historical writing: metaphorical plots create a sense of organic unity; metonymy exposes the role of circumstance, the way history is shaped by chance events, details, and calculations which resist absorption into some overarching intention or meaning. When we look at Dame Elizabeth Partridge's legs, we focus on an overlooked, insignificant detail, metonymical in that it forces us to think in terms of juxtaposition (we follow the light beam from legs to the rest of her, to her surroundings, forcing us to see history as a collection of disparate details). We are also, of course, looking from the bottom up (from legs up to throne), from the female to the male (from Dame to King). Shift the angle of vision away from the powerful, and history as a self-justifyingly organic movement into the future dissolves into an open-ended story that refuses to coalesce.

The German writer Christa Wolf, in her 1981 novel *Cassandra,* offers a feminist methodology for historical fiction that grows quite logically out of Woolf's suggestion. Wolf privileges words over actions, random details over synthesis, anything overlooked or anticlimactic over plot, with its ultimate closure, death. "Use the word to oppose necrophilia," Wolf writes, "to name the inconspicuous, the previous everyday, the concrete" (270). Historical discourse for Wolf *is* necrophilia; it loves death because it loves endings.[5] No matter how sad, the ending always feels good, because it is what the reader has been waiting for. As Hayden White points out, "Insofar as historical stories can be completed, can be given narrative closure, can be shown to have had a *plot* all along, they give to reality the odor of the *ideal*" (*Content* 24). Events that are told as formally satisfying stories take on an aura of inevitability. Given that these stories generally either leave women out of the picture entirely, or include them as silenced objects of exchange or conflict, it is in the interest of women writers to rob them of that "odor of the ideal."

One way they do this is through their emphasis on the "previous everyday," the detail, as a metonymical unraveling of historical synthesis and closure. Naomi Schor has written of the traditional association between women and detail: minutely detailed paintings are seen as "feminine"; abstract or imaginative art is "masculine" (*Reading* 19–20). Unlike the "fragment," which serves synecdochically to represent the whole of which it's a part, the "detail" is tangential, everyday, fictive-sounding (66–69). Everyday details don't serve to represent a historical epoch; they are gratuitous and disruptive, hinting only at an endless chain of additional details that could have been included. In conveying the "previous everyday," historical novelists are thus performing a traditionally feminine task, but they are simultaneously challenging the completeness of any historical plot.

This "feminine" submission to detail suggests Margaret Homans's discussion of the nineteenth-century dichotomy between "male" imagination and "female" realism. The nineteenth-century ideology of womanhood, Homans argues, made it permissible for women writers to be "bearers of the word": transmitters of male knowledge who did no inventing of their own. To a certain extent, they are thus "imitation sons," reinforcing the values associated with that knowledge (20). But they are also women who, precisely because they are women, have not undergone the same process of differentiation from their mothers as men. Combining Lacanian theory with that of feminist Nancy Chodorow, Homans argues that as a result a woman "retains the literal or presymbolic language that the son represses at the time of his renunciation of his mother" (13). Our culture values figuration, Homans argues, because it facilitates flight from the mother, but "women must remain the literal in order to ground the figurative substitutions sons generate and privilege" (9). This puts women in an ambivalent position, inevitably absorbing their culture's devaluing of the literal, but also able to value the literal differently. At particular moments in the text, this differing valuation of the literal may become evident: moments when a metaphor is literalized or women characters or the text itself translate or transmit the language of other authors (30–31). Homans describes the subtle ambivalence that results:

> Even though the novel in question always keeps on going in the symbolic order . . . these are moments nonetheless in which there is an implicit contradiction between the novel's continuous representation of female

experience and the text's seeming suddenly to become aware that the implication of such representation is, from the perspective of the symbolic order, the silence and objectification of women. (32–33)

Homans's discussion, despite its nineteenth-century context, illuminates writers like Mitchison, Bentley, and Bryher who, because they are stylistically conventional and respectful of their sources, are themselves "bearers of the word." Not only do they transmit others' knowledge, they often thematize the act of transmission itself by depicting within the plot a struggle for interpretive control. At such moments, these writers' identification with the literal becomes clear.

This notion of "bearing the word" might well be another reason these writers chose historical fiction as their genre. Certainly there was the need to reinterpret the past in gendered terms and a new opportunity to do so now that women could study ancient languages and even get a university education. But for women raised as Victorians, the very modesty of historical fiction as a genre might well have been inviting as well. The gathering of data was a form of submission to authority; its transformation into novel a "bearing" of the word. A glance at the acknowledgment pages of their novels reveals how literal this submission was; Mitchison, in particular, tends to thank the male historian friends who guided her through her research, while all take time to explain their relationship to previously available materials. Both Mitchison and Bentley expressed at various times the tension between their ambition and their fear of hurting their families' feelings; the submission to authority required by historical fiction allowed them to rebel and submit simultaneously.[6]

Both Schor and Homans offer ways of being "feminine" with a vengeance: taking the role assigned them, women play out that role in such a way as to expose the way it operates. Because the writing of historical fiction seems on the surface so submissive an activity, it is an especially appropriate forum for what Irigaray calls "mimicry," the deliberate assumption of a feminine role. This mimicry is the opposite of immasculation, for while immasculation means identifying with the male subject, mimicry aligns the writer with the silence and marginalization of women:

> To play with mimesis is thus, for a woman, to try to recover the place of her exploitation by discourse, without allowing herself to be simply reduced to it. It means to resubmit herself—inasmuch as she is on the side of the "perceptible," of "matter"—to "ideas," in particular to ideas about herself that are elaborated in/by a masculine logic, but so as to make "visible," by an effect of playful repetition, what was supposed to remain invisible: the cover-up of a possible operation of the feminine in language. (76)

Laura Riding's Cressida and Mary Butts's Cleopatra are mimics, in Irigaray's sense. As they play their "feminine" roles, these women are vilified precisely because they are always in excess of the identity assigned them, irreducible to what Irigaray calls the "economy of the Same," which defines all reality in terms of a "masculine subject" (74).

There are other ways as well in which these writers resist the pressures of historical discourse. Even those writers who do seem to identify with the masculine subject—Bryher, for example, with her male adventurers and Renault, with her glamorous depiction of Theseus, conqueror of matriarchy—do so in such a way as to draw attention to their narrative cross-dressing, so that their apparent immasculation becomes an act of transgression against gender boundaries. As lesbians, Renault and Bryher serve as reminders that sexuality as well as gender inflects these women's lives and writing. Both depict male-male relationships of particular intensity; both narrate at times as "male impersonators" (Hugh Kenner's term for Renault); and both depict gender-bending characters who resemble the "mannish lesbian" discussed by Esther Newton, Teresa de Lauretis, and others.[7] Their emphasis on nonheterosexual relationships also subverts the romance plot that so often lends closure to historical novels. When Bulwer-Lytton, Whyte-Melville, or Kingsley, for example, marry off their heroes at novel's end, conflating personal and historical happy endings, they doubly reinforce their readers' sense that how it was, was right. Plots that refuse to privilege heterosexuality are thus undercutting that tendency to read history as romance.

While Riding and Butts are the most radical in their redefinitions of historical fiction, all the writers I discuss here problematize narrative authority and closure, through their use of conflicting sources for and variant perspectives within their novels, and through their emphasis on what has been left out: on silences that resonate beyond the end of the novel and on details that resist absorption into it.

As Celeste Schenck points out in discussing women's epithalamia, generic boundaries often have the effect of excluding women's voices. Confronted with the epithalamion, a genre that "by definition objectifies the feminine," women writers produce variant responses to marriage that necessarily challenge generic definitions (110). The historical novel, too, if less obviously, has been codified in terms that exclude female experience. The pervasive insistence on its historicism, defined by Shaw as "a new awareness of the systematic otherness of society in the past" (26 n), by emphasizing the differentiation of past and present, suggests a past that is completed, objectified, accessible to scholars, unchangeable. By setting their works in the past,[8] in a particular locale, and by simulating period dress and concerns and names, the novelists I discuss announce their acceptance of historical probability as a structuring principle.

But they also work out the problems such a notion poses for them. Just as H. D.'s aim was to "open a place for herself in a tradition that may have seemed closed and completed" (DuPlessis *H. D.*, 19), women historical novelists of this century have sought ways to open up, as well as convey, the past. As they do so, their greatest enemy is the privileging of closure and distance that underlies Shaw's "historical probability" (22) and Lukacs's "historical authenticity" (50). For Lukacs, any experiences that are not historically determined are unsuitable subjects for the historical novel; he mentions sexual abnormality (113) and extremes of feeling (220), but as Shaw points out, much of daily experience is untouched by history (44)—or at least eludes those versions of the past that reach us.

It is precisely this daily experience—Wolf's "previous everyday, the concrete"—that women's historical fiction seeks to evoke. But it cannot do so directly, for there are no data. So for women, resisting the past means reading erasures. Writing the past means making palimpsests: texts that carry traces of that which has been suppressed. The novelists I explore, bound by generic conventions and their sources, preserve much of the patriarchal overwriting—the stories of "politics, events, dates, and great personalities" from which women's passage has been erased (Cantarella 5). But they leave also traces of another story—traces I will seek to read in the pages that follow.

NOTES

1. While I am aware of Judith Butler's convincing discussion of the way *gender* has been hypostasized in feminist criticism (7–13), I find the word an irreplaceable way of describing the pattern of behavior expected of middle class British women raised in the late nineteenth and early twentieth centuries. Given a sexually dichotomized culture, the way in which one's body is categorized—as either female or male—inevitably shapes much of what one experiences as a social being.

2. Barbara Foley criticizes Lukacs in somewhat similar terms, rejecting his "reflectionist model" as outmoded (18). Defining ideology as the "nexus of concepts by which individuals represent to themselves their situation in the social world" (87), Foley argues that an unproblematized mimesis would tend to reinforce the culture's dominant ideology. The role of mimetic fiction, then, is to show the conflict preceding synthesis (98), exposing ideological contradictions rather than rationalizing them. "The knowledge that fiction conveys," Foley writes, summing up her argument, "is the knowledge of the contradictory subjective appropriation of an objective social reality" (96).

3. For Lukacs the historical novel has no generic identity (242). Ideally, the writer will have the same relation to past eras that he does to the present. Thus the "classical historical novel" is not essentially different from the novel of social conditions. But in practice, the historical novel does exist as a distinct genre

because the 1848 revolutions and the triumph of the bourgeoisie cut writers off from the populace and from any sense of an organic, meaningful line of historical development (206–50).

4. "The first act of the feminist critic," Judith Fetterley writes, "must be to become a resisting rather than an assenting reader and, by this refusal to assent, to begin the process of exorcizing the male mind that has been implanted in her" (xxii). Fetterley's use of the term *resistant* obviously differs from Freud's. I would argue that both kinds of resistance—the repetition wrought by repression and the exposure wrought by feminist self-awareness—operate in the subjects of this study.

5. Laura Riding seems to be thinking along similar lines when she calls historical fiction "ghoulish" (*Trojan* xvii).

6. Ironically the genre also allowed for a more explicit treatment of sexuality than would otherwise have been acceptable. Mitchison comments that sex "in wolf skins and togas" seemed to be acceptable, where any explicitness in her contemporary fiction triggered objections from her publishers (*You May Well* 179). Its historicity presumably distanced the material and gave it a scholarly context that made it more acceptable. Anthropology seemed to operate under a similar dispensation in regard to sexual explicitness.

7. See Garber's *Vested Interests* as well as Newton and de Lauretis.

8. With Shaw, I would exclude novels of the recent past from the category "historical fiction." Fleishman suggests the following set of characteristics: historical novels are set at least 40–60 years in the past, involve historical events which affect the characters, and include at least one "real" person and a realistic background (3).

CHAPTER 2

Greece, Gender,
and The Golden Bough

To mid-nineteenth-century European thinkers, ancient Greece—by which was meant fifth-century Athens—was all that a culture should be. Its architecture, sculpture, literature, and men possessed grandeur, dignity, and nobility. At the heart of Europe's idea of Greece was human beauty, conceived as "eminently orderly, symmetrical, and tender" (Ruskin 80). According to Pater's version of the Hellenic ideal, "man is at unity with himself, with his physical nature, with the outward world" (177), while Arnold quotes approvingly the saying that the "Athens of Pericles was a vigorous man, at the summit of his bodily strength and mental energy" (*Tradition* 23).

Crucial to these characterizations is the sense of constraint, order, generality, masculinity. "Breadth, centrality, with blitheness and repose," writes Pater, "are the marks of Hellenic culture" (181). There is no room here for the peculiar or extreme. Nor is there any sense of a less "civilized" pre-Periclean Greece.[1] Smith's 1844 *Dictionary of Classical Mythology and Biography* stated firmly that Troy and Knossos were imaginary and the world began in 4004 B.C. Nor, of course, is there any room for women. The "supreme beauty is rather male than female," Pater writes of Greek art (153).

This version of Greek history and values served the interests of the British ruling classes throughout the nineteenth century. During this time, Frank Turner points out, most scholarship on ancient Greece "invoked prescriptive images of Greek civilization that supported the social and moral values of the traditional British elites as models for the new middle class leaders of the nation" (448). Earlier, more aristocratic leaders had preferred Sparta, finding Athens "wanton, too 'merry,' and given to pederasty" (Culler 15), but Britain's rising upper middle class found in the Athenian qualities of dignity, self-control, patriotism, and individualism virtues to which they themselves could aspire (Payne 183). Linda Dowling attributes the growth of Hellenism at Oxford in particular to the quest for values to transcend midcentury materialism (*Hellenism* 31). Intellectuals such as J. S. Mill found an alternative in a notion of self-development derived from eighteenth-century Hellenism (Dowling *Hellenism* 60). The nineteenth-century taste for "energy," "individualism," and "diversity," she argues, is a product of Hellenism (59). Even the athleticism so valued by nineteenth-century educators derives from the Greek ideal; J. G. Cotton Minchin reminisces in his 1898 *Old Harrow Days*, "Was there ever a race more intellectual than the ancient Greeks, and did they not worship the human form divine?" (qtd. in Haley 207). Thus for Great Britain, the world of classical antiquity played a particularly vital role in the national self-image. "Much of the intellectual confidence of the ruling classes," according to Frank Turner, derived from their "knowledge of the classical world" (5).

Inculcating this knowledge was the essential goal of the British educational system. With it came the sense of belonging to an elite group of men, set apart from the less educated and the female. Throughout the nineteenth century, knowledge of Latin and Greek—required until after World War I for admission to Oxford and Cambridge—set young men apart from their female counterparts. The British boarding school, Walter Ong points out, took boys from their mothers in order to initiate them into a competitive male world where learning Latin and Greek meant learning to imitate the values the original Romans and Greeks incarnated. Among those values—at least as Greek and Roman history was understood at the time—was the marginalization of women. Greek women were relegated to their women's quarters and denied any public role; Roman women, if freer in their social life, were under the control of a male guardian and married off as convenient. The intimate connection between classical learning and the British educational system served to reinforce upper-class male cultural hegemony.

Nineteenth-century Hellenism was not monolithic. Linda Dowling points out the "competing discourses" that constituted "Greece" in midcentury Britain (*Hellenism* 59), among them a "homosexual counterdiscourse" which found in Athenian homoeroticism the idealization of male love that has helped define homosexuality as a modern social identity (31, 4). This counterdiscourse, embraced by J. A. Symonds, G. L. Dickinson, Oscar Wilde, and Edward Carpenter among others, was repudiated by Oxford don Benjamin Jowett, who attempted to teach Plato while denigrating homoeroticism (*Hellenism* 129). What Dowling calls the "Socratic ideal of mental intercourse between male friends" (124) was thus a contested notion, embraced for its very ambiguity by Wilde as a defense at his 1895 trial.

While this association between ancient Greece and homosexuality opened up discussion as to what "Greece" was, it did not make Greek culture any more accessible to women, who were still largely excluded from universities and the study of classical languages, and for whom classical culture represented a world of male power and collegiality denied them. Nineteenth-century literary women longingly watched their brothers master Latin and Greek and studied the languages themselves "with a touching faith that such knowledge would open up a world of male power and wisdom to them" (Showalter, *Literature* 42). Initially accessible only to those who had mastered Greek and Latin—to a male elite, in other words—the ancient world signified female absence from power and hence from history, and reinscribed women's exclusion from the dominant cultural vocabulary.

Then, as Hugh Kenner writes, "Schleimann had been to Troy, and a cosmos had altered" (42). Throughout the second half of the century, archeology, anthropology, psychology, and political science all conspired to change Great Britain's sense of what Greece was, including its sense of the role of women in ancient Greece. J. J. Bachofen's 1861 *Das Mutterrecht*, Sappho's poetry, Heinrich Schliemann's excavations at Troy, William Dorpfeld's at Athens, and Arthur Evans's on Crete, as well as the work of James Frazer and the Cambridge Ritualists (among them Jane Harrison and Gilbert Murray) uncovered a Greece that offered little support to the social and moral values of the British elite (Jenkyns 343; Payne 184).

Excavations revealed a Mycenean Age quite distinct from the fifth-century Athenian culture that gave rise to Arnoldian Hellenism (Turner 180). There was now evidence that thousands of years of Greek culture had in fact preceded Periclean Athens. The archeological evidence uncovered in the 1880s and 1890s by Dorpfeld led Jane Harrison to write her 1890 *Myths and Monuments of Athens*, the "first book of the Cambridge ritualists" according to Ackerman ("Jane Ellen Harrison" 225). The so-called Ritualists emphasized the irrational, Dionysian side of Greek history. The Greek myths originated not from a love of order and logic, they said, but were distorted versions of the rituals predating them—rituals involving sex and sacrifice to influence crops and seasons. Greek tragedy, Gilbert Murray argued, arose out of the yearly sacrifice of a Year God—hardly a reassuring notion to those for whom the Greeks incarnated sweetness and light.

Also in 1890, James Frazer published *The Golden Bough*. This compendium of myth and ritual from all over the world posited a single pattern underlying all: a periodically dying and reborn god whose cycle of life and death matches the seasonal cycle of planting and harvest. Rites in honor of god and goddess thus ensure the continuation of this cycle—the return of spring and the growth of crops. Frazer published three different editions of *The Golden Bough*, expanding and qualifying until it reached twelve volumes in its final (1911–1915) version. His theoretical discussion of how myth originated—whether in ritual or otherwise—is inconsistent, but the massive evidence provided by *The Golden Bough* suggests that ritual played a vital role. While Frazer may not have directly influenced Harrison, his work certainly provided evidence for her ideas.[2]

Frazer's work also served to bring together two disciplines previously separate: anthropology and classicism (Ackerman *Frazer* 63). This interrelationship was initially shocking, for it forced the hitherto idealized classical world into the same intellectual context as so-called savages. It also shifted the kind of data classicists could use in drawing their conclusions. For Jane Harrison this was particularly crucial; she felt she had come to classical languages too late to feel completely confident in her knowledge of them. Once anthropology (and archeology as a source of knowledge about anthropology) became an accepted adjunct to classical scholarship, she could gather data from vase paintings and inscriptions, from archeological sources in other words, as well as from textual analysis. Lewis Farnell—on this issue, at least, in agreement with Harrison—writes of the difficulties involved in persuading classicists to accept the relevance of nontextual data. Fighting to introduce classical archeology to Oxford, he fought the "prejudices of Jowett and the early Victorian scholars, whose souls were closed against art-study" (*Oxonian* 267).[3] Along with Frazer's treatment of ancient ritual, then, his joining of classical and anthropological studies radically shifted the perspective his contemporaries brought to bear on classical antiquity. This shift also has implications for historical fiction as a genre; if anthropology has data to offer classical historians, presumably it can also contribute to the work of historical novelists.

The early Greeks, then, according to Frazer and others who followed him, apparently participated in unseemly religious rites. Even more unsettling to the nineteenth century's image of antiquity, artifacts found on Crete suggested that ancient Minoan culture might have even been matriarchal. Among the finds on Crete was a clay sealing portraying a Great Mother. Jane Harrison describes the discovery as a crucial turning point in her intellectual life (*Reminiscences* 72), for it hinted at a pre-Olympian matriarchy. The association of pre-Olympian Greece with ancient matriarchy had first been made in Bachofen's *Das Mutterrecht*. When the initial clay sealing was followed by the discovery of other Mother Goddess figurines, Joseph Campbell points out, Bachofen's theory of an early matriarchy appeared to be confirmed (Campbell lv). Throughout the late nineteenth and early twentieth centuries, anthropologists, ancient historians, and political philosophers continued to hypothesize a matriarchal stage in the development of human society (Cantarella 4).[4] Susan Stanford Friedman, noting the influence of Bachofen on H. D., writes that among those she read who accepted his theory were "Arthur Weigall, Jane Harrison, Margaret Murray, Havelock Ellis, W. J. Perry, Sigmund Freud"

(266). Engels, whom Mitchison certainly read, and Jessie Weston, whom Bryher regarded as a role model, also shared some of Bachofen's assumptions. The notion of a previously unimagined prehistory in which goddess-worship and women prevailed over gods and men thus became a crucial factor in the development of modernism. That there could be power, even domination, associated with specifically female body parts working in alliance with nature was an appealing notion to many women, who then found in their identity as woman a source of strength, symbolized by their relation to a Magna Mater. Sandra Gilbert suggests the impact this image had, and the fear it inspired in such male modernists as D. H. Lawrence and Robert Graves (130–41).

Attitudes toward this ancient prehistory tended to divide along gender lines. While male theorists such as Bachofen, Frazer, and Freud regarded the movement from matriarchy to patriarchy as an inevitable movement toward civilization, feminist Jane Harrison was transparently nostalgic for the older culture she describes. Harrison's 1903 *Prolegomena to the Study of Greek Religion* seems to revel in the evidence that preanthropomorphic deities of the underworld dominated early Greek religious life. She describes festivals and rites—often led by women—whose aim was to placate nonhuman *Keres* and animal-gods, the grotesque hybrids despised by later Greeks.[5] She opens her book by quoting Ruskin's description of the Greeks:

> There is no dread in their hearts; pensiveness, amazement, often deepest grief and desolation, but terror never. Everlasting calm in the presence of all Fate, and joy such as they might win, not indeed from perfect beauty, but from beauty at perfect rest. (1)

Harrison then gleefully exposes the fear and irrationality that came before and after—in Orphism and the Dionysian mystery religions—that calm. In debunking Ruskin, she is attacking a century's worth of European male self-satisfaction.

In *Themis*, Harrison attacks the values of "Classical Greece" even more explicitly. "Classical," of course, refers to Greece between about 800 and 400 B.C., a Greece that worships the Olympian gods, as known to us through Homer and Hesiod: the familiar patriarchal pantheon reigning from Mt. Olympus, dominated by Zeus, incarnating all that is most human in human beings. For Harrison, the order imposed by the Olympians is death. She mourns the loss of the "beautiful courtesies" of totemism (*Themis* 449). Totemism, in constrast to the Homeric, anthropomorphic pantheon, posits kinship between people and animals and requires an attitude of awe and worship toward nature. "All this," she writes of totemism in *Themis*, "all life and that which is life and reality—change and movement—the Olympian renounces. Instead he chooses

Deathlessness and Immutability—a seeming immortality which is really the denial of life, for life is change" (468). For Harrison pre-Olympian ritual reflected collectivity, Bergsonian *durée*, Dionysian group consciousness (Stewart 92)—qualities in stark opposition to male individualism, abstraction, and objectivity.[6]

Harrison's thesis, needless to say, brought her enemies. Interestingly, those most opposed to her theories about ancient Greece also disliked her feminism—for she was an ardent feminist, writing in support of women's education and suffrage. Harrison's biographer, Jessie Stewart, writes that the apparently scholarly fight between Ritualists and non-Ritualists over the existence of the Year God was embittered by Ridgeway's "anti-feminist politics" (18). Lewis Farnell, another prominent academic opponent, reviewing *Themis*, harps on all that most offends his own values, blaming Harrison's dislike of a "personal individual God" and her "matriarchal prejudice" for its failure (455). "Her sympathetic delight in savages," Farnell concludes, "is dimming her eyes and distorting her judgement of much Greek literature and art" (458). Somewhat more circumspect in his 1934 memoir, Farnell writes mournfully, "One may discern how the writings of . . . Jane Harrison, the leading woman scholar of the time, were marred by the spirit of feminist propaganda" (*Oxonian* 281).

Sigmund Freud, if more tolerant of "savages" than Farnell, was certainly less so than Harrison. The notion of a newly discovered prehistory became a crucial metaphor in his thinking about women's sexual development. Attributing lesbianism to the failure to progress beyond a pre-Oedipal attachment to the mother (Friedman 125; Freud 21: 226–30), Freud compares that pre-Oedipal mother-fixation to pre-Hellenic culture: "Our insight into this early, pre-Oedipus, phase in girls," Freud writes, "comes to us as a surprise, like the discovery in another field, of the Minoan-Mycenean civilization behind the civilization of Greece" (21: 226). He made a similar connection in analyzing H. D., who wrote Bryher of her 1933 psychoanalysis, "F[reud] says mine is absolutely FIRST layer, I got stuck at the earliest pre-OE stage, and 'back to the womb' seems to be my only solution. Hence islands, sea, Greek primitives and so on" (qtd. in Friedman 132). What Freud criticizes in H. D. as a dangerous "desire for union with my mother" (H. D., *Tribute* 65) sounds a lot like Harrison's pre-Olympian culture in which there is a "lack of differentiation, of subject and object" (*Themis* 128). While these thinkers differed in their valuation of the motherlands they hypothesized, they clearly shared a conceptual vocabulary; Bachofen, Freud, and Harrison all posit a primordial past shared by the individual psyche and by the human race, a past dominated by the female, by nature, by the nonrational, by indeterminacy.

Interest in these concepts pervaded feminist and literary circles.[7] Virginia Woolf refers with awe to Jane Harrison several times in her diary and letters as well as in *A Room of One's Own,* and owned all her major works (Maika 8). Naomi Mitchison, introduced to *The Golden Bough* by her grandmother, based much of *The Corn King and the Spring Queen* on its accounts of agricultural rituals. And she writes in *All Change Here* of her excitement when, as a child, she attended a party at Sir Arthur Evans's house—of whose Knossos discoveries she was well aware (34). Mary Butts writes repeatedly of *The Golden Bough* in her memoir *The Crystal Cabinet,* referring to it as a "tree of knowledge" (43). For women studying the past, this intellectual climate set up a chain of associations from which they could draw in recreating a revised version of ancient Greece, one in explicit opposition to traditional, male-originated versions, one that gave far greater prominence to women and that questioned such traditional Western values as rationality, detachment, and individualism.[8]

Male modernists, of course, were also attracted to this newly reimagined world. The link between modernism and myth has long been a critical commonplace. While using mythic material is not quite the same thing as setting a novel in ancient Greece, the same reservoir of cultural phenomena is being drawn from in both cases; what has not been sufficiently noticed is what a vexed sea it was: writers could choose from a wide range of allusions and sources and so generate a range of different meanings. T. S. Eliot, writing of James Joyce's *Ulysses,* was the first to define what he calls the "mythic method," which has ever since been a hallmark of modernism:

> Psychology . . . ethnology, and *The Golden Bough* have concurred to make possible what was impossible even a few years ago. Instead of narrative method, we may now use the mythical method.
>
> In using myth, in manipulating a continuous parallel between contemporaneity and antiquity, Mr. Joyce is pursuing a method which others must pursue after him. . . . It is simply a way of controlling, or ordering, or giving a shape and a significance to the immense panorama of futility and anarchy which is contemporary history (177–78).

For Eliot, myth is a means of making coherence out of the meaningless phenomena of contemporary life. It is a way of shoring up fragments against ruin, to paraphrase "The Waste Land," of making order out of chaos.

Such anxiety in the face of dissolution and disorder has long been regarded as typical of modernist writing and one reason for the modernist fascination with myth. Recently, however, feminist critics have suggested that women writers felt no such anxiety. Judith Kegan Gardiner, for example, contrasts the self dissolved by Dorothy Richardson, Gertrude Stein, and Virginia Woolf into a "female choral and collective voice" with the "self-pitying pieces" of the male modernist's fragmented

self (115). Women writers could not mourn the loss of the coherent indi-
viduated self they had never fully experienced, nor could they wax nostalgic about a lost cultural coherence which had been premised on their
exclusion (Ostriker 330).[9] Nor would the use of myth to evoke the "primitive" bear quite the same meanings for women as for men. As Marianna Torgovnick has pointed out, "Familiar tropes for primitives" are
also "the tropes conventionally used for women" (17). If the appeal of the
primitive is that it appears—as Torgovnick argues—to have "escaped
the confines of masculine identity as we know it" (236), women writers'
relation to its "flirtations with boundary dissolution" (151) may well be
different from men's.

Women writers did, of course, use myth.[10] John Vickery, though his
study of the *The Golden Bough*'s literary impact focuses on the familiar
figures of Yeats, Eliot, Lawrence, and Joyce, does mention a smattering of
female writers as well who were influenced by Frazer: Caroline Gordon,
Kathleen Raine, H. D., and Naomi Mitchison. But female modernists—at
least those discussed here—tended to use it differently, not to order reality or evoke a universal underlayer in human experience, but to explore
and challenge their culture's assumptions about gender. Crucial to this difference is the recognition that myth is not just myth, that ritual can exist
without a system of narratives to explain it.

All the Cambridge Ritualists argued for the importance of this distinction and insisted that in fact ritual came before myth; the telling of stories emerges at the same time that gods are anthropomorphized and the
early, intimate relationship of humans to the natural world is severed.
This notion of "ritual"—as opposed to "myth"—allowed women writers
a radically different sense of how mythic material could be used. Butts, in
particular, seems to have been heavily influenced by Jane Harrison's
notion of a Greek religion based on the propitiation of nonanthropomorphic forces (*Prolegomena* 7). To understand pre-Olympian religion,
Harrison writes, we must give up analysis, and "think back the 'many' we
have so sharply and strenuously divided, into the haze of the primitive
'one'," a haze of "protoplasmic fulness and forcefulness" (164). And in
Themis Harrison continues to describe this underlayer in Greek religion,
linking it to matriarchy, collective emotion, and totemism, describing a
pre-Olympian world of "fusion . . . [and] non-differentiation" (122).
Such formulations don't provide "a way of controlling, or ordering, or
giving a shape and a significance to the immense panorama of futility
and anarchy which is contemporary history"; on the contrary, Harrison
seems to be advocating a rejection of analytical detachment altogether.

These, then, are the concepts with which male and female modernists
proceeded to debate gender. The world of ancient Greece had been transformed from a static model imitated by young men aspiring to power,

into a sea of conflicting images. In the pages that follow, I will explore the ways in which Mitchison, Butts, Riding, Renault, and Bryher locate themselves within this discussion of Greek culture as each takes on the task of reinterpreting what "Greece" means. For each, gender is a crucial consideration in that reinterpretation; for Mitchison, Renault, and Bryher, sexual orientation is a consideration as well. The "counterdiscourse" Plato offered late-nineteenth-century homosexuals emerged for lesbians with Sappho, and in fact one reinforced the other, making Greece a conceptual space in which alternatives to heterosexuality could be explored. Particularly for Mitchison and Renault, both of whom lived and studied at Oxford, Greece meant Plato and Plato meant male love. Edward Carpenter writes that all those who have most successfully recreated ancient Greek life—he names Winckelmann, Goethe, Pater, and Symonds—have had a "Uranian" (homosexual) streak (103–4); certainly a number of the writers I discuss are either themselves lesbians (Renault and Bryher) and/or strikingly sympathetic in their depictions of homosexuals (Mitchison and Butts).

For centuries, ideas about "Greece" had shaped the way people talked about human nature, government, and the meaning of life. Most recently, Greece had become a way of talking about gender and sexuality. In writing historical novels set in Greece, these writers were plunging into contested waters, setting up their own "Greece" to compete with those constructs that in the past had served, implicitly if not explicitly, to disempower women. Mitchison, Butts, Riding, Renault, and Bryher were responding to ancient sources, to recent historians and anthropologists, and to the way their fellow novelists—particularly Conrad, Eliot, Lawrence, and Robert Graves—had used turn-of-the-century anthropology. It is in the context of that interpretive struggle over "Greece" and its implications for women that I will discuss their novels.

NOTES

1. The exception here is Pater, who in his discussion of Winckelmann in *The Renaissance*, acknowledges the wilder side of Greek religion, suggesting, "The Dorian worship of Apollo, rational, chastened, debonair, with his unbroken daylight, always opposed to the sad Chthonian divinities, is the aspiring element, by force and spring of which Greek religion sublimes itself" (162). But Pater, too, finds the Hellenic ideal in "repose and generality" (170).

2. William Robertson Smith's 1888–1891 lectures, published as his 1890 *Religion of the Semites*, were also a crucial factor in the development of ritualism. Smith, close friend to Frazer, saw primitive religion as the result of ritual (Ackerman, "Frazer" 118–20). Harry Payne, however, suggests that Harrison's ideas about ritual emerged simultaneously with Frazer's and Smith's, and were not

directly influenced by them (188); Ackerman, on the other hand, argues for a direct line of influence ("Frazer" 115).

3. Joan DeJean describes the influential role of philology during these years, when romantics assumed that a particular racial or national essence could be understood through analysis of the national language.

4. The possibility of an ancient matriarchal culture remains a vexed question. Lerner writes that there is no evidence of any society where women as a group ruled men, suggesting that in the strictest sense, there has never been a matriarchy (30), and Cantarella concurs. But some anthropologists have found evidence of societies which are decidedly nonpatriarchal. See, for example, Ruby Rohrlich-Leavitt and Eleanor Leacock.

5. A *Ker* is a winged being generally associated with death, according to Harrison.

6. In her preface to the second edition of *Themis*, however, Harrison radically alters her attitude. During World War I, she dropped her study of Greece; when she returned to *Themis* after the War, she felt new respect for the restraint represented by the Olympian gods. Her critics were right, she says, in attacking her attack on the Olympians (viii).

7. American feminists Charlotte Perkins Gilman and Elizabeth Cady Stanton were influenced by Bachofen (Lerner 26). During the 1960s and 1970s, a number of feminists returned to the notion that the earliest human societies had been at the very least "matri-equal" (Evans 89) or "partnership societies" (Eisler), less hierarchical, and involving less violence and more reverence for nature.

8. These images also entered the popular imagination, linking feminist activism to Greek atavism. While suffragettes had long carried banners depicting Artemis and Boadicea, and Nike served as the emblem for *Votes for Women* (Kestner 12–13), frightened spectators of the suffrage movement now linked feminists to pre-Olympian revelers. When a suffragette attacked a Velasquez painting of Venus, Edmund Gosse compared her to a maenad, while he himself struggled to maintain an "Olympian" calm in the face of such crimes (Kestner vii). Similarly Vera Brittain, wondering why the British public distrusted the presence of women at Oxford, writes, "Are we pictured as Maenads dancing before the Martyr's Memorial, or as Bacchantes revelling in the open spaces of Carfax?" (qtd. in Leonardi 47).

9. "At both the psychic and social level," Cora Kaplan writes, "always intertwined, women's subordinate place within culture makes them less able to embrace or be held by romantic individualism with all its pleasures and dangers" (59).

10. Alicia Ostriker has described the "revisionist mythmaking" of recent women poets: their rejection of male modernist nostalgia, their experimentation with style and form, their undercutting of the values implied by the myths they use (330). And Rachel Blau DuPlessis examines H. D.'s uses of myth. But for the most part the impact of Frazer on female modernists has been overlooked.

CHAPTER 3

History, Ritual, and Gender in Naomi Mitchison's Greece

Steeped in Greek culture from an early age, Naomi Mitchison was born in 1897 into the well-educated, upper-middle-class Haldane family. Until adolescence, she went to the same school as her beloved brother Jack, where she was, she writes, "for all practical purposes a boy until the awful thing happened," the awful thing being menarche and her subsequent removal from the school (*All Change* 11). As a result, she got a "boy's" education until the age of twelve. Thereafter she was only an onlooker to her brother's excellent education; she, with four other girls, was put in the hands of a governess (13).

Even after her removal from the Dragon School, however, Greek culture remained an essential part of Mitchison's intellectual framework. Her grandmother introduced her to Frazer's *The Golden Bough* (*All Change* 28); she read Jowett's translation of Plato and imagined herself one of the Guardians, specially trained to rule Plato's ideal republic (40). She attended a party at Sir Arthur Evans's house after his Knossos discoveries and discussed anthropology with family friend Andrew Lang (34; Benton 7). Greek history provided her, throughout her life, with an indispensable vocabulary for the discussion of politics. Any utopia is a "Cloud Cuckoo Borough," after the ideal community established in Aristophanes' *The Birds*. Body-proud athletes are Spartans (*All Change* 71). And civilization itself is Athens; Mitchison mourns, at the start of World War II, the loss of "all that we care for, *all that we mean by Athens. . . . The ending of a civilization*" (Sheridan 42, my emphasis).

Mitchison knew, however, that the sexual role into which puberty pushed her was in conflict with her love of Greek culture. The ancient world—Roman as well as Greek—was a lifelong preoccupation, but inseparable from the problems posed for her by her identity as a woman. Born during the same decade as Bryher (1894) and Mary Butts (1890), Mitchison writes, like them, of the conflict between her desire for action—expressed through her identification with male historical figures—and her culturally defined role as a young woman. Immersed in a culture at once hers and not hers, she imagined herself one of Plato's Guardians, but

"In my inside stories," she writes, referring to her childhood fantasies, "I don't suppose I was ever a Greek woman" (*All Change* 40). She admired Roman Mithraism—a mystery religion closed to women—and read Franz Cumont's *Les Mysteres de Mithra* soon after its 1913 publication precisely because it allowed entry into a wholly male world. "One attractive aspect of this," she writes of her interest in Mithraism, "was that I always imagined myself a man" (98). She loved the ancient world, in other words, at once despite and because of its exclusion of women. To enter it was a kind of cross-dressing. To depict it was a delicate act of negotiation, in which, in the act of repeating her historical sources, she also challenged them.

Mitchison's years at the Dragon school appear in her autobiographies (*All Change Here*, *Small Talk*, and *You May Well Ask*) as a time of magical freedom, when brother and sister had the same opportunities, before rigid sex roles divided them. They were also the years when she received the same classical education as her brother. The classical world is thus not only a permanent part of her intellectual apparatus, but also offers access to an exclusively male world she could hardly help associating with a power and cultural authority for which she longed. Elaine Showalter points out that for the middle-class Victorian girl, the moment when her brother left for boarding school was a "painful awakening to her inferior status" (*Literature* 41); for Mitchison the awakening must have been particularly painful, since it meant her own removal from already-tasted pleasures. "What then, would happen after the end of being a boy at the Dragon School?" she asks herself sadly in *All Change Here* (12).

Mitchison's adventures were decidedly different from those of the virile heroes she admired in her childhood reading—which included Zane Grey, Kipling, Wells, Bulwer Lytton, Poe, and Whyte-Melville's *The Gladiators*, among others (*All Change* 35–37). Mitchison married Dick Mitchison, a friend of her brother's, at the opening of World War I, nursed him through a head wound, bore his children, took lovers, became a socialist and feminist, and wrote more than seventy works of fiction, nonfiction, and children's literature (Spender 278). She is most famous, however, for her historical fiction—particularly the two major novels set in and around ancient Greece, *Cloud Cuckoo Land* (1925) and *The Corn King and the Spring Queen* (1931). Both these novels recapitulate earlier versions of Greek history: *Cloud Cuckoo Land*, set during the Peloponnesian War, relies on Xenophon and Alfred Zimmern, among others, while *The Corn King and the Spring Queen* draws heavily from Plutarch and Frazer. Both novels allow Mitchison entry into a predominantly male world and seem aligned with the movement of plot toward its inevitably male-controlled conclusion. But the tension between imagining herself male and feeling herself female is also very much in evidence. If androcentric history invites Mitchison to see her male-dominated plots as simply the way it was—as neutral, ungendered stories about the human past—her body's history would remind her that her own access to the ancient past had ended with menarche.

Existing at once within and outside of her own culture, Mitchison seems intensely aware of the way in which culture serves ideology. "We can no more stand alone in time than in society," Mitchison writes in *The Moral Basis of Politics,* pointing out the extent to which we are conditioned by our historical moment (11). The production of "art, science, and political and moral thought" by a cultural elite aids in the preservation of the social status quo. One's own culture, she suggests, severely limits one's vision (89). Awareness of oneself as the product of these constraints is thus an essential aspect of self-knowledge and a prerequisite for social change. Writing, for Mitchison, is always an "attempt to clear my own mind" (vii); her historical fiction especially serves to work through, in a Freudian sense, the contradictory aspects of her own relation to history and in the process expose the repression of female experience by historical discourse.

Published in 1925, *Cloud Cuckoo Land* exemplifies the problems faced by the feminist historical novelist. Interested in the impact of the Peloponnesian War on an ordinary person, Mitchison tells her story mainly through Alxenor, a young man from the Greek island of Poieessa. Alxenor serves her purpose well: fleeing Poieessa, he takes us to Athens just as that city falls definitively to Sparta, then to Sparta, then, as the book closes, he is moving east, to join Cyrus's army in Persia. Through his experiences, the reader learns of the major political and military events of the time. Alxenor defines himself as "ordinary"; in a world of ideological conflict, he has no strong opinions and wants mainly to survive and to protect the young wife, Moiro, he takes from Poieessa and the son born to them in Athens. His best friend, Moiro's brother Chromon, is a pro-Athenian democrat; his older brother Eupaides is a pro-Spartan oligarch. Alxenor's basic sympathies seem democratic, but his drive to survive leads him, after his flight to Athens, into military service for Sparta, where he nearly leaves his son to be educated. He is able to see what each side has to offer, and finally leaves his son in Poeeissa to be brought up by his two uncles, sharing time equally between the oligarchic Eupaides and democratic Chromon. "I want to be just, I want to see both sides of things!" he tells Chromon (318).

But what of women? Looking at their roles in the novel, I see clearly why, in her "inside stories," Mitchison never saw herself as a Greek woman, and why she uses a young man rather than woman as her central character. Given the roles of women in Greek society, she would be risking implausibility were she to introduce into a woman's thoughts the political issues, the broad experiences, the wide range of social contacts through which we absorb the time and place: through which "historical probability" is established.

In *Cloud Cuckoo Land* the women lead shadowy lives of suffering, increasingly marginalized during the course of the novel. At the novel's start, Alxenor is passionately in love with fourteen-year-old Moiro, and in fact his main reason for fleeing Poieessa is to save and protect her. As the novel progresses, however, Moiro's importance fades. Young, inexperienced, appealing but hopelessly passive and stereotypically "feminine," she is not allowed to grow, change, or learn. Alxenor, his life full of events, grows alienated from her, as does the reader.

Moiro's fate is to suffer and die. She becomes pregnant immediately, and suffers so giving birth to her two children that she fears further sex. Her second child, a girl, is exposed at her husband's orders (the socially acceptable method of disposing of unwanted female infants being to leave them outside in earthenware vases until they were either adopted or, more likely, died). She and Alxenor grow apart; he's away on military service for long periods of time, in any case. She then falls passionately, self-abasingly in love with the Spartan who had several years before killed her father. She dies when her maid attempts to abort the fetus conceived with the Spartan. Moiro is defined by and destroyed by her gender, which dictated, from the moment she was born, that she was more likely than a boy to be exposed, and, once allowed to live, that she be kept inside, isolated from public life, and married young. Throughout her life she would be restricted to the women's quarters, the innermost section of Greek houses that becomes powerfully claustrophobic in *Cloud Cuckoo Land*.

Mitchison offers little in her novel that deviates from standard versions of the Peloponnesian War. Other than the starkness (with its hint of suppressed authorial rage) with which the women's lives are portrayed, there is little resistance evident. Moiro's trivial interests and her groveling masochism before her Spartan lover, in fact, reinforce traditional notions of femininity and female sexuality. There are, however, little knots of resistance—spaces in the text where there is room for Mitchison to work through her relation as a woman to the version of history she reinscribes.

One such space is provided by brother-sister relationships, which play a prominent role in many of Mitchison's novels. Brother and sister often resemble each other, but contrasting sex roles dictate contrasting fates. Moiro closely resembles her brother Chromon, but while Moiro leads her limited life then dies, Chromon lives on at novel's end. The Athenian Nikodike provides another such brother-sister contrast. She impresses her younger brother Hagnon with her intelligence and curiosity, but when she attempts to join him in a revolt against the Athenian oligarchs, he sympathizes laughingly with her husband, who beats her. The women respond with shame and self-abasement. Moiro grovels before her Spartan lover Leon, loving him the more for his brutality; Nikodike cries with her mother over the "utter baseness of being a woman—two women together clinging on to one another, oh shamed again and always!" (229). Her mother's response to the beating she received from her husband is even more disturbing: "At least it does mean he wants you" (229).

The women's unlived lives haunt their brothers, who respond by repressing the memories they share and moving on. Hagnon, on his way to join Cyrus with his friend Alxenor, imagines his sister "shut up there in her house, sitting disconsolate with her hands in her lap, and her heart closed against him for ever" but rejects the image as "nonsense" (237). Gradually he attempts to erase her from his consciousness: "after one is grownup, one does not talk to women, not even one's sister—what good would it be?" (345). Self-rejecting, silenced by the plot itself—for at novel's end, we are in the wholly male group of Greek soldiers setting off to serve Cyrus—Moiro and Nikodike lead quite different lives from the brothers they resembled at novel's start. The brother-sister relationship thus exposes the brutally different rules to which men and women are subject.

Cloud Cuckoo Land's title is part of this process of exposure. In Aristophanes' *The Birds*, "Cloud Cuckoo Land" is the land between earth and heaven which Pisthetaerus persuades the birds—led by the hoopoe Tereus—to establish. Strategically placed between the burnt offerings of men and the gods in heaven, Cloud Cuckoo Land blocks the delicious smoke from rising and so starves the gods into submission. In this way Pisthetaerus wins Basileia (at once goddess and Power) as his wife and at play's end is to rule from Zeus's palace.

Pisthetaerus and his friend Euelpides and the birds' leader Tereus thus triumph over the gods. Not mentioned within the play is Tereus's past: the story of how he became a hoopoe. Tereus, of course, raped his sister-in-law, then cut out her tongue so she couldn't tell anyone. She wove the story into a tapestry, however, which her sister Procne deciphered. Procne avenged her sister by killing and cooking her own son and serving him to Tereus, his father. All were then transformed into birds. In *The Birds*, however, Procne is just a stunningly beautiful nightingale asked to sing by her husband Tereus and lusted after by Pisthetaerus and Euelpides. Female suffering is simply not relevant.

Cloud Cuckoo Land's role as a reminder of women's powerlessness becomes clear in Mitchison's 1935 nonhistorical novel *We Have Been Warned*.[1] Near the end of this novel, the protagonist, Phoebe Bathurst, has a climactic vision in which hallucinated seals drive home to her her insignificance as a woman:

> Women, said the seals, can't catch Basileia; she needs a man to marry
> her. No women in Cloud Cuckoo Borough, only shadows, only wives,
> only the shadow-nightingale for King Hoopoe! . . . Oh no; oh no,
> Phoebe Bathurst, said the coughing jumping seals, you will never get to
> Cloud Cuckoo Borough. (165)

Ironically, the novel *Cloud Cuckoo Land* depicts precisely those horrors
of war from which Aristophanes was providing an escape in his play
(which was written and performed during the Peloponnesian War). But
the irony is doubled when gender enters, for that is when we see that
for women, the dream of an alternative reality is already tainted by the
repression of female experience.

Through her depiction of siblings and her choice of title, Mitchison
thus manages to insert some anger into her faithfully "realistic" treatment
of the Peloppenesian War, turning it into a palimpsest from which the
overwritten experience of women threatens constantly to emerge. It is
through her depiction of Sparta, however, that Mitchison most fully
explores the relation of women to history.

Sparta was admired by eighteenth-century Britons for its order; but its
oligarchy, its helots, its austerity, and anti-individualism appealed to few
in the nineteenth century (Rawson 356). Only occasional British socialists
such as Godwin, who favored the property redistribution of Lycurgus,
saw Sparta differently (Rawson 354). Alfred Zimmern, one of Mitchison's
sources for *Cloud Cuckoo Land*, is typically nineteenth century when he
contrasts the "skill and energy" of Athens with the "dull, dogged,
unthinking courage and discipline of Sparta" (424). Mitchison, however,
was more ambivalent; her attitude toward Sparta is entangled with her
attitude toward socialism. Elizabeth Rawson points out that Mitchison's
treatment of Sparta reflects the discomfort of socialist antitotalitarians
(365), who admired the communality of Spartan life while distrusting
its oligarchic political organization. Thus, in one work, Mitchison admiringly compares the Soviet Union's lack of materialism with Sparta's
(*Moral* 70), while in another, she associates Sparta with the Bloods, aristocratic, brutally anti-intellectual athletes (*All Change* 70). In *Cloud
Cuckoo Land*, written before Mitchison's deepest involvement in socialism, she depicts Sparta as appealingly egalitarian, but ultimately heart-
less—an ambivalent depiction complicated by Mitchison's feminism as
well as her antitotalitarianism.[2]

For Mitchison, the crux of women's suffering was the division
between private and public life. The Greek tradition of "women's quarters," set in the innermost section of the house, epitomized for her the
restriction of women to private roles. She followed Engels in believing
that the oppression of women was intimately associated with private property and capitalism, and that when work and property became communal,

women would gain equality with men. Engels's *The Origin of the Family, Private Property, and the State* is an appealing text for a socialist feminist, for he insists on the temporary nature of female submission to male control. Accepting Bachofen's notion that women had dominated the most primitive societies, ruling a "communistic household" based on matrilinear descent, Engels argues that "The lady of civilization, surrounded by false homage and estranged from all real work, has an infinitely lower social position than the hard-working woman of barbarism" (80). The accumulation of wealth led to the privatization of property, which in turn led to the need to regulate inheritance. The exclusion of women from the workforce and the rigid control of their reproductive powers are thus part of the "victory of private property over primitive natural communal property" (95). The first step toward liberating women, according to Engels, is to "bring the whole female sex back into public industry" (105).

The issue is relevant to the Peloponnesian War, for if a communal state treats women better than one with private ownership, Sparta would logically treat women better than Athens. And in fact Engels writes of Sparta that there women were "much more honoured" (94). Mitchison seems to agree with him in *The Home and a Changing Civilization*, where she argues that any culture that separates public from private life works to women's disadvantage by sequestering them in a "home" which the society as a whole devalues. In Sparta, women as well as men identify with the state, not family—precisely that identification sought fruitlessly by the Athenian Nikodike when she seeks to join the democrats' revolt against the oligarchs. "It's my Athens too," Nikodike asserts, but she is beaten by her husband and ridiculed by the City; clearly it's not her Athens. The Spartans Kleora and Dionassa, on the other hand, are encouraged to put the state's interest before their families. As a result, they have far more physical freedom, more shared interests with their husbands, and little in common with Athenian wives:

> Kleora never seemed to want to talk about the ordinary things of life, details of marriage and children, what to do with one's slaves, dresses and scents, marketing, charms and cures—or at least she did talk about them, but not, somehow, as if she took any interest in the things themselves, but as if they all had to be made to fit into some scheme of life, and were only worth thinking of in as far as they did (242).

But is this equality desirable? Is it even genuine equality? The women of Sparta have gained their freedom at the expense of their difference. Thinking of "things themselves" only as they "fit into some scheme of life," they are living metaphors, absorbing experience into a single, organic plot. Identifying with the state and its history, they are complicit in precisely that "elevation of male difference into universality" described by Schweickart;

they have been, in Fetterley's terms, "immasculated." Moiro's concerns, on the other hand, "slaves, dresses and scents, marketing, charms and cures," the "ordinary things of life," if trivialized by Athenian ideology, at least offer an alternative to the dominant, brutally militaristic culture.

The plot of *Cloud Cuckoo Land* thus places the "ordinary things of life, details of marriage and children," in opposition to absorption in historical plot—the sense one gets, in acting as part of some larger entity, that one is "making history." Alxenor himself is tempted by Sparta's coherence, its offer of shared purpose. Describing the lure of surrender to the state, he thinks, "It beats on one's soul like being under a great wave" (121). But then he turns away to see, with relief, a lizard escaping Hagnon's hand: "It was good to be reminded that there were things like lizards in the world too" (119). The freedom Sparta offers its women, is, *Cloud Cuckoo Land* suggests, illusory, because it is freedom only to sur-render the self to a larger, already androcentric entity: the city-state of Sparta and the story it tells about itself. Alxenor's turn to the lizard is a rejection of that self-surrender, a privileging of the insignificant detail over the meaningful whole, a choice of metonymy over metaphor. In *Cassandra* Christa Wolf urges her readers to reject "necrophilia" (270), by which she means precisely the love of closure, of plot, of history that Sparta represents for Mitchison. Arrayed against it, for Mitchison as for Wolf, is the naming of "the inconspicuous, the previous everyday, the concrete" (270)—whatever testifies to the exclusionary, partial nature of historical plots. In *Cloud Cuckoo Land*, the "previous everyday" is that lizard escaping the hand of the state.

What the lizard is to Alxenor, the details of everyday life are to Moiro and her servant Thrassa. But they are also the product of pre-cisely that separation between private and public that devalorizes women. Follow Engels's suggestion, in other words, and you get freedom for women but also women who identify fully with the state, women who have no separate culture and require no separate history. Follow the Athenian example, on the other hand, and you get women who suffer and die: women as victims. Alxenor's island identity alone allows for oscilla-tion between participation and withdrawal.

In the world of *Cloud Cuckoo Land*, women are so silenced by the extremes of their inclusion (in Sparta) and exclusion (in Athens) that Alxenor's uncertainty must serve as a textual refuge for the feminine, evoking what Margaret Homans calls "the special ambiguity of women's simultaneous participation in and exclusion from a hegemonic group" (205). A major characteristic of women, for Mitchison, is precisely their uncertainty: amid another war, she writes in her diary that women are more sane than men, "less certain of themselves, less arrogant, more able to see two sides to any question" (Sheridan 63). She admits that such flexibility may be the result of their removal from power. But it is clearly a state she values, one she evokes again later in her speculations about a compass with five points rather than four, and "so no complete opposite to anything" (Sheridan 253).

Cloud Cuckoo Land dramatizes fifth-century Greece, the period Eva Keuls calls the "reign of the phallus." Mitchison's 1931 *The Corn King and the Spring Queen* explores a different era and does so far more ambitiously. Juxtaposing a fictional culture derived from Frazer's *The Golden Bough* with a Sparta straight out of Plutarch's *Parallel Lives*, Mitchison undercuts any stable sense the reader might have of what history is while also challenging the way her fellow modernists—particularly D. H. Lawrence—had used Frazer to define sexuality.

The Corn King and the Spring Queen depicts two contemporaneous cultures: Marob and Sparta. Marob is "fictive," though plausibly based on archeological evidence about Scythian life and, most extensively, on Frazer's speculations about the religious life of primitive peoples. Sparta, on the other hand, is "historical"; the major events Mitchison retells all come from Plutarch. Mitchison is following Frazer's lead in combining classicism and anthropology, but her aim is not to synthesize, as Frazer does, but to use anthropology to open out history and historical fiction. In the process she also questions the use to which her fellow novelist and sex reformer Lawrence has put Frazer. The result is a two-stage process: Frazer displaces Plutarch; then Frazer undoes himself. For *The Corn King and the Spring Queen* is another palimpsest: an apparent reproduction in faithful detail of the kind of tribal ritual Frazer describes, but a reproduction that also highlights all the implications Frazer played down. In borrowing from Frazer, Mitchison was in some ways acceding to a male-authored version of a male-dominated past, but she was also hinting at an alternative Frazer, which was also an alternative Lawrence: allowing to surface the story both Frazer and Lawrence disavowed, a story of female power, autonomy, and fecundity.

In *The Corn King and the Spring Queen*, Erif Der, the Scythian Spring Queen, lives in Marob, on the shores of the Black Sea. She and her husband Tarrik, chief and Corn King, lead the rites that ensure successful plowing and harvesting of the corn. They represent the harmonious interrelationship of tribe, nature, and "godhead": "I am not separate from the grain and the cattle and the sap creeping up the green veins of the plants," Tarrik declares, explaining his power over the crops. "Whatever I do goes out like a wave to the rest of my place" (458).

Tarrik and Erif Der, however, in part through their contact with Sphaeros, a Stoic philosopher shipwrecked in Marob, become uncomfortable with their roles and decide (at different times) to seek wisdom in Sparta. There they become involved in the novel's other plot: the rise to

power of King Kleomenes. Erif Der becomes friends with Philylla, a
young Spartan girl who supports Kleomenes' plans for social reform,
and Erif Der's artist brother Berris falls in love with her. Philylla, however,
marries Kleomenes' lover Panteus and flees to him in Egypt after the
defeat of Kleomenes. In Egypt, Kleomenes leads a failed revolt; he and his
followers, including Philylla, are executed.

While the Spartans fail to achieve their goals, the Scythians succeed in
theirs. Through their involvement in Spartan history, Erif Der and Tarrik
attain a new awareness of the mythic patterns that give meaning to their
lives and are successfully reintegrated into their society. Ironically, these
patterns also turn out to be the only vehicle through which the Spartan
experience will endure; Kleomenes' story, we're told in the book's final
pages, is known to the defeated and enslaved Spartans only through
Berris's paintings, which emphasize the analogies between Tarrik's sacrificial role, Kleomenes', and Christ's (who will not be born, of course,
for several hundred years). History is thus superseded by myth, for it
endures only as the repeated cycle of "kings who die for their people."[3]

History is represented for Mitchison by Plutarch, by Sparta, and by
Sphaeros. Sparta is history because it defines itself through its relation to
the past: Kleomenes' goal is to bring back the values of Lycurgus. Integral
to these values is Stoicism, the submission of the body to the mind.
Sphaeros teaches how man's will may be "made to go the way of nature,
of things-as-they-are, not crossing the purpose of life" (*Corn* 103). This
acquiescence of the mind to "nature" (defined as "what happens," nature
as law, not liberation) suggests that stoicism means the submission of
body to plot. Body submits to mind which submits to "the purpose of
life": each part vanishes into the larger whole. Having witnessed the failure of their uprising, Kleomenes and his followers kill themselves. The
Spartans seem to pride themselves on leaving no loose ends, on granting
closure to their own plots.

This is most striking in Plutarch's descripion of the Spartan Queen
Aegistrata and of Panteus's wife—whom Plutarch, unlike Mitchison,
leaves unnamed. Aegistrata, mother of Agis (Kleomenes' predecessor and
role model), carefully lays out her mother's and son's bodies before presenting her own neck to the noose (Plutarch *Lives* 47–49). Panteus's wife
(Mitchison's Philylla), similarly lays out her companions after their execution, then arranges her own body so carefully that her executioners
are spared the awkwardness of covering her. She "maintained to the
end," according to Plutarch, "that watchful care of her body which she
had set over it in life" (139).

Philylla's austerity and decorum, like the suicides of Kleomenes and
his followers, indicate her acquiescence to history. Mitchison, however,
subverts that acquiescence by enclosing Plutarch's Sparta within the story

of Marob. If the Spartans, proud and self-reflective, epitomize historical consciousness, the Scythians epitomize historical unconsciousness. Living only in the present, they reenact yearly the death, fertilization, and rebirth of their cornfields, their gods, and their chief, who are one. Their life is undocumented, innocent even of stories about heroes or gods. Yet while, in actuality, we generally hear more about the documented than the undocumented past, Mitchison insists that Marob take precedence over Sparta: a Spartan slave tells the Scythians at the end of the novel, "We didn't matter enough to be told about" (717), their story known even to themselves only through the barbarian Berris Der's paintings. Paradoxically, then, the nondocumented, ritualistic world of Marob gets the last word in Mitchison's novel; Frazer, in other words, displaces Plutarch.

But is this a triumph for women?

History in Mitchison's work is associated with the suppression of the female body—through Athenian exclusion or Spartan decorum—and its subjugating of all behavior to an overarching plot. But while ritual provides a release from Philylla's repressive decorum, it is nonetheless problematic for the feminist. For Frazer's rituals—especially as interpreted by Mitchison's fellow modernists—were saturated with a phallus-worship unlikely to liberate female participants.[4] In reading Frazer, then, Mitchison had to deal with Frazer's phallicism; and even more particularly, she had to deal with D. H. Lawrence's ferociously phallic Frazer. Thus, *The Corn King and the Spring Queen* is in part an effort to supplant Lawrence's Frazer with Mitchison's own.

Mitchison's effort was particularly urgent because human sexuality was a vital topic during the 1920s. Women's right to sexual pleasure had at last been recognized, as is suggested by the proliferation of marriage manuals during these years. But this recognition coincided with an attack on female autonomy. In the light of Freud, careers were for neurotic spinsters—who were derided by Mitchison's own sister-in-law, Charlotte Haldane, in her 1927 *Motherhood and its Enemies*.[5] Psychoanalytic sexologists like William Stekel—a supporter, along with Mitchison and Lawrence, of the World League for Sex Reform—equated female orgasm with submission: "Orgasm means to give in, to be the weaker one, to acknowledge the man as master" (qtd. in Jeffreys 170).

Mitchison, however, wanted to have it both ways: female sexuality and female autonomy. Given her stance, Lawrence was an admired oracle who had, it became increasingly clear, gotten things slightly wrong. In 1930, when Mitchison published *Comments on Birth Control*, she made her respectfully adversarial relation to Lawrence explicit: "This was written," she concludes, "before the death of D. H. Lawrence, one of the great men and liberators of our time. My criticism of his ideas hoped for an answer" (32). The years leading up to the publication of *The Corn*

King and the Spring Queen were thus characterized by a public dialogue about female sexuality—a dialogue in which both Mitchison and Lawrence were major participants, and for which Frazer often provided the vocabulary and imaginative context.[6]

Lawrence finds, in Frazer's link between human and natural worlds, an appealing, alternative consciousness: "There is another seat of consciousness than the brain and the nerve system," Lawrence wrote in a 1915 letter to Bertrand Russell about *The Golden Bough.* "There is a blood-consciousness which exists in us independently of the ordinary mental consciousness" (*Collected Letters* 1: 393). For Lawrence, Frazer supplies a thesaurus of terms with which to evoke this blood-consciouness, this submersion of consciousness in sexuality.

Where was a feminist novelist to place herself in relation to these concepts? What Mitchison liked about Frazer was what she liked about Lawrence: his evocation of a world where boundaries between person and world were not recognized, where ritual and sexuality played vital, social roles. What worried her about Frazer was what worried her about Lawrence: an implicit linking of a "blood-consciousness" she admired to a phallus-worship she feared.

If the "primitive" is characterized by "phallic power," it provides women little more power than the invisibility generally offered by "historical" cultures. The problem is posed early in the novel, when Tarrik, unable to contain his sexual passion, rapes Erif Der, his bride-to-be. Not only can she not prevent him, the rape is sanctioned by the community. Mitchison seems to see the sexuality released by ritual through a Lawrentian/Freudian lens; sexuality is inseparable from the exercise by men of power over women.[7] Erif Der herself, for a time in her relationship with Tarrik, finds peace in "giving herself up altogether to him" (227).

Frazer himself was no feminist. While he admitted that the dying gods were linked to goddesses who were often more powerful, and certainly less vulnerable, than their male sons or lovers, he is careful to disassociate the Dying God from matriarchy. In the beginning, he admits, "Isis was, what Astarte and Cybele always continued to be, the stronger divinity of the pair" (6:202). But this, he argues, was the result merely of matrilinearity, not at all the same thing as "mother-rule." "Indeed," he continues, "so far is the system from implying any social superiority of women that it probably took its rise from what we should regard as their deepest degradation, to wit, from a state of society in which the relations of the sexes were so loose and vague that children could not be fathered on any particular man" (6:209). He concludes that, as a rule, "human society has been governed in the past and, human nature remaining the same, is likely to be governed in the future, mainly by masculine force and masculine intelligence" (6:210).[8] Frazer invokes the horror that his culture must feel at women's sexual promiscuity to mask his own obvious discomfort with female power—whether human or divine.

Lawrence, similarly uncomfortable with female autonomy, in retelling the story of Isis in *The Escaped Cock*, makes male sexuality central. Lawrence's Isis is "not Isis Mother of Horus," but "Isis Bereaved, Isis in Search," seeking the scattered parts of her lover, finding all but his genitals "that alone could bring him really back to her, and touch her womb" (38).[9] Lawrence depicts the priestess of Isis as a woman similarly in search, who finds in Jesus her Osiris and conceives by him. As Gerald Lacy points out, the original Isis conceives her son Horus supernaturally, by the dead not-yet-reassembled Osiris (Lawrence, *Escaped* 125). Lawrence's version, in contrast, by conflating resurrection, erection, and conception, gives Osiris and his phallus a crucial role. "I am risen!" Lawrence has Jesus say, as he "felt the blaze of his manhood and his power rise up in his loins, magnificent" (57).

Reading Frazer and Lawrence would have left Mitchison wondering: Is the story of Isis and Osiris about Isis's power, or about her need for her lover's missing phallus? Does the Dionysian "savagery" innate, according to Frazer, "in most men" (7:3), enhance or limit the power of women? Can the sexuality evoked by these Dying Gods be separated from the phallus?

In *The Corn King and the Spring Queen* Mitchison performs this separation: she redefines sexuality as a pervasive sensory responsiveness which is not only separable from the phallus but often inimical to it. She does this by borrowing from Frazer extensively but selectively. Tarrik, as Chief and Corn King, is a patriarchal figure, but the world of ritual as portrayed in Marob, by sanctioning magic, ornate costumes, and an intensely sensual awareness of sexuality and procreation, does grant women space in which to escape male hegemony. The story of Osiris as dying god/king is central, but hovering palimpsestically behind it is the story of Demeter's rescue of Persephone.

Early in the novel, when Tarrik abducts and rapes Erif Der, he echoes the rape of Persephone by Pluto, a rape enacted, according to Frazer, as part of the Eleusynian Myteries (7:66). For Demeter is yet another incarnation of the Isis-Osiris story, this time as mother-seeking-daughter rather than wife-seeking-husband. Frazer touches only briefly on the parallel between Demeter/Persephone and Isis/Osiris (6:117); Mitchison uses the parallel to transform a story of male rivalry and self-sacrifice into one of female bonding. If Tarrik must recognize his identity as Osiris, Erif Der must go through the more complex process of first finding her mother (as Persephone to her mother's Demeter), then recognizing her mother as Isis, and then recognizing Isis as herself. Only then—after she has been purified and empowered by her mother—can she regain her identity as Spring Queen to Tarrik's Corn King.

In Mitchison's version of Frazer, the world of ritual not only grants women a vital public role, but also, by sanctioning magic and ornate costumes and more open sexuality, grants them a way of expressing their difference, gives them a way of expressing what Mitchison calls the "she" side of things. Even when she is raped by Tarrik, and even though the rape is sanctioned by her society, Erif Der retains the means to fight back and heal herself. Instrumental in the healing process are clothes, magic, and other women. After the rape, Erif's mother and nurse bathe and dress her and put ribbons in her hair of "rainbowed shining silk" (62). She wears a white dress "woven with coloured, fantastic lions" (63) and walks with a cane "carved into narrow leaf shapes, and a fruit under her hand" (62). She also gets back her magic star—grabbed by Tarrik during the rape—which seems "some part that was virgin in spite of him [Tarrik]" (152). Clothes and star suggest the power that Erif and her fellow magician-women have to step outside time, to resist absorption into the plots men set for them. Erif's character is defined by her resistance to these plots—by her ability (as Sphaeros complains) to make life run counter to its "natural" order. In one of the novel's most haunting moments, Erif Der, having broken a thread she is spinning, turns the two pieces to little worms which bleed, then rejoin, in her hand (215). Magic—practiced in the novel only by women—is a weapon against time, against history. "I hate the time when I shall be dead" Erif Der says, explaining her dislike of all things beyond human power (76). Erif Der's necrophobia is yet another anticipation of Christa Wolf's rejection of "necrophilia." Erif Der hates death because she refuses to be absorbed into a system of historical meaning that recognizes female experience only as submission and rape.

Closely allied with magic are clothes as a weapon against male power. Clothes are important to all the Scythians because of their role in seasonal rituals, but they also serve to destabilize the line between body and not-body, to undercut the Greek idealization of the naked male body as cultural norm. Thus a visiting Greek ridicules the Scythians' "ridiculous clothes that muffled them up, kept them pink and modest like women" (51); for him, the Greek habit of naked exercise is responsible for the greatness of Greek culture. For Erif Der in particular, however, clothes are powerful, threatening Scythian male power as well as Greek. She punishes her murderous mother-in-law by throwing her clothes in the water;[10] she teases her brother by making him strip off his own clothes. And she finds in her own a way to escape the narrow role set for her by others. Most striking about Erif Der's clothes is their unspecifiability. The rainbow ribbons she wears in her hair after her rape are too multicolored to be caught by language. Similarly, on the night Tarrik goes to her father to ask for her in marriage, she wears a dress made of "a very delicate, silvery linen web, crossed again and again with dozens of colours, yellows and blues and greens, and sometimes a metal thread, copper or gold, that held the blink of the candles" (47).

Linked with clothes and magic as alternatives to male power is a female sexuality portrayed as diffuse and multifaceted, implicit in the pleasures of friendship and maternity as much as in heterosexual sex. Erif Der's name itself—Red Fire spelled backwards—suggests a female counterpart to the phallic "sparkiness" Lawrence associates with male sexuality. Increasingly as the years passed, Mitchison saw Lawrence's view of sexuality as inimical to her own. Writing in 1934 of Lawrence and others like him who praise sex but oppose birth control, Mitchison writes, "Above all, they are afraid of women getting power" (*Home* 131), particularly sexual power: "It must be fairly obvious that Lawrence could never stand the idea of a woman enjoying herself sexually" (*Home* 141). Erif Der, however, pleasurably participates in the sexual ritual marking the Spartan helots' harvest. Asked by her brother how many partners she had, she says she doesn't know, "But it was fun!" Mitchison even supplies the revelers with a postcoital birth control pond, in which Erif Der is advised to immerse herself (372).

In her 1930 *Comments on Birth Control*, moreover, Mitchison insists on the need for variety in sexual expression. "What happened," she asks, "to Lady Chatterley and Mellors three years, or, still more, ten years after the end of the book?" The desire for sexual intercourse, she insists, is not constant, and is easily deadened by habit. Nor do couples always want to use contraception. The answer? "There are many kinds of mutual caresses and pleasures," she suggests.

Mitchison did not expand on this brief hint of nonphallic pleasures until *The Corn King and the Spring Queen*; historical fiction, like anthropology, allows unusual freedom in the portrayal of sexual behavior. In *The Corn King and the Spring Queen*, relationships between women, and between mother and child are charged with a powerful sexuality. Even the Spartan Philylla responds sexually to Queen Agiatis and Erif Der (611), and to her wet nurse, who touches the "soft, very sensitive growing points of her body":

> Philylla shut her eyes and began breathing in the queer, shiveringly alive country smells, of green things pushing and growing, and tight, rustling corn sacks and meal sacks, of old wood and hot dung and places where honey had dripped. . . . Waves of feelng poured over her as she waited, shut-eyed, centering, centering. (155)

With a similar emphasis on the variety and intensity of women's sexual responses, Mitchison describes Erif Der's sensations as she anticipates nursing her newborn baby. The tips of her breasts "turned upward and outward, and the centre of the nipple itself grew velvet soft and tender and prepared for the softness of the baby." Mitchison goes on to describe the process in minute, sensual detail:

> For a moment she teased him, withholding herself; then, as she felt the milk in her springing towards him, she let him settle, thrusting her breast deep into the hollow of his mouth, that seized on her with a rhythmic throb of acceptance, deep sucking of lips and tongue and cheeks. (304)

This is a world of women apart from men, a world at least as sensorily intense as the heterosexual world, and offering equal access to nature and blood-consciousness.[11] This is what Mitchison calls the "she side of things . . . a great fish leaping out of dark water" (667). The image suggests that such interactions between women take place at the deepest level of consciouness, in "dark water," and are charged with an energy all their own.

This "she side" is a shared reveling in fecundity and maternity, as represented by an Isis who is not in search of anything, but is in possession of her own child, who is at once Horus and Persephone. At novel's end, Erif Der finds her mother, who has died, in the form of a bird on Lake Mareotis. Demeter and Persephone are reunited then, conflated, as Erif Der accepts herself as a human avatar of Isis, "the women's goddess, the pure mother" (361).

The Golden Bough, by focusing on the role of male scapegoats, turns fertility into a story of phallic prowess, death, and rebirth. *The Corn King and the Spring Queen*, on the other hand, portrays fertility as a matter of womb and breast. Isis is herself a kind of palimpsest, "one of the tamed and hurt," Mitchison calls her, "one of the group of whisperers, of women-together" (361). Written over by Frazer's story and Lawrence's, she bears traces still of her past power.

Mitchison's relation to Frazer is perhaps best conveyed by the moment in the novel when Erif Der, in the guise of Spring Queen, is to mock-kill the Old Corn, played by her father. Angry with him because he killed her first-born baby, instead of miming the murder she actually kills him. In doing so, she does no obvious violence to the ritual; Tarrik, as the New Corn, rises up again. But her action exposes the latent threat to men contained in the story of *The Golden Bough*, a threat both Frazer and Lawrence recognized and suppressed by privileging phallic struggle. Mitchison, like Erif Der, is faithful to her anthropological source, even as she underlines the female power he suppressed.

Notes

1. In 1934, after a visit to the Soviet Union, Mitchison made an elaborate comparison between the Communist U.S.S.R. and Aristophanes' "Cloud Cuckoo

Borough"; here the comparison seems to be intended in a wholly positive way ("New Cloud" 36–38).

2. Jill Benton, in her biography of Mitchison, writes that she was not politically active until 1926, and only read Marx's *Capital* when she was writing *The Corn King and the Spring Queen* (63–64).

3. Francis Hart writes similarly of *The Corn King and the Spring Queen* that in it, "finally history is less real than myth." He sees the novel's fascination with myth as typically Scottish; among traits it shares with the Scottish novel in general: first, it makes a marginalized, conquered place its locus; second, history, a "record of betrayal and defeat," is superseded by myth; and third, a god-man provides the means of cultural survival (188).

4. Jill Benton writes that Mitchison opposed what she calls Frazerian "phallic worship" (64).

5. Susan Squier, in *Babies in Bottles*, reads Haldane's work quite differently, as introducing, amid the devaluation of the feminine shared by modernist literature and science, the "birthing woman as *embodied subject*" (131).

6. Mitchison actually traveled to Taos, New Mexico, and stayed with Mabel Dodge Luhan there, as had Lawrence some time before (*You May* 200). In *You May Well Ask*, she writes that all her later books sound like Lawrence (163).

7. Margaret Jackson attributes this equation between sexuality and male power to the work of Havelock Ellis; she convincingly argues that the "sexual revolution" instigated by his work and culminating in the 1960s in fact reproduces "both the values and the practices of male supremacy" (83).

8. One 1913 writer in the *New Freewoman*, while generously supposing that Frazer was not "actuated consciously by masculine prejudice," complains of his failure to recognize the matriarchal societies predating those he describes (F.R.A.I. 69).

9. Judith Ruderman makes this point as well (165).

10. Frazer writes that primitive magic posits a sympathetic tie between a man and his clothes, which allows Burmese magicians, for example, to drive someone mad by throwing his clothes, along with appropriate charms, into the water (1:205, 62–63). This is precisely how Erif Der drives her mother-in-law crazy.

11. In *The Delicate Fire*, Mitchison again portrays the magical sensuality of an all-female world when she depicts Sappho's circle in Mytilene. Describing the attraction between two girls, Kleis and Stryme, she writes, "It seemed as though Kleis had some magic in her that sucked up the younger girl, off the cushions, on to her feet, and a step or two forward till they touched hands, and urgently, very shyly, kissed" (29).

CHAPTER 4

Mana and Narrative in Mary Butts's Greece

Like Mitchison, Mary Butts was born into a distinguished family. Her great-grandfather was a Swedenborgian and a friend of William Blake, and her father was a well-educated gentleman who valued culture, caring for the family's collection of Blake memorabilia. Butts identified fiercely with her father, feeling that she alone understood his relationship to the past and to the arts.[1] "I am his fulfilment," Mary Butts wrote of her father, "fulfilment of the name he gave me and the race that bred me" (*Crystal* 39). Paternal inheritance is an obsessive theme in Mary Butts's work and one reason Butts chose to write historical fiction, for the very act of writing historical fiction is a way of asserting inheritance over the past. As a woman, however, Butts found the taking up of her inheritance problematic. The classical education, the class identity as gentleman, the money and experience that made Mr. Butts an elegant amateur of culture were all unavailable to his daughter—or at least, unavailable without struggle.

In many ways profoundly conservative, Butts could nonetheless not inherit as she wished to without challenging traditional female roles and values. In her memoir, *The Crystal Cabinet*, written during her last years and published posthumously in 1937, she finds herself mired in contradictions as a result. She did not want to be a boy, she writes, "but I wanted to learn the things boys learned. In the way boys learned. Properly" (68). But sent to a boarding school based on just this premise, where "the girls were taught Latin and Greek like boys" (*Crystal* 126), she felt it *too* like a boys' school, with its emphasis on sports, competition, what Martha Vicinus calls the "corporate life" of the school (183). Finding herself an outcast for her love of poetry, she is led to a "dislike and distrust of my own sex" and envies the greater freedom and individuality of her brother's Eton (*Crystal* 198).

Butts's situation epitomizes the identity problem facing young women of her generation. Rejecting the traditional role her very conventional mother played, she is offered only limited alternatives by her culture. St. Leonard's, Butts's school, was one of the "reformed" girls' boarding schools established in the last quarter of the nineteenth century. Established by impressive, autocratic women intent on providing girls with a good education, these schools were nonetheless quite conservative in the roles they suggested their graduates might fill: the unmarried career-woman investing all of her sexual and emotional energy into her vocation; or the educated wife of an even more educated husband (Dyhouse 78). St. Leonard's in particular discouraged emotionalism and the devoted attachments that often formed between mistress and student, favoring "physical fitness and public duties rather than gentility and academic work" (Vicinus 169). Intent on not challenging traditional notions of "feminine respectability" (Vicinus 134), the school offered the learning Butts sought but in an atmosphere of aesthetic and emotional austerity she found traumatic. Careers for women were acceptable to the extent that they fit the traditional female role of "service"; pure ambition was unacceptable (Dyhouse 73–74). For Butts, starved for beauty and achievement, St. Leonard's had so little to offer that she entitles the chapter about her school experiences "Regiment of Women," borrowing the name of Clemence Dane's homophobic novel about lesbianism in girls' schools. The name she opposes to it, as a positive contrast, is Cheiron, whose teaching reflected an "antique balance of deep love with sound discipline" (Butts, *Crystal* 200). But Cheiron was primarily a "bringer-up of heroes," not women; and the fear of stimulating girls' excessive emotionalism forbade—at St. Leonard's at least—his use as role model.[2] The grace and ease of her father's education and genteel intellectualism were simply unavailable to young women of her generation.

Like others of her generation, Butts blamed her mother, for it was the mother who passed on the joyless values of "service and self-sacrifice" (Dyhouse 26) and perpetuated her daughter's sexual ignorance at the same time that she placed a high value (without naming it as such) on sexual attractiveness. William Plomer writes that Butts "hated her mother" (269), and indeed this hatred surfaces in all her work. In her transparently autobiographical novel *Ashe of Rings*, Butts speculates that her mother began an affair with her stepfather-to-be before her father's death. In *The Crystal Cabinet* she mentions neighborhood gossip that her younger brother was not, in fact, her father's son (174). In the *The Death of Felicity Taverner*, another novel, there is again a younger brother not his father's son. Worst of all, in *The Crystal Cabinet* (and thus presumably in actuality), after her husband's death, Mary's mother sells the family's Blake paintings and burns her husband's valuable collection of supposedly pornographic books. Shortly after, Mary is sent to boarding school and her mother remarries (175). Finally, her mother accuses her of inviting sexual attention from her stepfather and younger brother Tony.[3] The alienation of daughter from mother is complete.

In her place, there is only a much-loved but dead father and the cultural inheritance she associates with him, but to which she has only partial access. She has, however, a sudden insight into how she can at once fulfill her father and herself: how she can mend the break between herself and her past. One teacher at St. Leonard's has given her a key. About to leave school, Butts remembers what she has learned from this teacher:

> The first Isaiah and the Second, Edmund Spenser; Amos the Shepherd, John Milton and King Arthur and his and Aristotle's magnificence. Colin Clout (who might be me), Ezekiel, the great noble in Babylon. The Diamond Shield and Queen Elizabeth, who was England, who was Britomartis. And Britomart came from Crete, and from Crete you stepped like the legs of a compass to Egypt, and from Egypt round again to Cambyses, between Darius and Cyrus the Persians.
>
> All parts of a pattern, the web on which the world is strung. My seeings were part of it, and you had to go on filling in the pattern as she had taught us to do. (233)

This vision of the connectedness of all of history and her own role as filler in of the pattern underlies her sense of her role as novelist, most specifically as historical novelist.

In love with continuity, Butts in her personal life was doomed to break with the past: to live an experimental life of partying, drug use, and multiple relationships undreamed of by her mother. She was doomed also to lose her inheritance: her father's belongings burned or sold after his death, the land around Poole subdivided into suburbia. In response, Butts created a life for herself that was an odd mixture of traditional and revolutionary values. She loved the land, old country houses, and old families. Memoirs of the time recall her as pale, red-haired, forceful, and odd. She used drugs and believed in magic. She partied intensely and fell in love with self-destructive men. She tended to mother young homosexual aristocrats in flight from the Russian Revolution. "A rather handsome, angular lady, breathing erudition, with a gentle family background," according to Elsa Lanchester (65), Butts was also, in Lanchester's words, "strong meat" (70), a cocaine user who introduced her to Krafft-Ebing "for laughs" (65).

Married to John Rodker in 1918, Butts left him for Cecil Maitland in 1920 (Wagstaff in Butts, *Crystal* 278–79). Douglas Goldring writes of Butts at this time: "she was a living embodiment of surrealism, with a flair for everything queer in art and life, a tremendous zest for parties and a child-like delight in all the more exotic forms of sin" (*South* 147–48). She and Maitland spent several months at Aleister Crowley's abbey at Cefalu, on Sicily.[4] In 1930, Butts married Gabriel Aitken, who left her several years later; in 1932, she moved to Cornwall, where she died in 1937.[5]

Butts published her first book, a collection of short stories, in 1923. She also wrote poems and five novels (including two of historical fiction), as well as her memoir.[6] Throughout her work, she attempts to come to terms with her relation to the past, seeking moments of transcendence, of vision, when all of experience, the seen and the unseen, seems to cohere. Her historical fiction is part of her effort to lay claim to her father's inheritance, but also to rewrite the past and find there images of power that transcend gender. Women, according to Simone de Beauvoir, still "dream the dreams of men. Gods made by males are the gods they worship" (132). In her later works—*The Death of Felicity Taverner* (1932), *The Macedonian* (1933), and *Scenes from the Life of Cleopatra* (1935)— she seems to me to have dreamed women's dreams—in ways that force us to rethink the relations among modernism, mythology, and women.

Like Mitchison, Butts was immersed in the classical world by her father and by her childhood reading. In *The Crystal Cabinet*, she quotes big chunks of Macaulay's *Lays of Ancient Rome*, which she recited while walking around the garden "waving an old scimitar" (40). She loved Shelley's "Hellas," in which she found "the beginning and the end and the significance of it all" (114). When she writes of her most intense childhood insights, she uses ancient analogies. "If Troy fell," Butts wrote about herself on the verge of adulthood, "(and our fathers had sold the gates) we would get out, not with them but with our lares and penates on our backs. Save our *sacra*. Save Helen" (261). The past worth preserving is for Butts synonymous with the world of classical scholarship. Latin itself she regards as a link between herself and her father: "what 'came out' of my father was something that carried with it a wholly satisfactory satisfaction. . . . 'Like' the turned words of Latin I sometimes heard on his lips. First intimation of the secret knowledge we shared" (*Crystal* 17). To preserve that secret knowledge she must play the role of Aeneas, who carried his father from Troy on his back. But Butts is Aeneas with a difference. While Aeneas saved his father but lost his wife in the flight from Troy, Butts deserts "our fathers" (who had in any case already deserted her, having "sold the gates") but preserves the sacra, preserves Helen. Butts is concerned with preserving a past traditionally seen as male dominated, a past she associates with her own father, but she construes it with a difference: this past sends us out of Aeneas's teleological narrative of the founding of Rome, into moments of mystical vision. The sacra turn out to be moments of transcendence triggered by magically charged spots—in this case Badbury Rings, where Butts undergoes a kind of cosmic initiation (*Crystal* 265–66). Returning home afterwards, she picks up her *Iliad* and reads about Helen on the walls of Troy.

Butts shares her interest in the ancient world with other modernists, but her exclusion as a woman from an easy accession to that past defines her use of Eliot's "mythic method": the use of classical allusions and patterns to structure depictions of modern life. Like Eliot, Butts was steeped in Frazer's *The Golden Bough*, and all her work reflects its influence. Butts admired Eliot (Barbara Wagstaff 281), but comments, "Mr. Eliot's cold water is by no means the entire answer" (Butts, *Crystal* 264). Butts's mythical method differs from Eliot's, most crucially in the use it makes of Jane Harrison.

For Butts, myth is aligned with women, against men, and it is based on a notion of myth shaped not only by Frazer but more importantly by Jane Harrison. Harrison, in her 1903 *Prolegomena to the Study of Greek Religion*, argues for a pre-Olympian stage of Greek religion, based on chthonic rituals "ignored or suppressed by Homer" (vi). These rituals, addressed to nonanthropomorphic "ghosts, and sprites and bogeys" (163), predated mythic narrative. Harrison describes pre-Olympian religion as prerational, preanalytical, evoking a world at once unified and diffuse. To understand it, she writes, we must give up analysis, and "think back the 'many' we have so sharply and strenuously divided, into the haze of the primitive 'one,'" a haze of "protoplasmic fulness and forcefulness" (164). Published nine years later, *Themis* describes a pre-Olympian world of "fusion . . . [and] non-differentiation," where nature and human beings alike are charged with *mana* (122), a "vague force . . . trembling on the verge of personality" (67), a "world of unseen power lying behind the visible universe" (68). In this notion of a diffuse yet all-pervasive energy, in mana, Butts found both a theme and a narrative method, a way of articulating the correspondence she'd experienced on the Rings "between the seen and the unseen" (266).

Harrison's positive portrayal of mana and ritual were crucial to Mary Butts's writing. For it is with the totemistic haze of "protoplasmic fulness and forcefulness," with mana, with a sense of flow between individual and group, among person, animal, plant, that Butts comes increasingly to align her narrative voice.

Butts evokes the contrast between male and female versions of antiquity as early as 1924, in "Pythian Ode," where she describes the transition from a Pythia- to an Apollo-dominated Delphi, a shift, she says, "from fact to reality" (236). Apollo is a "good policeman with the sun for flash-lamp," gilding the earth, moving history toward Christianity and the "western world." Before his arrival the "divine mind"

> drifted up through a crack in a stone, and out from
> the mouth of a woman.
> The wind that blows and blows crooked.
> There was the Pythia, and under her a three-legged stool,
> a lid on the earth's mystery.
> A stone wreathed in raw wool
> Not a portrait statue of the god. (236)

The shift in control of Delphi from Pythia to Apollo, from female to male, from earth to sky, is chronicled by Jane Harrison in *Themis* (387–94). There also Harrison explores the significance of the *omphalos*, the stone marking the grave of the sacred snake slain (according to myth) by Apollo, a stone, she insists, originally "not commemorative, but magical" (400). "Pythian Ode" suggests to me that Butts had already read *Themis* in 1924 (its first edition was published in 1912) and that she had absorbed its contrast between an early, female-controlled religion based on magic and a later, male-controlled religion based on anthropomorphic gods and myth. Butts's Pythia, serving only as a "lid on the earth's mystery," offered "Lights and wings, and blood, and tides where there is no more sequence," pieces of vision that make no logical sense. Apollo, on the other hand, offers "reality": an anthropomorphic religion suited to people's desire for order and meaning, a religion that aligns itself easily with history, that turns Delphi into a "little old town with a too large cathedral" (238). The contrast echoes that which Harrison makes between two interpretations of the omphalos at Delphi: For the Pythia, the omphalos is a magical stone charged with power in its own right. For Apollo, the stone's significance is narrative, not magical: it commemorates a past battle for control of Delphi (Harrison, *Themis* 400).

Butts had certainly read Harrison by 1928, when she published her novel *Armed with Madness*. There a character named Picus is based on Harrison's description in *Themis* of the ancient bird-king (*Themis* 105).[7] Based on the Grail legend, *Armed with Madness* resembles Eliot's "The Waste Land" in its use of mythical analogues to add resonance and structure. But while Butts had read Harrison by 1928, it is only with the 1932 *Death of Felicity Taverner* that Harrison's pervasive influence becomes clear. Here, as in *The Macedonian*, published a year later, myth is not a gender-neutral substructure to human experience, but an ally of female intuiton against male rationalism, of silent vision against narrative voice. By 1933, when Butts cites Harrison's *Prolegomena to the Study of Greek Religion* and *Themis* as sources for *The Macedonian*, Butts's Harrisonian mythic method—her fascination with ritual (versus narrative) and mana (versus individual heroes or deities)—determines her choice of setting, subject, and narrative technique.

In *The Death of Felicity Taverner*, Scylla Tracy (formerly Taverner) wonders how her much-loved cousin Felicity died. This question becomes unimportant, however, when Felicity's widower, the evil Nicholas Kralin, arrives with a plot to buy Felicity's land and develop it. He threatens to publish Felicity's letters and diaries unless her Aunt Julia sells him the Taverner land, which he envisions as the start of a profitable seaside resort. Felicity's family is horrified; selling the land is unthinkable, but so is allowing publication of Felicity's letters and diary, for Kralin plans to turn them into an "erotic classic" (131), an illuminating study of the Elektra complex (162).[8]

Kralin is at once storyteller and mythmaker, a follower, in fact of Eliot's "mythical method." He has a story to tell about Felicity that is also a plot to acquire her land, and it is based on mythical analogues: Felicity becomes Elektra, who, in helping to kill her mother for love of her father, exemplifies the child's sexual attraction to her opposite-sex parent. Psychology, which, like ethnology, seeks out similar underlying structures in apparently different people or cultures, was one of the disciplines listed by Eliot as making a mythical method possible. But Kralin's use of myth makes it clear that the "mythical method" doesn't just borrow a preexisting structure; it orders and controls and provides distance from the "primitive" material it evokes.

In *The Death of Felicity Taverner*, this Freudian narrative is murderously false, obscuring the facts with its compelling but false patterning of experience. In fact, Felicity's distrust of her mother is justified, not the product of a neurotic passion for her father. Her brother Adrian was the product of her mother's sexual infidelity, and Felicity herself was deprived of her rightful inheritance. Butts's treatment of Kralin suggests that she recognized the threat to women posed by this use of myth—to distance and control—a use she associates with myth as storytelling, as opposed to ritual.

This distinction between storytelling and ritual was crucial for the Cambridge Ritualists, Harrison among them. All the Cambridge Ritualists believed that ritual preceded myth: what began as an effort to insure fertility through magic became with time a ritual, then a mythic narrative telling the story underlying the ritual.[9] Harrison associated ritual with pre-Olympian Greece; the storytelling stage of myth arrives with Olympian religion, and with it comes a valuing of order, objectivity, and hierarchy. In the *Prolegomena* she writes, "As soon as the story-telling, myth-making instinct awakes you have anthropomorphism and theology" (80). Making a story means making connections that in turn impose the human drive toward systematization on a formless world. Ritual, on the other hand, acts on the world without trying to make it mean something in human terms.

Kralin himself recognizes the antipathy between his plots and a mythology (in my terms closer to ritual) he associates with Felicity. Remembering Felicity's sensibility, her occasional transformations into something "transparent, glorified," he complains to himself, "Dead, she was at her tricks again, making him dance to her tune. . . . There were images in his mind—learned out of the cursed mythology they had sucked in with their milk, and he could never get right" (69). These images finally

destroy him. The Taverners' friend Boris leaves Kralin to drown, uncon-
scious in an underwater cave as the tide comes in. Cave, tide, sea,
mother's milk—all images associated with the female body—destroy him,
triumphing over his Freudian narrative. Not coincidentally, his death
rewrites the story of Odysseus, who this time is destroyed in the cave of
Polyphemos, to the joy of Scylla, his adversary and opposite.[10]

Scylla, like Kralin, is writing a book; like his it uses mythical material.
But it does so differently. Scylla's book is about the land, and by exten-
sion, it is the only true account of Felicity herself, for Felicity *is* the land.[11]
Butts writes, "Scylla's passion . . . was—spending if necessary her life
over it—to leave behind her the full chronicle of their part of England"
(183). Scylla researches her chronicle by consulting books, people, but
especially the land itself:

> there were times when the trees and stones and turf were not dumb, and
> she had their speech, and the ruins rose again and the sunk founda-
> tions, and copse and clearing and forest changed places, and went in and
> out and set to partners in their century-in, century-out dance. There
> were times, out on the high turf at sun-rise and set, when in the slanted
> light she saw their land as an exfoliation, not happening in our kind of
> time, a becoming of the perfected. She did not know how she knew, Kil-
> meny's daughter, only what it looked like—the speechless sight of it—
> her thread to the use of the historic imagination, Ariadne to no Mino-
> taur in the country of the Sanc Grail. (183)[12]

Scylla sees herself as a transmitter of the land's speech, a recorder of the history inscribed palimpsestically in its landscape. This speech is conveyed
not linguistically but ritualistically—through dance: a dance that has meaning because landscape and Scylla alike share the same totemistic universe—
a world that merges animate and inanimate, human and nonhuman.

The land's dance not only attributes animation to an inanimate landscape; it provides entry into an alternative time-frame. It is an "exfolia-
tion, not happening in our kind of time, a becoming of the perfected"
(183). The description of Scylla's chronicle—which opens by telling us she
consults history books and closes by describing her hallucinatory fusion
with a landscape outside time—moves from the linearity Julia Kristeva
associates with male time through cyclical into monumental time—the latter two both forms of "women's time" (Moi 191). "Cyclical time" Kristeva describes as "cycles, gestation, the eternal recurrence of a biological
rhythm which conforms to that of nature and imposes a temporality
whose stereotyping may shock, but whose regularity and unison with
what is experienced as extra-subjective time, cosmic time, occasion vertiginous visions and unnameable *jouissance*" (191).

In explaining "monumental time," Kristeva writes: "one is reminded
of the various myths of resurrection which, in all religious beliefs, per-

petuate the vestige of an anterior or concomitant maternal cult" (191). Frazer focuses on the cyclical process of male death and resurrection; Harrison's interest, in *Themis* at least, is in the fusion, the group-consciousness, the nondifferentiation of subject and object she associates with an "anterior maternal cult" (128).

This vision is Scylla's "thread to the use of the historic imagination, Ariadne to no Minotaur in the country of the Sanc Grail" (183). That the thread leads to no Minotaur suggests a rejection of teleology; this historic imagination perceives cosmic parallels for their own sake, not as they connect to each other or lead toward greater coherence, but as they provoke a Kristevan jouissance (Moi 191). In *The Death of Felicity Taverner* these moments are epitomized by the silence at the core of the text: the silence of Scylla's speechless vision, her land-book, which alone could tell the true story of Felicity Taverner.

Scylla's land-book, it seems to me, provides the key to Butts's own methodology. In *The Crystal Cabinet* Butts describes her "seeings"— moments when the land seems charged with magic, and time collapses. They are crucial to her sense of herself as a historical novelist for whom everything is a "web on which the world is strung," and whose purpose is to fill in the pattern (233). Butts's "mythical method," then, involves ritual not story, and is associated with with fluidity, nurturing, and jouissance. It evokes a totemistic world whose passing she, like Harrison, mourns.

If storytelling is the enemy, however, and what we need is a return to what Butts calls "primitive animism with all its bogys" (*Crystal* 134), Butts's task of novel writing becomes problematic. How write a novel without telling a story? How conjure up a nonverbal world through language? How serve as her "father's fulfillment" while embracing a mythical method steeped in maternal imagery?

Butts's answers are evident in her next novel, *The Macedonian*. Here she tells the story of Alexander the Great—a story so familiar she need not tell it. She chooses as her setting Hellenistic Greece, a time when Greek power was fading and Roman power not yet established, when the old religions had lost their credibility and people knew enough, according to Butts, to be scared (*Traps* 19). It is a period characterized by what Gilbert Murray—one of Butts's sources for *The Macedonian*—calls a "failure of nerve": a loss of faith in rationality and a shift toward mysticism.[13] It is this shift toward mysticism that fascinates Butts.

Instead of events recounted by an authoritative narrator, there are scenes, in which thoughts, dreams, hallucinations, prayers, and events mingle. Instead of psychological insight into a human being, we are shown only the ebb and flow of mana. Butts herself uses the term, calling it, in *Traps for Unbelievers*, the "wild, enchanting incalculable force in nature . . . the non-moral, beautiful, subtle energy in man and in everything else, on which the virtue of everything depends" (47). And in her preface to *The Macedonian* she defines mana as "the sheer force that lies behind the manifestations of life" (xi). In *The Macedonian*, mana is both narrative method and main character.

Butts aligns her narrative voice with mana. She does so by providing so little continuity or explanation that the reader must become writer, constructing the novel for herself out of her own knowledge of history. *The Macedonian* focuses on ten scenes from the life of Alexander: his parents at the time of his birth and on his fourteenth birthday; Alexander's mystical experience at Siwa; the Persian influence on Alexander, as perceived by Mardios, a fictional Persian satrap; the murder of Clitus; the pages' plot against Alexander's life, as reported in a letter from Callisthenes to his uncle Aristotle; the departure from India; the trip homeward and reunion with Nearchus; the death of Alexander in Babylon. Why these scenes and not others? Butts seems to be following the mana—going wherever the energy is most intense, where human motives seem least relevant, the incursion of nonhuman forces most probable. The focus is very much not on Alexander's personal self; the shifting scenes and characters indicate the nonexistence of such a self, except as a site where various energies merge. Rather than depict Alexander's death, for example, Butts reproduces the dreams of his friends and the prayers of priests—these are pieces of Alexander's essence more certainly than any physical body or psychological persona could be.

Butts's style reinforces this effect. She tends to separate verbs from their subjects and her many relative clauses from their referents: the "who" or "which" stresses connectedness but forces the reader to supply the link. "He knew he was alone," Butts writes of Alexander, "who had never minded himself for company" (63). To make sense of such sentences, the reader must join in the flow of objects, minds, gods, of characters, narrator, and reader.

Butts thus underlines the similarity between mana's role in the universe and the reader's and narrator's roles in the novel: all are a kind of omnipresent energy. This becomes clear as Alexander moves toward Siwa, where he will visit the temple of Amen-Ra and there identify himself as the god's son—the novel's climax. Feeling that he is not alone, he decides that there is something near him— but not a god:

> It was not that. It was not a person. It was something that shaped equally the Universe and an acorn, and It called him friend. (65)

Reader and narrator, Alexander's other companions on the way to Siwa, are thus aligned with that "something," with mana.

Alexander's awareness of an unseen force, that "something" that accompanies him to Siwa, shapes his behavior from then on. At Siwa he enters what Harrison calls the protoplasmic haze: Feeling himself under the sea, "in moisture and a darkness of green light" (67), Alexander feels an oceanic oneness with the world: "And God was there, in an emerald, on a boat. Boat and emerald and temple, pylon and colonnade, engraved figures upon another emerald, the oasis-green" (66). He worships no anthropomorphic god, but Amen-Ra in the form of a lamb, and the revelation involves no goal but an ecstasy clearly valuable for its own sake, for its glimpse into eternality. The vision is premised on the melding of incongruities, the rejection of polarities, so that finally Alexander is unwilling to distinguish between himself and godhood: "I may not be man. I have been shown what God is until it has changed my blood. I have gone into the forms that are shapes of god" (135).

Alexander's religious feeling aligns him with his mother, Olympias, whose *enthousiasmos* contrasts sharply with the rationalism of her husband and his friend Aristotle. The contrast is underlined by the allusions to *The Bacchae* in the book's opening pages. Olympias thinks of Agave, who "killed her son because he could not see god" (13) and feels herself Semele, mother of Dionysos (14). Her thoughts are rhythmic, fragmentary, incantatory:

> *While the earth shows . . . the earth shows . . . The earth is showing . . .*
> *the earth is making . . . the earth is making . . . the earth is showing . . .*
> *The earth is making god and son . . . Making my son god.* (13; ellipses in
> original)

Philip and Aristotle, on the other hand, are Pentheus, self-righteous and deluded in their skepticism. The antithesis is linked to gender by Aristotle, who insists on the inferiority of women (5) and blames Olympias for her "barbarian lawlessness and unreason and desire and certainties" (23) and by *The Bacchae*, which pits the religion of women against male repression. Alexander may identify with Achilles (28), but Olympias will always be too pre-Olympian—and in Aristotle's terms too female—to be a proper Thetis (45).

At Siwa, the pre-Olympian side of Alexander emerges, as does the peculiarly Harrisonian stamp of Butts's mythical allusions. In *The Prolegomena* Harrison contrasts Homeric and pre-Homeric religion. In Homer, the gods are anthropomorphic and act according to humanly understandable rules, most obviously what she calls "*do ut das*": I give that you may give. Religious ritual is a shared feast aimed at getting something from the gods or at giving them the honor that is their due. Earlier ritual she characterizes as "*do ut abeas*"; I give that you may stay away. These earlier gods are nonhuman—kers, sprites, bogeys, demons—and incomprehensible. Ritual is aimed at avoiding disaster rather than at attaining any humanly determined outcome. To understand these spirits, Harrison writes, requires a nonanalytic state of mind: we must "think back the 'many' we have so sharply and strenuously divided, into the haze of the primitive 'one'" (164). That haze she sees not as blinding superstition but as a "protoplasmic fulness and forcefulness" (164). One must, in other words, abandon the teleological, analytical thinking of Olympian religion (and nineteenth-century rationalism) and reenter the "fulness and forcefulness" of the haze. This is precisely what happens to Alexander at Siwa, when he feels himself under the sea, "in moisture and a darkness of green light" (67).

Alexander's religious feeling aligns him with his mother, Olympias, with the Egyptians, and with the Persians against the rationalistic Greeks, who oppose any blurring of boundaries between god and man: Clitus, for example, who argues that the Hellenes found out man is not god (99), Aristotle, and Aristotle's nephew Callisthenes.[14] Those for fusion, then, are women and conquered peoples—those the Greeks are intent on defining as "other"—as Aristotle indicates when he attacks Olympias's "ecstasies and her savageries, her barbarian lawlessness and unreason and desires and certainties" (23). But it is Olympias's barbarian lawlessness that the narrator seems to endorse and echo. The religious ritual in which Olympias's life has been steeped derives from a view of the world as interconnected, a rejection of the concept of incongruity, because of the way mana links all things. Olympias tells Alexander:

> When I was born, I was my father and my mother's child, but at the same time I was made out of the earth, and given back to it the hour I drew breath. When I was a maid, I was married to a tree. A fish hung round my neck. (38)

In her 1932 *Traps for Unbelievers* Butts writes that behind magic—which preceded religion—lies "a very peculiar kind of awareness. . . . It has something to do with a sense of the invisible, the non-existent in a scientific sense, relations between things of a different order: the moon and a stone, the sea and a piece of wood, women and fish" (24). Increasingly throughout her career, Butts used writing to forge those connections, disconcerting though they are. In doing so, she was not creating an alternative structure through which to perceive experience, but destabilizing the ordinary categories into which we sort phenomena. The concept of mana, with its hazy, shifting definitions and impalpable nature, suited her aim. By insisting that mana, not man, shaped history, she was aligning herself with formlessness and jouissance against plot, purpose, and male hegemony. Butts started writing historical fiction to fill in the gaps, to make manifest the underlying coherence she sensed in the universe and thus enable herself to serve as a part of that web, as her father's heir. In the process, her sense of what that past was grew farther and farther away from anything her father would have recognized. In making her escape from Troy she had indeed left her father behind but preserved Helen, her sacra, not his.

NOTES

1. Butts matches the pattern Elaine Showalter detects in nineteenth-century "feminine" novelists, who tend to identify with their fathers and feel alienated from their mothers (*Literature* 61). Bryher and Mitchison also mention a similar admiration for—and desire to identify with—their very successful fathers.

2. Sappho would have served as an alternative image for an educator of women; Joan DeJean points out that the English Greek scholars "led the way in promoting Sappho the schoolteacher" (284). But the fear of lesbianism underlying the ban on student-teacher attachments at St. Leonard's would serve also to make such an identification undesirable.

3. Tony, under the name William D'arfey, wrote a book about his family entitled *Curious Relations*. Here their mother appears quite sympathetically. Tony and Mary were at odds from the late 1920s on.

4. Goldring writes that they returned from their visit "considerably shaken and in poor health; . . . Neither of them discussed their experiences, and when Mary was asked, by ribald friends, 'what happened about the goat', she always changed the subject" (148). Aleister Crowley was a practitioner of magic who attracted followers of fanatic devotion, to whom he was known as The Beast 666. He renamed his followers (Butts was Sister Rhodon) and expected from them obedience and participation in mass-like rituals involving pentagrams, invocation of demons, and the occasional animal sacrifice. His esoteric *Book of the Law* derives from the work of such earlier mages as Abramelin and Eliphas Levy. His abbey, based on Rabelais's Abbey of Thelemes, was to be a great social experiment, but it fell apart when Italy expelled him.

5. See Christopher Wagstaff for a detailed chronology of Mary Butts's life, as well as an invaluable bibliography.

6. During her life, her work was admired by Ford Madox Ford (Goldring 147), Ezra Pound (Wagstaff, in Butts, *Crystal* 279) and Bryher, who gave her substantial financial support.

7. This connection is also made by Robin Blaser (193).

8. *The Crystal Cabinet*, Butts's memoir of her childhood, provides an interesting gloss on *The Death of Felicity Taverner*, revealing its autobiographical basis. Butts's adored father died when her brother Tony was four and she was fourteen. Tony may, according to neighbors, have actually been the son of the man her mother then married, a possibility she explores in the autobiographical novel *Ashe of Rings* as well as in *The Death of Felicity Taverner*. In all three—the memoir, *Ashe of Rings,* and *Felicity Taverner*—she portrays a mother who rejects her daughter and dominates her son, and a daughter who adores her dead and betrayed father.

9. According to Ackerman, Frazer may have gotten this idea of ritual from his friend William Robertson Smith's 1888–91 lectures on Semitic religion

("Frazer" 120). There is no evidence, however, that Jane Harrison heard these lectures; her 1890 *Myths and Monuments of Ancient Athens* argues similarly that ritual precedes myth (Ackerman, "Jane Ellen Harrison" 227).

10. Kralin is of Russian-Jewish descent, a Bolshevist sympathizer, an anti-Christian rationalist—everything Butts dislikes. His murderer, Boris, is a white Russian, an impoverished aristocrat in flight from the Revolution, and a homosexual, a figure who appears throughout her writing, generally named Boris, as a sympathetic figure. Butts's politics were conservative; she admired old families with a long tradition of land-owning and culture, and seems to have disliked Jews. Though she flirted with socialism as a young woman (*Crystal* 254), Bryher writes that the two women never agreed on politics (161) and suggests we ignore the "occasional sentences in her last books that seem surface reactionary" (163).

The name Scylla, the reader is told in *Armed with Madness*, is a shortened version of Drusilla, chosen because she is "sometimes a witch and sometimes a bitch" (4)—a name that reinforces the opposition between Butts's myths and traditional myth, or the "dreams of men," as Simone de Beauvoir puts it (132).

11. Women and landscape are inseparable throughout Butts's work. In *Armed with Madness*, Carston thinks of Scylla, "The wood and the woman might be interchangeable" (15). And in *The Death of Felicity Taverner* Scylla tells Boris of Felicity, "The hills were her body laid down. Think of a shape of bright darkness, blowing out flowers" (40).

12. Kilmeny, in Hogg's poem, ventures into an alternative fairylike world from which she sees the horror of earthly reality. She returns briefly to earth to tell what she has seen, then returns to that other, spiritual plane.

13. In *The Crystal Cave* Butts writes that the influence Gilbert Murray had on youth in the early 1900s is worthy of study (264).

14. Gilbert Murray points out that while fifth-century Athens insisted on the "difference between Man and God" (146), Hellenistic Greece moved "under Oriental and barbarous influences towards the most primitive pre-Hellenic cults" (144).

CHAPTER 5

Cressida's Complexity: Laura Riding Unwrites the White Goddess

Frazer's *The Golden Bough* and Harrison's *Themis* obviously had a tremendous impact on early-twentieth-century British writers, but not all responded with enthusiasm. While women writers such as Mitchison and Butts appreciated the pre-Olympian pantheon thus revealed, with its powerful female deities and its close interrelationship of man, woman, and nature, other women writers found these images problematic. For one thing, the world of religious ritual—whether Frazer's or Harrison's—remains a world of dichotomized sex roles, where bodies are categorized as either female or male, and these categories in turn define human possibility. For another, some of the most enthusiastic followers of Frazer and Harrison were men, who found fertility goddesses less threatening than women who achieved power in less traditionally "female" ways. D. H. Lawrence and Robert Graves, for example, two of the writers most entranced with Frazer and Harrison, granted women enormous powers—at the expense of their voices and wills. H. D., friend and admirer of Lawrence, confronts the problem in her autobiographical novel *Bid Me to Live*, in which Lawrence himself appears as "Rico": "There was also the woman," H. D.'s persona complains in *Bid Me to Live*, "not only the great mother-goddess that he [Rico] worshipped, but the woman gifted as the man, with the same, with other problems" (136). For the female artist, for the "woman gifted as the man," such a mother-goddess represented the wrong kind of creativity: it aligned women with their bodies at the expense of their intellects and artistry.

Mitchison countered with her feminist version of Frazer in *The Corn King and the Spring Queen*; Butts countered with her feminist version of Harrison in *The Macedonian*. Both objected to the way history had excluded female experience, but neither challenged the assumption that sexual identity was a given, defined by the body and bearing with it particular possibilities for achievement and self-fulfillment. Laura Riding, on the other hand, anticipates contemporary feminist theory in her insis-

tence that the "feminine" is not a physical attribute but a linguistic phenomenon. Perhaps because, living with Robert Graves, she had the most
urgent need to repudiate the lessons for sexual identity he derived from
Frazer, Riding launched the most radical attack on the way late-nineteenth-century assumptions about fertility goddesses had shaped her contemporaries' notions of gender. Her vehicle was *A Trojan Ending* (1937),
a historical novel about Cressida and the Trojan War.

For Laura Riding, an understanding of gender based on identification
with ancient earth goddesses was a particular problem, in part because it
was so troubling to her own understanding of herself, but more importantly because it disregarded what she saw as the real issue underlying talk
about gender: language. "Let it be a care" she writes in her poem "Care
in Calling," "How man or child / Be called man or child, / Or woman,
woman" (Jackson [Riding], *Poems* 175). To turn to a pre-Olympian
earth goddess as a source of strength was to risk losing one's own identity
and voice; it meant buying into a male-created dichotomy between sky
and earth, culture and nature, male and female, mind and body, and
embracing the silenced half.

Unwilling to silence herself, to denigrate her own intellect, Riding
explores the relationship between language and a female power derived
from goddess worship in "Back to the Mother Breast":

> Back to the mother breast
> In another place—
> Not for milk, not for rest,
> But the embrace
> Clean bone
> Can give alone.
>
> (Jackson [Riding], *Poems* 53)

She writes of a "vague infant cheek" which, in earlier years, "Turned
away to speak"; the movement suggests a shift from maternal intimacy
toward the Symbolic, an inevitable maturational step, in Lacanian terms.
But the poem's speaker, now older and distanced enough to face the
maternal without risking loss of language and selfhood, urges a return,
though not to quite the same place. She goes back to the mother breast
"*In another place*": This is no return to pre-Oedipal merging with a soft,
nurturant female, but a clear-eyed encounter with discipline and death,
"the embrace / Clean bone / Can give alone." The echo of Donne's
"bracelet of bright hair about the bone" suggests the mother breast
teaches the harsh reality of mortality. But most important, the encounter
is a lesson in a different kind of language:

> Now back to the mother breast,
> The later lullaby exploring,
> The deep bequest
> And franker singing
> Out of the part
> Where there is no heart. (53)

The speaker is rejecting the position from which she has been speaking, presumably aligned with the father, with the authority of symbolic discourse. But the place from which she now prefers to speak is defined only in relative, transitional terms—"back to," "another," "later," "franker," a place "where there is no heart." The speaker herself, in fact, exists only as a movement; there is no "I"; instead there is a movement from present to a past knowable only as difference.

Riding's effort throughout her work is to sing a "later lullaby," to use language not to soothe but to trouble. To embrace the "mother breast" unproblematically is to ignore the way language itself has contributed to the oppression of women. Her answer: to point continually to the gap between "The Word 'Woman,'" (the name of her long essay on the subject) and woman. By 1937, Riding had long been aware of the role played by ancient Greek culture in defining female identity through such figures as Pandora, Helen, Cressida, and Klytemnestra. She had already written several poems about Helen and was working on her essay "The Word 'Woman.'" Her companion at that time, Robert Graves, had published an immensely successful historical novel, *I Claudius*, in 1934, and would, within a year or two, begin writing (as *The Roe in the Thicket*, later published as *The White Goddess*) his theories about the relationship between goddess-worship and poetry. *A Trojan Ending*, which focuses on Cressida's behavior during the Trojan War, is Riding's response to these issues. In this chapter, I want to look at how *A Trojan Ending* works to counteract the kind of thinking evident in Graves's *The White Goddess*, and implicit in the work of writers like Harrison, Mitchison, and Butts: a thinking that grants women power, but accedes too easily to binary oppositions that align them also with physicality, fertility, and silence.

A "violent feminist, an original poet, a more than original thinker, a personality of seductive and overmastering force": these are the words Randall Jarrell used to describe Laura Riding—just before calling her the "White Goddess incarnate" (473). The term *White Goddess* comes from Robert Graves's 1946 book of that name, in which he attributes all poetic inspiration to a primal moon goddess he suggests was worshipped in matriarchal, pre-Olympian Greece.

Graves was very much a part of the reimagining of ancient Greece that took place during the first part of this century. Obviously influenced by Bachofen, Frazer, and Briffault, Graves believed "as early as 1924" that matriarchy characterized the earliest human societies (Richard Graves 104). In the 1938 *The World and Ourselves*, Graves wrote, "History proper begins everywhere with the suppression of matriarchal culture by patriarchy, of poetic myth by prosaic records of generation—how this hero begat that hero and he another—with notes of the battles and laws which made each hero famous" (qtd. in Richard Graves 268). These beliefs about ancient history found their way into his historical fiction and *The White Goddess* as well as his 1955 account of *The Greek Myths*, which was to influence Mary Renault. Throughout, the assumption is that on the most profound level, men are vulnerable and time-bound, in service to a powerful, terrifying-yet-beautiful goddess, their muse.

This notion of an early, goddess-worshipping matriarchy appealed to many during the first part of this century. Male thinkers who accepted it—among them Freud and Marx—tended to see the movement from matriarchy to patriarchy as part of an inevitable progression. Female thinkers—most prominently Jane Harrison—tended to regard the change more unhappily. Graves, however, breaks this pattern of contrasting male and female views: unusually, for a man, he calls for a return to the great truth of goddess-worship. In a 1961 talk, Graves commented, "A dedicated poet sees history as a dangerous deviation from the true course of human life—an attempt to deny women their age-old moral ascendency" (*Oxford* 73).

What did Laura Riding think of all this?

A Trojan Ending, her 1937 novel about the fall of Troy, is a response to these ideas, and, as such, is a valuable contribution to the ongoing debate about gender and history taking place during the first half of the twentieth century through reconstructions of the ancient world. In particular, it dramatizes the problems posed for female writers by goddess-worship. In *A Trojan Ending*, Riding tells the story of Cressida, transforming her from a fickle, sexually irresistible object of male desire to a strong, articulate woman whose actions are freely determined by her will. Aligning Cressida, Cybele-worshipping Troy, and the feminine against a masculine, Apollo-worshipping Greece, Riding may seem to be replaying yet again the defeat of matriarchy by patriarchy. But in fact her novel works to deconstruct any such straightforward opposition. In its treatment of characterization, language, and plot, *A Trojan Ending* is a careful response to Graves's oversimplified thinking about gender.

Riding's response to Graves was particularly urgent because between 1926 and 1939 she was living with him. But this is precisely what makes reconstructing their dialogue so difficult. Particularly during the time they lived together on Majorca, between 1929 and 1936, they were constant collaborators, always reading and editing each other's work, constantly exchanging ideas. While *The White Goddess* was published well after *A Trojan Ending*, which therefore could not have been a direct answer to it, Graves and Riding surely would have discussed these ideas throughout the 1930s. Riding herself accused Graves of having stolen ideas for *The White Goddess* from her own essay, "The Word 'Woman,'" left unfinished on Majorca in 1936. In her 1975 response to *The White Goddess*, Riding—by then known as (Riding) Jackson because of her marriage to Schuyler Jackson—wrote that Graves stole her

> ideas of the relation of poetry to the spiritual instincts of truth and the spiritual intuitions of articulate human participation in the cosmic reality; . . . my findings of significances concerning cosmic forces in the character of personal difference exemplified in woman-identity and man-identity, and my principles of moral value for the poetic linguistic effort, and my visionary description of the universal story in terms of personal sense of being of it, and *in* it. (Jackson [Riding], *Word* 209)

The question might arise that if Graves stole these ideas from Riding, why would Riding want to argue with Graves's thinking in *A Trojan Ending*? He has linked poetry to myth and gender, he has given it moral importance, and perceived humanity in relation to a "universal story," just as she did. But Riding goes on to accuse Graves not just of stealing but also of distorting her ideas, of violating the integrity of her thinking and defaming her personally:

> The wickedness of the "White Goddess" performance is not just in the large-scale appropriation of my ideas. . . . The centre of the wickedness is the effort it is, in its inception and sustained purpose, to murder the actuality of my thought, my living reality of being, my knowledge, comprehension, of the general human and cosmic realities; to possess the bodily substance of all this in literary transmogrification, distort the personal character of myself in the malignant version of revered, loyally hated, goddess muse, convertible from the vilifying and worshipful distortion into different aspects according to his giantistic enthusiasm for his project. (Jackson [Riding], *Word* 209)

For Riding, anthropological interpretations of ancient Greece suggested that women had access to the language and insight necessary to save humanity. For Graves, they suggested women could inspire men, but it was the men whose language mattered. The "literary transmogrification" that so enrages Riding is in effect a silencing: Riding's notion of woman as articulate moral agent becomes Graves's "white goddess," a muse dependent on human, generally male poets to give her voice.

    A Trojan Ending emerges out of the gap between "The Word 'Woman'" and *The White Goddess*. It is an attempt to dramatize the ways in which men misconstrue women and the ways women can retaliate.

Graves's thesis in *The White Goddess* is that poetry grew out of cer-
emonies honoring the Moon-goddess, who is thus synonymous with the
poetic Muse (9). This Moon-goddess is one avatar of the White Goddess, who is herself the female principle incarnate: the source of both
life and death, of fear and desire, immortal inspiration of mortal men. The
poet writes out of his obsessive love for the Goddess, who is also "Truth";
"his heart breaks with longing and love for her" (448). Any true poem
invokes this Muse, which he describes as the "ancient power of fright and
lust—the female spider or the queen-bee whose embrace is death" (24).
This Goddess, according to Graves, was worshipped exclusively until
the Achaeans brought their patriarchal pantheon to Greece in about
1,900 B.C. (62). Since then her power has been forgotten or misunderstood, and it is the role of the poet to remind the world of her power.
Graves is certainly not belittling the importance of women, and in his
emphasis on women's moral ascendency, he seems to echo Riding.

But it is when he describes the role of the poet that his views become
most disturbing to the female writer. For the role of the poet is to contrast
male mortality with the immortal female whom he serves. There is,
Graves writes, a "single grand theme of poetry: the life, death and resurrection of the Spirit of the Year, the Goddess's son and lover" (422).
Graves's aesthetic thus links poetry to the mortality that men alone experience. "Woman," he writes, "is not a poet: she is either a Muse or she is
nothing" (446). He does allow for the occasional woman poet, such as
Sappho (447), but clearly the most urgent song belongs to men, whose
vulnerability gives them more to sing about. Women are the ones with the
answers, for Graves, but they are by their very nature suprahuman, "wild,
ruthless, awe-inspiring, their progress like a forest fire" (*Oxford* 81).
Like Jarrell, Graves identifies Riding with the White Goddess. For in
describing the White Goddess as a demanding muse, requiring tremendous effort from the poet, he quotes a poem by Laura Riding:

> Forgive me, giver, if I destroy the gift.
> It is so nearly what would please me
> I cannot but perfect it. (*White* 444)

Equating Riding's speaker with the White Goddess puts Riding herself in an anomalous position—both poet and muse. Graves defines the
proper tone for such a female poet; she is either to remain silent or to
write, like Sappho, as the "visible moon: impartial, loving, severe, wise"
(447). While the description matches Riding's narrative voice, it puts
Riding in the same situation as her heroine Cressida: both are shadowed
by a confining, male-originated version of themselves to which they feel
pressured to conform. *A Trojan Ending* can be read as self-defense: an

attempt by Riding to clarify her own ideas about gender, language, and history in the face of Graves's reinterpretation of them. Central to their disagreement is their conflicting notion of the relation of language to truth, a relationship which, for Riding at least, is expressed by the word *God*.

Riding certainly believed in the superior spiritual insight of women and was even said to have equated woman (and thus herself) with God, so that one might think that the notion of the White Goddess would appeal to her. Tom Matthews, a friend of both Riding and Graves during the 1930s (later to turn rabidly anti-Riding) said that Riding's "Idea of God" was part of her crusade against masculinity: "Theology for her is man's dodge away from the inevitable admission that the solution to all his problems . . . lies in the woman. Woman is God" (Richard Graves 197). Horace Gregory and Marya Zaturenska write of Riding that she had, in her house on Majorca, "in large gold letters on her bedroom wall: God is a woman" (380). But while, like Graves, Riding saw poetry as an effort to get at God, she differed greatly from him in what she meant by God. When Riding works through these ideas in her poetry and in *A Trojan Ending*, the result is far more postmodern than mythic. Graves articulates a mythic substructure that pins women to a monolithic identity with Truth. Riding, in contrast, is concerned with the liberation of women from any such monolithic identity.

In "The Word 'Woman,'" Riding writes that because men dislike difference, they see women only in terms of themselves; "woman is identified with man, and where she seems to resist identification she is disliked" (Jackson [Riding] *Word* 26). But there is, she argues, an "untranslatable residue" (27)—an aspect of female identity that escapes masculine terms, but which man "regards, nevertheless, as ideally translatable into himself; and the conquest of this residue forms the spiritual objective traditionally represented by 'God'" (27). God, then, is the run-over of meaning: that which cannot be articulated because it is knowable only as difference. God is thus aligned with the feminine; both God and women are elusive others which "resist absorption in the meanings with which man elarges his nature" (18–19):

> Man, in giving the meaning of himself to everything, grows conscious of "something else" to which his meanings do not easily adhere. And the "something else" is divided into two notions—"God," the "other" thing as a passive subject of thought to which he makes his meanings adhere by force of will, and "woman," a closer, more co-operative kind of "otherness." (19)

As "other," women parallel God in lying outside the framework of male discourse; because of this position, they have a unique capacity for "truth-telling: the elucidation of man and the coherent unification of him with herself" (73). But Riding's "truth-telling" is more a dialogic process than divine revelation. As Jerome McGann has recently pointed out, "the revelation of truth through language occurs, so far as (Riding) Jackson is concerned, only as an interactive event" (459).

Graves turns Riding's notions of woman, God, language, and poetry into sources of transcendence. His measure of a good poem, which he attributes to A. E. Housman, depicts poetic receptivity as a male-oriented thrill: "Does it make the hairs of one's chin bristle if one repeats it silently while shaving?" (*White* 21). Nothing could be farther from the cerebral, strenuously moral and interactive relationship Riding creates between speaker and listener as they attempt, through language, to approach an understanding of the world.

To approach truth means to expose the slippage between language and "reality," and nothing dramatizes this slippage better than the lives of women. Riding's Cressida, like Riding, is a woman who sees she is being transmuted by male accounts into Woman; in *A Trojan Ending*, Riding tells her story in such a way as to draw attention to this process. Retelling the final months of the Trojan War, Riding focuses mainly on Cressida, who leaves Troy not as an object of exchange, at her father's request in trade for the Trojan Antenor (the traditional interpretation), but of her own free will, in order to survive as a witness to her town's death. And she leaves Troilus for Diomedes not, as Shakespeare has her say of herself and all women, because "The error of our eye directs our mind" (V:ii), but because she genuinely likes Diomedes, who must agree to a sexless marriage before gaining her consent. Action, descriptive detail, chronological precision, and climactic movement are neglected in favor of endless, often abstract, conversation. Instead of coherence and closure there are interruptions, gaps, uncertainties.

From the start, Troy is itself equated with the feminine through its preference for Cybele over Apollo, its family-loving King Priam, its at-homeness, even its possession of Helen. Troy has—and in a sense *is*—the woman Greece wants. But Troy is "feminine" most of all because of its indefinability. The novel opens with Cressida's analysis of the Trojan position:

> Consider: we are Troy, Trojans. Other peoples make a mystery of us. They nod their heads knowingly and say 'Trojan, I think,' when one of us comes into their midst, as a fisherman might guess at some monster brought up in his net. (3)

Trojans are strangers wherever they go, just as women, according to Riding, are strangers in the land of men. At one point Achilles, explaining why he prefers boys to women, explains, "I feel so young, and women seem so old—old as the rocks the earth rests on" (194). The echo of Pater's description of the Mona Lisa as "older than the rocks among which she sits" is apt (Pater 103); the image evokes the long tradition of monstrously powerful females out of which Graves's White Goddess emerges.

Where Graves and his male forebears see a sexual monster, however, Riding depicts a textual monster. Crucial to her novel—and her conflict with Graves—is her transformation of Cressida, the notorious sexual monster, into what Mary Jacobus calls "the monster in the text": the "ambiguity of subjectivity itself which returns to wreak havoc on consciousness, on hierarchy, and on unitary schemes designed to repress the otherness of femininity" (Jacobus 5). Irigaray writes similarly of the "*disruptive excess*" that is "possible on the feminine side" (78). Cressida terrifies because she defies coherence. Mirroring the reader's own repressed fragmentation and uncertainty, she is that which can't be contained by a language based on sexual polarity. Women in general, because they are not simply the opposite of men, will always exceed the meanings attached to them by a phallogocentric language. Thus women always involve, in Riding's terms, an "untranslatable residue," which men insist on attempting to conquer. Cressida is the excess, the "untranslatable residue" that got away: the part of women—or Troy—that resists male—or Greek—schemata.[1] Since the conquest of this residue is, according to Riding, "the spiritual objective traditionally represented by 'God'" (27), it makes sense that this residue unconquered would be associated with God's opposite, which, in the Western tradition, is often the sexually dangerous female—Eve, Pandora, Lilith, Circe, Medusa. The Western literary tradition thus turns an incomprehensible Cressida into a transparently understandable personification of Fickleness. But the monster fights back, as Jacobus and Irigaray suggest. While comfortable lies may be more convincing than truth, as the Greek Sthenelus tells Cressida, there is always Nemesis, which "becomes Truth" in such cases and takes its revenge. Cressida equates "she whom you call Nemesis and we, Cybele the Provider" (314) because both are the revenge the repressed feminine "truth" takes on "lies": exploders of false texts, the pressure point at which pretense unravels. If every woman is part of Cybele (322), then Riding has certainly created a kind of "White Goddess," or at least an equation between Woman and Godhood. But the equation is premised very much on woman as textual phenomenon, not as incarnation of an essential truth. Riding, in other words, sounds more like Mary Jacobus and Luce Irigaray than Robert Graves.

Cressida knows that her actions will be interpreted in terms of hackneyed notions of female sexual infidelity. But she prefers male misinterpretation to death because even if misunderstood, her survival ensures the continuation of her conversation and thus of her memories of Troy, while her "monstrosity" ensures that these memories will live on in others after her death. If she dies in Troy, Troy dies with her. By going to Greece, on the other hand, she prolongs both her own memory of Troy and that of others, for the shame with which her name will be equated will also serve as a trigger to memory. Her monstrousness in the eyes of others ensures the setting off of a chain of associations of which Troy will at least be a part. She anticipates that Dictys, the Greek scribe, or Dares the Trojan will write: "Cressida, daughter of the traitor Calchas, this day left us, departing with a shamed name the Greek camp":

> Let it be shame; the shame, called after her, would be a means of memory. Poets would revile her; then, the story, done, the listeners would look at one another and ask, "What was Troy?" And the image of Troy would flicker unforgettably in the shadows of their curiosity. . . . Troy would remain Troy in the depths of the mirror of self-resemblance, the haunting unification of what had been with what was to be. (215)

Cressida's name doesn't trigger automatic revelation of the "true" Troy, for Troy in an absolute sense remains unavailable, flickering "unforgettably in the shadows of their curiosity" (215). Troy can be remembered only through language, which inevitably displaces that which it would represent. Troy can "haunt" human consciousness but cannot be fully present to it. But Cressida's name at least sets off questions, uncertainty, conversation.

What makes Cressida a textual monster is precisely this power to *haunt*: to unsettle meanings by suggesting there is another, truer one somewhere else; to trigger dialogue by exposing ambiguities and uncertainties. Like Troy, she is above all a voice, creating the conversations that can never connect those two realms, but can bring the conversers closer to a true understanding of the distance between them.

Cressida, like all Trojans according to Riding, is obsessed with *truth* (76), but it is a strangely tentative, interactive truth, expressed through the dialogue that constitutes the novel. As the Trojans face inevitable defeat,

> The voice of Troy spoke above the wordless clamour of matter, and above the ghastly silence of the gods: "We are neither the matter of the earth nor the spirit of the heavens, but the mind between; we are ourselves, and these are our likely things, and those our impossibilities" (206).

Language cannot convey truth, as even the Greek Achilles can see, when he tells Patroclus, "We try to tell the truth, but we only speak in riddles we don't know the meaning of. No matter how little we say, it's always more than we understand—the words form into large, unrecognizable shadows of ourselves" (194). Helen points out the tendency of language to be at once excessive and insufficient; the custom of identifying oneself by naming one's father, she says, has been so abused that if you want people to think you were born in wedlock, you have to avoid using the patronymic (117). This is the *shadow* cast by language, a problem best understood by Cressida, who chooses to act in such a way as to live out this riddle, the gap between herself and the shadow of herself cast by stories about her.

If language is inadequate, conversation is nonetheless the best hope offered for an approach to understanding. Talk, for Riding, is the most important thing that people do. Such plot as there is in *A Trojan Ending* takes place through conversation: we seem to relive the epic events entirely through the medium of gossip. Riding's version of the famous *Iliad* scene in which Helen names the Greek warriors for Priam as both watch the fighting from the Scaean tower is instructive; in Riding's version they talk about what is happening while barely able to decipher it. When the action becomes too disturbing, a friend of Helen's says, "Look away Helen—I'll tell you what happens!" (47).

Talk supersedes action and even offers a more humane alternative to it. Language for Riding, while always social, presses against the temporal and spatial specifics by which human activities limit themselves. "If we call the world a story," Riding writes in *The World and Ourselves* (1938), "we have to choose between calling its material changes the whole story of ourselves, and making of ourselves another story that is all of inactive characters as the world story is all of characterless narration" (184–85). Ignoring the "material changes," which leave women's roles obscure, she makes of history a stream of words—"characterless narration"—and turns historical individuals into speakers, whose characters are defined only by what they say. Riding's Achilles is less killer than talker, and, Riding implies, his words are far more useful—in their effort to approach truth—than his actions. His killing of Hektor is expected, even desired by both sides throughout the first two-thirds of the novel; when it finally comes it is gruesome and anticlimactic, the least significant of Achilles' actions.

Cressida removes herself from Troy to save it, she says, as a woman may leave a lover to preserve the perfection of her love: to "separate the knowledge of love from the time of love and all the corruptions with which time falsely amplified love" (264). For the same reason Cressida will not have sex with Diomedes, nor can she stay with Troilus; any entanglement in time corrupts her status as witness. She must gain the "saving distance" that will allow her to speak of Troy (407). Cressida's aim is "Finding the world not making it; knowledge, not hysterical creation" (265). Cressida rejects the standard female procreative role, the word *hysterical* suggesting her rejection of the womb as her defining quality. The very word *hysterical* evokes the long tradition of equating women with their uteruses, an equation countenanced also by archaic goddess-worship. *Hysterical* was also a word often used to describe Riding, herself a childless intellectual. The phrase *hysterical creation* is thus an act of revenge, making reproduction bear the charge of insanity more frequently leveled at women like her who reject it.[2]

By rejecting hysterical creation, one can begin "to seem what one was, and to know oneself without the mirror of appearance" (264).[3] Crucial to this self-knowledge is conversation; as McGann insists, Riding's notion of truth is always "interactive":

> for (Riding) Jackson truth is a "telling," an enactment. Her project . . . must not be seen as a *conceptual* project. Rather, it is the continuous execution of that story, which has an infinite number of (possible and actual) realizations. (459–60)

Cressida's effort is an endless, dialogic process, one that equates knowledge with *self*-knowledge and human interaction, not with some transcendent, universal truth.

Rejecting the temporal means rejecting the conventions of plot itself; Cressida will neither marry (in the conventional sense) nor die. She insists on living, in Rachel Blau DuPlessis's terms, "beyond the ending." Her whole aim is to circumvent plot, in particular to circumvent the inevitable movement of plot toward climax and resolution—in this case, toward the definitive death of Troy.

Ends in themselves are the enemy in *A Trojan Ending*. The very definition of a "Trojan ending," according to Riding, is a kind of anti-ending: when the participants in the death of something stop just short of the last moment to observe and recognize, what Cressida calls "stopping short in a difficult hour" (304). It is the moment when witnessing supersedes action, when witnessing is the only way to avoid the obliteration about to be wrought by continued action. It is a time when women, perennial witnesses to the acts of men, play a particularly important role. Helen comments: "It's the real work of women—to watch, watch, storing away in their minds what can be saved from the waste of life" (251).

This work of women—watching and talking—provides Riding with a counter to the death-ridden discourse of men and of the poets who chronicle their deeds. It also provides a key to the book as a whole, which is essentially a recounting of anthropological and legendary material through idle talk. When Polydamas complains that a ceremony in honor of dead heroes has been disrupted by a chatty discussion of comparative religion, Hektor responds, "The dead would surely not complain that their names fell among living gossip" (143). Talk whose only aim is the exchange of insignificant information becomes a discourse of life opposed to the ceremonial or didactic discourse associated with heroes, epic, and death.

Gossip, Patricia Spacks points out, reflects a communal consciousness, for it is a voice emerging from groups rather than individuals—a kind of folk history (447). What is sometimes denigrated as "idle talk," in fact is a "function of intimacy" (4). The public, solitary, authoritative voice of the ancient bard invoking his muse so he can tell the story correctly is here superseded by a medley of casual voices. This medley cannot be resolved into a single "true" story. History construed as group conversation resists assimilation into a single plot.

The standard accounts of male historians and bards are revealed as woefully insufficient, the results of misinterpretation and malicious distortion. Odysseus, Riding's villain, is obsessed with manipulating future accounts of his behavior during the war. The implication is that what we hear of him in the Homeric epics is the result of his intervention; he plots to gain control of Dares' notes, which "would tell all too little of him" (363) and has a fire set to destroy Dictys's records (364). Homer himself, Riding suggests, is descended from the traitorous Calchas and "his tales were ruins under which Troy was buried more profoundly than under its silent dust" (406). It is no accident that two of the most despicable characters as depicted by Riding—Odysseus and Aeneas—are those lionized by epic versions of the past.

Both epic and traditional history privilege the "material changes" over "characterless narration." In the process, they privilege male over female activities, closure over open-endedness, detachment over intimacy. Traditional history, according to Riding, excludes the immediate: "The more precise and 'scientific' history becomes, the more it leaves out, the less it reveals 'what actually happened,' the more dead its subjects become—formal figurines in the historically advanced mind" (*Word* 39). Defining itself against male-centered, culturally privileged epics, Riding's version is a rather formless narrative in which past and present, reader and characters, seem to merge in endless conversation. In her afterword, Riding complains that modern writers see human beings in terms of their "divergencies" rather than their "general quality of humanness" (439). Her aim is to let commonalities among characters and between readers and characters emerge. Riding's concern is with identification and sympathy, not detachment and objectivity; she contrasts herself explicitly with the archeologist digging for objects, whom to some extent as historical novelist she resembles, seeking a "consistent story-scheme for the legendary (the personal, the verbal) remains" (*Trojan* xii). This "consistent story-scheme" will not be found by piecing together evidence, though; Riding's aim is communication through "sympathy"—i.e., through identification with her subjects, not investigation of them.

"This—how we are now together—is the end of Troy, not whatever end the Greeks will deal us. The end we make ourselves" (*Trojan* 242). "How we are now together" emphasizes contextuality, interrelelationships, what Riding calls women's "appetite for intimacy" (258). The "truth," in other words, is not somewhere else, recorded by bards or historians or available to poets through divine inspiration. It is the unending conversation in which ordinary human beings try to make themselves understood to each other and to themselves and in the process find themselves constantly confronting and dealing with the ambiguities and silences of language.

A Trojan Ending has not yet found much of an audience, and Riding's commentary on her own work has often seemed calculated to alienate any group among whom she might possibly find adherents. She has denied that her work is "feministic" (*World* 27) and criticized the women's liberation movement for its emphasis on equality (Jackson [Riding], "Bondage" 25).[4] But Riding's work does anticipate recent literary and feminist theory in its insistence on the need for feminism to emphasize "equality" less and female "difference" more (Jackson [Riding], *Word* 53–54); on the peculiar relationship between women and language; and on the unavoidable interrelationship of literature and politics.[5]

Riding's commitment to social change is clearest in her 1938 volume *The World and Ourselves*, a compendium of letters solicited by Riding from various woman writers, accompanied by her own and Graves's responses. The book's purpose, she wrote, was to "apply a personal scale of values to an outer situation . . . grown destructively irrelevant to persons" (23). It is here that she argues her approach is not "feministic"; men, she says, are better at administering while women excel at the inner life (27). But the world has become "overexternalized" (27), with recent history giving "off a curious all-male odour" (17), the result of women having been ignored for too long. If Riding's thinking here seems dangerously dichotomized, it is important to keep in mind several factors shaping her thinking. First, she is arguing against an equality feminism that would simply welcome women into yet another war effort; troubled by the possibility that the entry of women into public life might mean "decharacterization" for those who do so, she points warningly at professional female politicians (17–18). Second, her dualistic formulation opposing male versus female abilities is not an essentialist contrast between men and women, but a historically determined use of language that defines "masculine" and "feminine" in contrasting ways. Riding states explicitly that she is not contrasting sexes, but abstract qualities, with her aim to right an imbalance in the way these qualities are valued, not to define gender-specific behavior (17). Finally, she is arguing for female activism. A year before Woolf's *Three Guineas*, she recognized that women's exclusion from the making of history gave them a unique intellectual standpoint from which to view it. But rather than prolong that exclusion, she suggested that women and other "inside" people remake the world in their own image.

The World and Ourselves was also an effort to create a sense of community among women writers. Riding solicited participation from Rebecca West and Storm Jameson and actually printed contributions from—among others—Christina Stead and Naomi Mitchison. The conversation that results is abstract, dialogic, unresolved—much like those of *A Trojan Ending*. Stead argues against Riding's male/female dichotomizing, rejecting the nurturant qualities Riding praises as those of a "servant" (68); Riding responds by emphasizing their importance as a "kind of personal guardianship and nurture which is on the same level of seriousness as poetry" (*World* 72). Mitchison argues women need economic equality in order to have an impact on world events (73); Riding warns again that women should not simply become like men (76). The first step in changing the world, Riding argues, is to define "woman power" (25). *The World and Ourselves* is such an act of definition. A collection of letters responded to but not synthesized by its author, the book suggests that meaning, for Riding, derives from dialogue.

In a 1972 commentary on her collected poems, Riding insisted that she wanted to have nothing to do with "goddess notioning" (Jackson [Riding], *Poems* 418). At that point, of course, she associated the term with the way in which Graves had, in her view, absorbed and distorted her views. But she was also responding to a culturally pervasive danger and temptation: the Earth Goddess as metaphor for female power. As an intellectual and a writer, as a childless and at times antisexual or perhaps lesbian woman,[6] such an image, glorifying physical rather than intellectual creation, was problematic. Where Renault would respond by basing her version of the ancient world on Graves while simultaneously challenging the rigidity of his gender boundaries, Riding redefines womanhood as the very opposite of "hysterical creation." To be a woman, for her, is to *un*-create, for by watching and talking women undo the certainties attributed by men to "reality." The ordinary historical novel, Riding writes in her preface to *A Trojan Ending* is "ghoulish" (xvii), for it kills off the living qualities of human beings in order to fit them into theories about historical periods and causality (xvi). By recreating her characters' conversations, she insists on their aliveness, on the inconclusiveness of their lives, and their resistance to assimilation into some larger historical schema. In *Progress of Stories*, Riding writes of thirty-two ages through which the world must pass. Of these, the final stage is "the age of learning that in the end the account which has the fullness of its wisdom shall never yet have been given" (337). This is Cressida's response to those who would label her "fickle" or "inconstant." It is also Riding's response to Graves's "White Goddess."

NOTES

1. Irigaray writes, in similar terms, that women experience themselves "as waste, or excess, what is left of a mirror invested by the (masculine) 'subject' to reflect himself, to copy himself" (31).

2. Similarly, Eve's function in Riding's *Progress of Stories* is not to be the mother of mankind but to "observe" (326).

3. Riding's language here is strikingly Platonic, and grows more so over time. In her 1972 *Telling*, she suggests that we use recall to get "spiritual knowledge" (24), suggesting that we all have a "memory of a before-oneself," the "common potentiality of imagining back to the all-antecedent reality" (25). Riding's poem "Back to the Mother Breast" could be read as a call to gain access to that "memory of a before-oneself." If Platonic in her rejection of appearances, however, Riding always emphasizes the *process* of return over the availability of transcendent truths.

4. In 1972 she insisted that she not be considered a "woman poet" (*Poems of Laura Riding* 418). And in a letter to the *Nation*, she rejects Judith Thurman's feminist reading of her *Collected Poems*, writing: "That the characterization 'feminist' alters the sense of my thought on the nature of woman-identity and woman-functionality I cannot here go into" (Jackson [Riding], "Reply" 322).

5. During the late 1930s, at a time when Robert Graves wanted to isolate poetry from politics, Riding was intent on using language to effect social change (Richard Graves 285).

6. Richard Graves writes in a footnote of Riding that during the years 1936–38, "The only person to whom LR is alleged to have made sexual overtures . . . was a woman, who did not reciprocate" (358).

CHAPTER 6

Masquing the Phallus: Genital Ambiguity in Mary Renault's Historical Novels

Famous for her sympathetic depictions of male homosexuality, Mary Renault, born Mary Challans in 1905, was rumored to be a man herself. She was, in fact, a woman, living quietly near Cape Town, South Africa, with her lifelong companion Julie Mullard. But the confusion about her sexual identity is revealing; throughout her work Renault focuses primarily on male characters, and in many of them her narrator—and her sympathies—seem male. Theseus, in *The King Must Die* and *The Bull from the Sea*, is a tough, womanizing hero who unites and civilizes Greece under the leadership of patriarchal Athens, and even makes an Amazon fall in love with him before he oversteps himself and tragically—through the machinations of a woman—causes his son's death. *Fire from Heaven*, *The Persian Boy*, and *Funeral Games*, about Alexander the Great, chronicle the noble if doomed attempts of men to bring order to a chaotic world. Setting her novels in historical periods that allowed women little power—the legendary Greece of Theseus, fifth-century B.C. Athens, and fourth-century B.C. Persia—and narrating for the most part in the first person from the standpoint of a male character, Renault seems enamored of male dynamos like Theseus and Alexander the Great, alike in their "precocious competence, gift of leadership, and romantic sense of destiny" (*King* 333).

Why would a lesbian novelist, in novel after novel, focus on male characters, with women playing only marginal, often stereotypical roles as either monsters or victims? The most obvious answer is that once Renault had chosen to write historical fiction set in the ancient world, she could hardly do otherwise and remain plausible. This is the answer of Marguerite Yourcenar, another lesbian historical novelist prone to assuming male narrative masks, when she explains her focus on male experience in

This chapter is a revised version of an earlier article, "Masquing the Phallus: Genital Ambiguity in Mary Renault's Historical Fiction," *Twentieth Century Literature* 42.2 (Summer, 1996). Reprinted by permission of Hofstra University Press.

Memoirs of Hadrian. Women, she said, could not possibly be plausible subjects for historical fiction because their lives were so secret and limited.

But then the question is: Why choose a genre and setting so uncongenial to the depiction of female experience? My argument here is that for Renault, as for Yourcenar, the choice is a strategy. Through her choice of subject, Renault was donning a male mask in order to trespass on particularly "male" turf; knowledge of the classical world had long served to define the British ruling class and to justify its position of cultural privilege. In the process, Renault's use of masks suggests that gender is itself more masquerade than biological essence and that the phallus, crucial indicator in Western culture of sexual difference, may not be as clear a gender marker as it seems. For while Renault's work at times echoes in troubling ways her culture's sexual stereotypes, it also works against them, depicting and celebrating sexual ambiguity. Renault does this in two ways: by depicting female characters who identify with masculinity rather than femininity and thus cross gender boundaries; and by depicting male and female bodies with such attention to their genitals that the exact location of those genitals becomes uncertain.

Renault's preoccupation with male characters led Carolyn Heilbrun to argue in a 1976 article that "Renault's work perfectly demonstrates the woman writer's deep need to affirm the patriarchal structure" (231). Ten years later, in *No Word from Winifred*, her 1986 detective novel, Heilbrun (writing as Amanda Cross) returns to the same problem when she has Kate Fansler complain of a Renault-like historical novelist:

> All the protagonists are men; the only women characters of substance are seen negatively, like Ariadne, for example, who is made to become the worst sort of monster of male imagination, gnawing on pieces of human flesh. (129)

Far from affirming patriarchy, however, I will argue that Renault's historical novels depict the human body in such a way as to undermine the sexual categories on which patriarchy rests. Underlying Renault's apparent exaltation of male achievement is an obsessive interrogation of the relationship between the human body and power. As a post-Freudian woman and as a lesbian, Renault was deeply concerned with the relation between phallus and power, between bodily taxonomy and personal identity. Heilbrun writes of Renault's fascination with "male wholeness" (231). In fact, Renault's novels examine—without endorsing—precisely that contrast between male wholeness and female incompleteness posited by her culture and deeply troubling to ambitious women.

Renault does this in part through her manipulation of incongruity: the intensely desiring gaze, a staple of heterosexual romance, is here turned solely on the male body; scholarly historical allusions mingle with grotesquely vivid depictions of bodily mutilation and veiled or absent genitals. But Renault's most subversive tool is the *mask*, more precisely what I call "masquing the phallus": a phallocentrism so dramatized that it is denaturalized, turned into masquerade, and a fetishism that masks the genitals themselves, undoing our certainty about where, in fact, that phallus is, and who has it.

Masquerade is a term frequently used by feminists to suggest the extent to which femininity is a culturally induced performance. Mary Ann Doane, for example, writes of exaggeratedly theatrical displays of femininity: "The masquerade, in flaunting femininity, holds it at a distance" (81). I am using *masquerade*, however, to refer to a flaunting of masculinity—as represented by the phallus. Like female masquerade, "masquing the phallus" suggests that gender is grounded not in the body, but in performance—and thus not securely "grounded" at all.[1]

Renault explores the notion of the mask most completely in her 1966 *The Mask of Apollo*. Worn by the actor Nikeratos when he impersonates the god, the mask also serves as a symbol for the god himself, in whose name tragedies are performed. The actor pours himself into the mask, allowing his performance to be shaped not by his own identity but by the demands of the play and the god. For Renault, the mask is what she wears when she writes; her writing, like Nikeratos's acting, means entry into the mind and body of another. For both, the personae can cross gender lines; Renault herself, as storyteller, repeatedly puts on a male mask, and Nikeratos often plays female parts. The mask offers transcendence of any merely human identity, and along with it, transcendence of gender as well. Or does it? Given that Greek women couldn't appear on stage, the mask is a giveaway that whatever the gender it depicts, the body behind it is male. The mask, then, while evoking the power to move from one gender to another, also implies masculinity, since historically, the person with the freedom to make these changes is likely to be male. When Renault puts on her male narrative mask, she is simultaneously asserting her masculinity (in her freedom to assume the mask) and her transcendence of gender (in that the mask could signify either gender). Thus the mask implies that she possesses a phallus at the same time that it suggests gender is itself a disguise, not determined by bodily taxonomy at all. Like the codpiece Marjorie Garber describes as a theatrical expression of female fetishism, the mask is "a sign of what might—or might not—be 'under there.'" (50).

Marguerite Yourcenar's version of the mask is more abstract, but serves a similar purpose. Just as Renault sees identification with the mask as the artist's goal, Yourcenar aims above all at what she calls "impersonality"; just as the mask is historically coded as male, so too is this "impersonality." "There is," according to Yourcenar, in some very great men, a tendency toward complete impersonality, of which Hadrian speaks to us: "A man who reads, reflects, or plans belongs to his species rather than his sex; in his best moments, he rises even above the human." Such impersonality is much more rare, at least up to now, in even the most eminent of women. (*Open* 227)

Both writers, then, are seeking a contradictory kind of transcendence—a space beyond gender that is nonetheless already encoded as male. In exploring that space, they cannot escape its culturally attributed masculinity, but merely by entering it, they turn masculinity itself into an act of mimicry and repudiate the "lack" by which it would define the feminine. Elizabeth Grosz has written rather tentatively of a "lesbian fetishism"—suggesting that some lesbians, like Freud's fetishist, disavow their own castration, finding in this disavowal "a form of protection . . . against the personal debasement and the transformation of [their] status from subject to object, active to passive, and 'phallic' to 'castrated'— Freud's 'definition' of femininity" (49). Renault's adoption of a male narrative mask is just such a strategy.

Freud's fetishist, of course, is the male who, unable to bear the reality of his mother's lack of a penis because of the implied threat to his own, posits a substitute in the form of a fetish (Freud 21:152–53). This fetish, then, by serving as the maternal phallus, both affirms (by its existence as a substitute) and denies (by disguising or hiding) the mother's castration (156). While Freud's fetishist is always male, feminist theorists have suggested that female fetishism may be a way of deconstructing sexual categorization. Sarah Kofman writes of the woman with the "masculinity complex" (one of the three developmental alternatives described by Freud in "Feminine Sexuality") that she "has the audacity not to hold herself in contempt, not to feel humiliated, not to feel any narcissistic wound." Identifying with the phallic mother, she refuses to "see" her own castration. Her blindness, Kofman writes, is the female equivalent of fetishism (203). In this context, the mask, with its ability to disguise gender contradicted by its availability only to male actors, is itself a kind of fetish. In *The Mask of Apollo* its role is almost literal: according to Nikeratos, his mother placed him as a two-week-old infant in a Gorgon mask, "to keep me from the draft . . . and found me sucking the snakes" (6). The Gorgon, of course, with her snake-laden hair, is an impressively phallic mother. But while for Nikeratos the mask provides emotional safety from the castration he might otherwise fear because he surpasses his father as an actor, for Renault the mask is a rejection of sexual dichotomizing. It is, as Grosz suggests, a disavowal of castration, allowing her to identify with male privilege and narrative authority, a fetish that seems simultaneously to *masque* or dramatize masculinity, and to *mask* or hide its absence, but one that constantly draws attention to its own artifice. It is not an attempt to become a male, but an effort to, in Emily Apter's words, pry "gender codes loose from the moorings of biological essentialism" ("Introduction" 5).

For Renault the attraction of the male mask is linked to Platonism, a philosophy that seems, through its emphasis on disembodied spirituality, to dispense altogether with the issue of gender. In *The Mask of Apollo*, both Nikeratos, the male narrator, and Axiothea, the female philosophy student, admire Plato, and both find in disguise a way of shedding gender-definitions. As an actor, Nikeratos must frequently play female roles; identifying with Axiothea's ambiguous sexual identity, he comments, "She was the same sort of woman as I was a man" (73), and tells her, "There are two natures in most of us who serve the god [Apollo]" (77).

While Plato worries about the social impact of theater and thus has a dampening effect on Niko's profession, he does endorse Axiothea's transvestism. She explains to Niko, "As for my clothes, he said one must be true to the mind before the body" (74). For Plato such an allegiance is not problematic: "the soul reasons best . . . when it is most by itself, taking leave of the body and as far as possible having no contact or association with it in its search for reality" (*Phaedo* 14 [65c]). In mentally shedding the body, Axiothea presumably escapes sexual definition by her body.

Axiothea is one of a series of female characters created by Renault who feel misplaced in their female bodies—a series that includes Colonna Kimball of *Purposes of Love*, Leo Lane of *The Friendly Young Ladies*, Hippolyta of *Bull from the Sea*, Eurydike of *Funeral Games*, and Renault herself. Renault writes that she considered herself an "honorary boy" for much of her childhood ("Mary Renault," *World* 1201). But when she found herself in a "conventional girls' boarding school," the pressures of gender became unavoidable. It was at that point that Renault became "riveted by Plato" ("Mary Renault," *Dictionary* 132), whose valuing of immaterial soul over physical embodiment would have an obvious appeal. Throughout her life, Renault read and reread Plato's work, alluding to *The Phaedo* in *The Charioteer*, and using Plato as a character in *The Last of the Wine* and *The Mask of Apollo*. For Renault, the Greeks, and especially Plato, appeared to offer a world in which self-transcendence was possible and gender irrelevant. "Greeks asked what a man was good for," she writes in her afterword to *The Friendly Young Ladies*, "and the Greeks were right. People who do not consider themselves to be, primarily, human beings among their fellow-humans, deserve to be discriminated against" (283). People should simply act free, she seems to suggest, and they will be.

But is the transcendence embraced by Axiothea possible? Is the call to be a "human being" worth following, or is it simply an invitation—

destructive to the female in body—to be a man? Greece's "tolerant individualism," after all, extended only to men; ancient Greece was, as Renault acknowledged, a "man's country" ("Mary Renault," *New York Times* B5). For such late-nineteenth- and early-twentieth-century thinkers as J. A. Symonds and Edward Carpenter, Platonic idealism was inseparable from the idealization of masculinity. The apparent escape offered by Plato thus seems to lead yet again to an equation between greatness and masculinity and hence to an affirmation of "patriarchal structure."

Like many other women writers who envied male power and freedom, Renault seems in her youth to have seen herself as more male than female. The young Willa Cather, who like Renault particularly admired Alexander the Great (O'Brien 82), identifed with boys and criticized women as weak, trivial, and self-involved:

> Women are so horribly subjective and they have such scorn for the healthy commonplace. When a woman writes a story of adventure, a stout sea tale, a manly battle yarn, anything without wine, women and love, then I will begin to hope for something great from them, not before. (Cather 409)

Similarly Leo Lane, the young lesbian in Renault's early nonhistorical novel *The Friendly Young Ladies*, wants above all else to be "a man with his friend, emotion-free, objective, concerned not with relationships but with work and things, sharing ideas without personal implication to spoil them, easily like bread or a pint of beer in a bar" (164).

In Renault's work, people with ambiguously gendered inner lives, particularly if they are intelligent and ambitious, choose to mimic the dress and behavior of men. Leo, a "slim, dark-haired youth in a fisherman's jersey" (55), has a feminine blonde lover named Helen and an idealized male friend, Joe, who "let her be what her mind had made her and her body refused" (164). Similarly, Axiothea begins by dressing as a man in order to participate on equal terms in Plato's Academy. "But," she tells her friend Nikeratos, echoing Radclyffe Hall's Stephen Gordon, ". . . having put them on I found they fitted my soul" (74). While these characters seem to be transcending gender, they are in fact, of course, aligning themselves with, rather than challenging, the power of masculinity.

But even when Renault writes of male beauty and male homosexuality in terms strikingly similar to Carpenter and Symonds, she is not simply idealizing male energy and power, nor does she wholeheartedly accept her culture's notion of sexual difference. Esther Newton uses the term *mannish lesbian* to describe those lesbians who, like Leo Lane or Radclyffe Hall's Stephen Gordon, adopt masculine traits as part of their identity, and she defends their existence—which to a large extent reinscribes traditional sex roles—as historically necessary. Such a "symbolic fusion of gender reversal and homosexuality was overdetermined," she writes (565). Sexologists like Krafft-Ebing and Ellis associated lesbianism with masculinity, and for them, "any gender-crossing or aspiration to male privilege was probably a symptom of lesbianism" (566).

Nineteenth-century sexologists associated male anatomy with male autonomy. Any woman who aspired to this autonomy was "masculine," in their terms. In creating and identifying herself with "masculine" characters, Renault was at least questioning the notion that her destiny was defined by her anatomy. For Leo Lane, who writes cowboy novels; for Colonna Kimball, a "mannish lesbian" in Renault's first published novel *Purposes of Love*, who reads cowboy magazines; and for Renault, whose own first attempt at fiction was a Western ("Mary Renault," *World* 1202), involvement in a masculine genre offers a freedom culturally defined as masculine. Amid the cowboys, Colonna becomes "her private picture of herself," the Dude of *Two-Gun Dude*:

> Clean-limbed, with sinews of steel and whipcord, she toted his silver-mounted guns, knotted his silk bandana, canted his elegant ten-gallon hat, confounded his hairy rivals, shot up his enemies, and kissed his pale-pink, incidental girl. (*Purposes* 323)

In *Purposes of Love*, Renault seems impressed by those who, like Colonna Kimball, cannot be easily classified: "There was an inevitable attraction about people who overlapped categories and threw down walls in the mind" (42). As Esther Newton insists, the mannish lesbian does not only assent to patriarchal sexual categories (male = ambitious, powerful, sexual; female = subservient, weak, passive); she also questions them, for by existing at all, she blurs them (573). This blurring disturbs ordinary men, for they perceive the threat it poses to their phallic-based hegemony. "Do you know," Axiothea asks Nikeratos, "you are the first man to be my friend who has not been a philosopher? The rest have thought me a monster" (77). By masquing masculinity, the mannish lesbian turns gender into a costume rather than a biological essence. Even as Renault's "masculine" females glamorize masculinity, they challenge gender boundaries simply by being as they are.

They also express, according to Teresa de Lauretis's view, lesbian desire. Both Garber and de Lauretis insist that women cross-dress not out of ambition or practicality, but because they take pleasure in it. The mannish lesbian, according to de Lauretis, is fetishizing not the maternal phallus, but the "denied and longed-for female body" (275). Lacking a "libidinally invested body-image" herself, she displaces this absence onto the male clothes she wears. She chooses male clothes not because she envies men their power or penis, but because "such signs are most strongly precoded to convey, both to the subject and to others, the cultural meaning of sexual (genital) activity and yearning toward women" (262, 263). Renault's ambiguously gendered women and her own narrative alignment with male experience thus challenge her culture's heterosexism as well as its gender categories.

So, too, do Renault's homosexuals. In novel after novel Renault depicts relationships between men with the intensity and sympathy more traditionally reserved for heterosexual romance. Alexis and Lysis in *The Last of the Wine*, Alexander and Hephaistion in *Fire from Heaven*, Nikeratos and Thettalos in *The Mask of Apollo*: all find in each other a source of deep physical and emotional satisfaction. Renault's treatment of homosexuality derives from her Greek sources—most obviously Plato—and their interpreters (Carpenter, Symonds, Hans Licht). Here it becomes clear that the late-nineteenth-century counterdiscourse of Hellenistic male love[2] was a resource even if it was problematically male. Pater, Carpenter, and Symonds, by defining Greek beauty as male, marginalized Greek women. But they also articulated a tradition of spiritual and physical homoeroticism that served Renault's larger purpose of destabilizing notions of sexual identity and behavior. Lacan points out that display is so much associated with women that even "*virile* display" seems feminine (qtd. in Garber 355). In these terms the Hellenists' very emphasis on male beauty was also an invitation to see men as feminized. Yet Carpenter, at least, also insists on the courage and military effectiveness of Greek homosexuals. The result is to challenge dichotomized ideas about sexual identity.

Again and again in Renault's novels, the male body is objectified by a desiring gaze. Alexis, posing for a sculptor as the dead Hyacinth, a boy beloved of Apollo, evokes the many precedents Greek culture offers for such desire. Women occasionally flit in and out of characters' beds but, at least in the non-Theseus novels, the young man is clearly the dominant standard of beauty. As a girl, Axiothea is all but invisible; as a boy, she is the object of admiring gazes and sexual innuendo (*Mask* 313). If Renault's depiction of men admiring male bodies suggests admiration for "male wholeness," it also, by turning the male body into an object of desire, shows men to be removable from their subject position.

Renault's depictions of homosexual eroticism echo the conventions of heterosexual romance: intense but allusive, focusing on desire, not consummation. The effect, however, is not to place one man in a consistently "feminized" role, but to question the process by which we gender these erotic positions. When Alexis, for example, tells us of a moment with his lover Lysis, his relative passivity is "feminine," but as the two men have just speared a boar together, the effect is disconcerting:

> My garland had slipped back on my hair as I ran; he put up his hand to
> it, and it fell behind me. I could hear the vine shedding its last heavy
> drops upon the terrace; the croak of a frog at the cistern beyond; and my
> own heart beating.
>   I said, "I am here." (*Last* 252)

The euphemistic shifting of attention from Alexis's body to nature projects
his desire onto vine and frog; only belatedly does he recognize the beating
heart as his own. A strategy typically used to evoke female sexuality is
here—unsettlingly—applied to a male.

When sexual excitement is not deflected onto nature, it is described in
ambiguously gendered terms, often as a process of melting. When Alexander looks into Hephaistion's eyes, for example, in *Fire from Heaven*,
"Hephaistion felt as if his midriff were melting" (181), an oddly nonphallic term for male desire. And when Lysis kisses a cut on Alexis's foot
in *The Last of the Wine*, Alexis comments, "My soul melted and fled; the
wound in my foot, which the water had opened, streamed out scarlet
over the wet rock" (143). The scene evokes simultaneously the deflo-
ration of a dephallicized Alexis and—the interpretation Lysis supplies—an
act of blood brothership. "The Thracians," he says, "when they swear
friendship mingle their blood, or drink it, I forget" (143). Alexis's body at
this moment can be read interchangeably as female (wounded, entered)
and male (sworn comrade-in-arms).

The moment of sexual consummation itself is always elided. Of
Alexander's relationship with Hephaistion, for example, we are told
only that their friends, who had bet among themselves as to the status of
the relationship, "read the signs with which their youth made them
familiar, and paid up" (*Fire* 253). The effect of all this indirection,
finally, is to "mask" the phallus—to underplay and overlook its presence. Renault's homosexual lovers, despite their occasional position-
ing as active or passive, do not fit into any stable hierarchy based on
their sexual organs or activity. If Renault and her "mannish lesbian"
characters are "masquing" the phallus, her depictions of homoeroticism "mask" it, depicting a sexuality in which the phallus seems, finally,
beside the point.

Even in her Theseus novels, Renault is able to create convincing
incarnations of gender-category overlappers who challenge our assumptions about sexual polarities. These novels, *The King Must Die* (1958) and
The Bull from the Sea (1962), are much indebted to Robert Graves,
whose extreme dichotomizing of human history in terms of gender would
seem counter to Renault's purpose. The overthrow of matriarchal religion
by patriarchy is, according to Graves, *the* story of Greek myths (*White*
10). For Renault, Graves's version of the matriarchy-patriarchy conflict
was crucial:

> Suddenly, everything fell into place. I could begin to guess at the way Theseus' mind was furnished, the kind of beliefs and aspirations and responsibilities which might have determined his actions; the tensions between victorious patriarchy and lately defeated, still powerful matriarchy, which could have underlain the love-conflict element in his legendary relations with women. ("Notes" 83)

Indeed there is much in the Theseus novels that is closely derived from Graves: the Moon-Goddess as term for an Artemis/Earth Mother; the presence of maid, mother, and crone at the goddess's rites (*Bull* 49); the inhuman quality of such White Goddess avatars as Ariadne and Phaedra, their evils even greater than in Renault's sources. (Renault's Jocasta, for example, is in the carriage with Laius when Oedipus strikes, yet agrees to marriage with the man she must recognize as her husband's murderer.)

Most similar, of course, is the central conflict between the old religion (matriarchal society worshipping a Moon Goddess) and the new, a conflict obviously based on Graves and Frazer before him and dramatized most intensely at Eleusis. There, until the arrival of Theseus, a woman, Queen Persephone, rules a land where descent is matrilinear, and males— whether human or divine—are powerless. "Only the Mother," Persephone tells Theseus, "who brings forth men and gods and fathers them again, sits at the hearthstone of the universe and lives for ever" (*King* 64–65). Zeus, on the other hand, dies yearly. Theseus, however, after defeating Persephone's consort in single combat (much like Frazer's King of the Wood and Graves's God of the Waxing Year) and becoming king, deposes his queen. Graves suggests in *The White Goddess* that after the defeat of matrilinear culture, myths were altered to justify the change (10); thus, Renault's Theseus employs Orpheus to create a rite celebrating the wedding of Athens's Zeus to Eleusis's corn mother, simultaneously defeating matriarchy and uniting the two states.

The eclipse of Persephone is echoed by numerous other eclipsed women: Theseus's mother (chief priestess of Mother Dia), his quasi-stepmother Medea, his near-wife Ariadne, and, in *The Bull from the Sea*, his Amazon love Hippolyta, and finally his wife Phaedra. All are worshippers of the mother-goddess; all find their religion and/or themselves weakened by their encounter with Theseus, who is everywhere aligned with Poseidon and Zeus. As all must be conquered if Theseus is to triumph, and as Theseus appears to have the gods as well as his own narration on his side, the reader tends to cheer their defeat. And Theseus's horror before the cruelty wrought by women—epitomized by the dismembered phallus he finds in Ariadne's hand after the Dionysian rites on Dia—suggests Graves's portrait of the hair-raising terror inspired by the White Goddess.

But while Renault's depiction of patriarchal Theseus defeating and transforming the matriarchal cultures of Eleusis, Athens, and Crete suggests a rigidly polarized view of sexual identity, Queen Persephone, Ariadne, Medea, and Hippolyta are not simply marginalized monsters, courageously suppressed by male heroes. While Renault borrows from Graves, she also undercuts his dichotomies. The entire island of Crete, in *The King Must Die*, and the Amazons, in *The Bull from the Sea*, offer realms of sexual ambiguity that threaten constantly to destabilize the distinctions by which Theseus and his culture maintain their identity.

Decadent and defeated by the end of *The King Must Die*, matrilinear, mother-god–worshipping Crete nonetheless maintains its hold on the former bull-dancers, who have been "rescued" from a place whose loss they mourn. In the Cretan bull-court, sexual differences are obliterated; "life and honor came before boy or girl" (*Bull* 6). The girls' and boys' bodies come to resemble each other: the ideal bull-dancer borrows qualities from each. At the start of *The Bull from the Sea*, Theseus is unrecognizable in his bull-leaper's guise; slim and smooth-shaven, he wears kohl around his eyes and a tight belt around his waist. Not until he dresses again as an Athenian can he be recognized as his "father's son" (4). Homosexual relationships are common and honored among women as well as men. In *The Bull from the Sea*, the female bull-dancers and lovers Pylia and Thebe die nobly together in their effort to capture the rampaging Cretan bull and to escape rigid Athenian sex roles. "They called us haters of men," Thebe says as she dies. "There is nothing left like the Bull Court. No honor" (34). While Medea and Phaedra are certainly seen in negative terms, those women who mingle traditionally male and female attributes—such as the bull-dancers Pylia and Thebe—offer alternative, genuinely destabilizing models of female power.

The Amazon queen Hippolyta in *The Bull from the Sea* has a similarly duplicitous sexual identity. She is as much Theseus's double as his opposite, insistently colleague as well as lover: "we learned as much of each other in battle as we did in bed," Theseus remembers (152). Nancy Huston has pointed out the historical incompatability of heterosexual love and war; intercourse was supposed to make both men and women unfit for war (129), yet Theseus and Hippolyta successfully merge sex and military prowess. When Hippolyta has an opportunity, just after her capture, to kill Theseus, she refuses not out of sentiment but because she cannot break her warrior's oath. Similarly, her decision to die for him is an example of "consenting sacrifice" to which Theseus himself aspires, not female masochism.

But the most impressive aspect of the Amazons' cross-gender identity is their bodily wholeness, which Renault implicitly contrasts with Freud's notion of woman as castrated man. Most of Renault's woman characters are described through fragmented glimpses of body parts or clothes. Only the Amazons are described in terms of their entire bodies. Theseus writes of recognizing Hippolyta from a distance, "I knew her by everything, though her face was too far to see: by her seat on her mountain pony, the set of her shoulders, the tilt of her light spear" (125).

The Amazons' wholeness is made manifest in their ritual worship of the Goddess, in which they pierce themselves with daggers, yet are not wounded. "Her skin was as whole as polished ivory before the carver scratches it," Theseus says of one Amazon dancer who has just driven daggers into her breast, as he watches, transfixed with desire and horror (*Bull* 128). In Freudian terms, Theseus's response is a classic male response to the female body: "Probably no male human being," Freud writes, "is spared the fright of castration at the sight of a female genital" (21:154), the wound, of course, being a standard image for female castration. But the emphasis here is on wholeness: these women are witnessed in the act of self-wounding, yet afterword appear as before. They are refusing, in Kofman's terms, to "see" their own castration. Naomi Schor uses Kofman's formulation in her reading of George Sand's fetishism, which, she argues, exemplifies her "insistent and troubling *bisextuality*" [sic]:

> The wounds inflicted on the female protagonist's body as a prelude to her sexual initiation are the stigmata neither of a turning away from femininity, nor even of a feminist protest against woman's condition under patriarchy, but rather of a refusal firmly to anchor woman—but also man—on either side of the axis of castration. ("Female" 369)

Emily Apter has pointed out the double message sent by Freud's own version of fetishism, which she describes as an "ambiguous state that demystifies and falsifies at the same time" (*Feminizing* 14). Renault's fetishism is even more profoundly ambiguous: in drawing attention to anatomy it reinforces the power of anatomy to shape experience. On the other hand, by dwelling on dismemberment, wounds, and veils, all of which evoke simultaneously the absence and presence of the phallus, she undercuts our sense of certainty about how to classify bodies. She at once draws attention to and blurs the "axis of castration."

In *The King Must Die*, for example, Ariadne after the Dionysian rites is described as follows:

> It [her hand] had lain closed on her breast, like a child's who has taken her toy to bed with her. Now when she tried to spread it out, the blood on it had stuck between the fingers, and she could not part them. But she opened her palm, and then I saw what she was holding. (*King* 323)

With characteristic elusiveness, Renault never states directly what Ariadne is holding, but presumably it is the sacrificial king's penis. Theseus, though experienced in horrors, is shattered:

> I turned away and leaned upon an olive tree, and almost threw the heart
> up from my body. I heaved and shivered in the chill of the evening; my
> teeth chattered, and water poured from my eyes. (323)

Theseus could be horrified at the implied threat that he, like the sacrificed
king, is in danger of losing his phallus; at the implied reality of the
mother-without-a-phallus, which carries with it the implied threat of castration (if she had one, she wouldn't need to take one; if she lacks one, so
might I some day); or he could be horrified at the sight of Ariadne as a
phallus-endowed woman—a phallic mother. Whatever the source, Theseus's horror forces the reader into a hallucinatory world where the possession of a phallus is by no means certain or unambiguous.

A similar scene occurs when Theseus loses his loinguard before fifteen
thousand spectators in *The King Must Die*:

> My belt held a moment, and I thought I was finished; then it gave way.
> Scrambling off without much grace, but none the worse beyond a nick in
> my side, I felt my loin-guard about my foot, kicked it away, and stood in
> the rink stark naked.
>   . . . there came from the men a shout of laughter, from the women
> flutterings and little squeals . . . I had all their eyes. (239)

Once again, an elided object stimulates an extreme response. In both
cases the emphasis is on the process of unveiling, with the actual object
unmentioned. Ariadne's hand and Theseus's loin-guard are like the "ath-
letic support-belt" fetishized by one of Freud's patients:

> Analysis showed that it signified that women were castrated and that
> they were not castrated; and it also allowed of the hypothesis that men
> were castrated, for all these possiblities could equally well be concealed
> under the belt. (156)

David Sweetman, in his recent biography of Renault, recounts an incident
playing out similar concerns in Renault's own life. In the garden of her
home near Cape Town, South Africa, according to John Guest, Mary
Renault had a metal statue of Hermes. Irritated by the decorous fig leaf it
wore, Renault had it removed, only to find there was nothing under-
neath it. She then commissioned a metal-worker to create and attach the
missing genitals (280). As a true fetishist, perhaps, Renault should have
preferred the fig leaf's ambiguity to the certainty of exposure, but her
very desire to meddle suggests a fascination with the idea that the phallus—ultimate signifier of sexual difference—can be removed and replaced.

The story of Renault's Hermes replays a much earlier story of mutilated Herms, when, on the eve of the Sicilian expedition in 415 B.C.,
Athenians of unknown identity broke the phalluses from such statues
throughout the city. Eva Keuls hypothesizes that Athenian women, aware

of their city's equation of male sexuality with military aggression and violence, expressed their revolt in the most symbolically vivid way possible (391). It is with precisely this night that Renault opens her first historical novel, *The Last of the Wine*, set during the Peloppenesian War. The Night of the Herms does much to explain Renault's choice of a Grecian setting, for the Greeks, too, were obsessed with the relation between body and power. In this "phallocracy," as Eva Keuls names it (1), the male body serves as cultural icon, the phallus signifying, in the most literal way imaginable, male dominance (2).

The gaze of thousands is again focused on—or, more accurately, deflected from—the genitals in *Funeral Games*, when boyish Eurydike, about to address the Macedonian troops, realizes her menstrual period has begun: "Already she felt a warning moisture. If she stood on the rostrum, everyone would see" (236). Speaking to the troops is the only way to establish herself as queen and her husband, Alexander's idiot brother Arridaios, as king. Eurydike had trained as a warrior, and admired Hippolyta; she "had known as long as she could remember that she should have been a boy" (118). She alone, of all the aspirants for Alexander's power, glows as he did, with a kind of superhuman energy (221). The men know, of course, that she is a woman, but seem at times willing to love and follow her. But for her to stand with the telltale blood on her clothes is impossible. It is all right to be a woman, but not to reveal the "fact" of one's castration:

> She had come, the morning being fresh, with a himation round her shoulders. Now, carefully, she slipped it down to her elbows, to drape in a curve over her buttocks, as elegant ladies wore it in fresco paintings. Getting to her feet, taking care over her draperies, she said, "I do not wish to address the Macedonians." (236–37)

Feeling herself "cheated by her body at a great turn of fate" (236), Eurydike exemplifies the issue at the heart of Renault's work. Preferring to see herself as essentially male, she seems to incarnate female self-hatred; women to her are an "alien species, imposing no laws upon her" (193), but her own body contradicts her freedom, leaving her, since all her allegiances are "masculine," nothing but a sense of bitterness and failed ambition. But in fact her two weapons, silence and the veil, allow her to sustain a saving ambiguity. She is not exposed; she rises to power one more time before her death, destroyed finally less by her gender than by her equally power-hungry rivals, all of whom will eventually die grotesquely.

Genital ambiguity reaches its height in Renault's work in the beautiful eunuch Bagoas, lover of Darius and Alexander in *The Persian Boy*. Bagoas's castration has placed him outside the categories of male and female: "There are eunuchs who become women, and those who do not; we are something by ourselves, and must make of it what we can," he is told by a fellow eunuch (40). As with Theseus and Ariadne, the simultaneous presence and absence of the phallus attracts the fascinated stare of others. Everyone wants to see him naked, and Darius would "stand [him] . . . by the bed, and turn [him] . . . here and there to take the light" (31).

Bagoas's world of mutilation and decadence contrasts, as does Crete in *The King Must Die*, with the Athenian notion of the perfect male body as cultural ideal. Bagoas tends Alexander's body, cleaning wounds and waste without disgust, kissing and admiring the various scars Alexander acquires (197, 334). Bagoas's father and numerous others lose ears and nose; thousands of Greek slaves lose a leg or two; a begging leper takes Bagoas's alms in a "palm without thumb or fingers" (14). This is a world of blurred boundaries, where a bodily appendage one day may be decaying matter the next.

The mutilated Greeks refuse to return to their home because there they would be ridiculed, as would Bagoas. Bodily deformation is the worst thing that can happen to a Greek (thus Theseus's horror of Procrustes and his famous bed, and of Sinois Pinebender, the robber of *The King Must Die* who ties his victims to two pine trees he has bent together, then lets them fly apart; thus also the outrage in Athens at the defacement of the Herms during the Peloppenesian War). To the Persians, on the other hand, deformation is on a continuum with bodily adornment (also despised by the Greeks), both being part of an infinite series of variations to which the body is prone. Crete and Persia suggest that the body's parameters may vary, and gender is a question of shading, not absolutes. Such variations decenter the phallus as source of power.

While Axiothea's Platonism is belied by her body, which inscribes her as female regardless of her own idea of herself, Platonism works more effectively—if less explicitly—in *The Persian Boy*, where Bagoas's body is as physically ambiguous as his self-image. Having been forcibly castrated, Bagoas must learn that procreating dreams is as satisfying as procreating sons. Here Bagoas echoes Plato, who writes in *The Symposium* that while women become "pregnant in body," "men who are more creative in their souls than in their bodies" conceive wisdom and virtue—offspring "fairer and more immortal than sons" (209e). At the opening of *The Persian Boy*, Bagoas's father tells him that unlike the evil, power-hungry eunuch who shares his name, *he* will be able to pass on the family honor—"you, and the sons of your sons" (5). Within a few pages, however, this Bagoas too has been castrated. Only gradually will he learn that reproduction can take place imaginatively, through the passing on of dreams rather than genes, as he shapes posterity's view of Alexander by helping Ptolemy write the history of Alexander that then serves as Arrian's source.

It is Bagoas, rather than Axiothea, who seems finally the most successful incarnation of sexual duplicity. For while Axiothea can imagine herself male and dress accordingly, her body still operates within a physical and social realm that defines her as female and can thus lead her—as it does Eurydike in *Funeral Games*—only to conflict and self-hatred. Bagoas, on the other hand, defies inscription as either male or female. David Sweetman points out that Bagoas, the only survivor of *Funeral Games*, "seems to represent for Mary a solution to the problem of gender by being, like T. S. Eliot's Tiresias, of neither, yet of both sexes at once" (294).

Finally, it seems to me, Renault's obsessive return to the relation between phallus and power forces the reader's attention so fixedly on the human body that she creates an uncertainty where none was before. Greek derision and shame at bodily mutilation in *The Persian Boy*, Theseus's intense horror before the Amazons' dance and Ariadne's bloody hand, Eurydike's and Axiothea's need to disguise their female bodies—all suggest a culture haunted by the possibility of castration. Renault's emphasis on this possibility, through her depiction of wounds, elisions, veils, and dismemberment, is finally a refusal (to quote again Schor's comments on George Sand), "firmly to anchor woman—but also man— on either side of the axis of castration" ("Reading" 369). Donning her male mask while repeatedly masking the genitals of the bodies she describes, Renault creates an unsettling world where bodies resist easy categorization as female or male, as "castrated" or not.

NOTES

1. Linked by some feminist theorists to the concept of a female or lesbian fetishism, this donning of masculinity as costume has been explored most recently by Elizabeth Grosz, Marjorie Garber, Naomi Schor, Emily Apter, and Teresa de Lauretis.

2. See Dowling, *Hellenism*, especially 104–54.

CHAPTER 7

History as Palimpsest: Gender and Narrative in Bryher's Gate to the Sea

Like Mitchison and Butts, Bryher (born Annie Winifred Ellerman) was attracted by adventure and frustrated by her gender. Unlike them, however, her connection to the past was mediated not just by the classical education of male relatives, but also by her lesbianism, and particularly by her lifelong relationship with H. D.

Bryher's upbringing was unusual. Her father was one of Great Britain's richest men, a shipping magnate. He did not marry her mother until 1909, when Winifred was 15 years old and her younger brother about to be born (*Heart* 114). Until 1909, the family traveled extensively, particularly in the Middle East, giving Winifred idealized memories of a rootless, adventure-filled childhood, a childhood she was later to call—in contrast to her postpubescent misery—"balanced, full. Unsplit" (*Two* 102).

Again and again in her autobiographical writings, Bryher writes of her yearning for the sea, for adventure, her desire above all to be a boy. "Her one regret was that she was a girl," she writes in *Development*, her 1920 autobiographical novel (6). For her—as for so many other ambitious women—being a boy meant access to adventure and achievement. From the age of eight, she devoured the historical fiction of G. A. Henty (*Heart* 94), attracted especially by the ancient world, which she saw as a "period of unrestrained freedom, a life of riding forth" (*Development* 31). She would make up her own stories about it, but always "A boy must occupy the centre of the story. To her [in *Development* she writes of herself in the third person], Carthaginian girls existed merely in a fabulous way" (*Development* 24). She yearned "not to watch but to battle with the waves. Yet the door was locked; she could only wait at the window, des-

This chapter is a revised version of an earlier article, "Multiplying the Past: Gender and Narrative in Bryher's *Gate to the Sea*," *Contemporary Literature* 31.3 (Fall, 1990): 353–72. © 1990. Reprinted by permission of the University of Wisconsin Press.

olate with lost adventure, desolate with a boyishness that might never put to sea" (*Development* 160).

Years later Bryher wrote in a letter of her discussion with Havelock Ellis about this longstanding desire to be a boy:

> Then we got onto the question of whether I was a boy sort of escaped into the wrong body and he says it is a disputed subject but quite possible and showed me a book about it . . . we agreed it was most unfair for it to happen but apparently I am quite justified in pleading I ought to be a boy . . . I am just a girl by accident. (qtd. in Hanscombe and Smyers 38)

Throughout her life Bryher thought of herself as in some way "male." Yet her autobiographical persona in *Two Selves* hates men (94), and, more significantly, Bryher identified with feminists and with other women, especially with other lesbians, throughout her life. Like Renault's "mannish lesbians," Bryher refused to define herself as "female" for reasons more complex than simple envy of or identity with male privilege. Esther Newton has suggested the disruptive potential of such gender-crossing; Teresa de Lauretis explains the "mannish lesbian" as a logical signifier of lesbian desire: since in Western culture only masculinity connotes desire for the female body, icons of masculinity are effective means of conveying that desire. The "fetish of masculinity," she writes, "is what both lures and signifies her desire for the female body" (243). Certainly for Bryher her sense of herself as both boyish and lesbian were interwined, and crucial to an understanding of her historical fiction.

Bryher's wandering, unconventional childhood was ended by her parents' marriage. Soon after, she was sent to a boarding school: Queenwood in her autobiographies, *The Heart to Artemis* and *The Days of Mars*; Downwood in *Development* and *Two Selves*, her two autobiographical novels. Bryher describes the experience in terms similar to Butts: as a nightmarish introduction to enforced conformity, a "violation of the spirit" (*Heart* 118). Already she saw her role in historical terms, identifying with a conquered people; entering Queenwood, she writes in *Days of Mars*, she felt herself a Saxon facing the Normans (165). For a time, in fact, she wanted to be an historian. She writes of history beckoning her, again in terms that echo Butts's:

> History from Tyre and Carthage to the Pillars of Hercules spun in front of me, waiting for an interpreter, not in separate, narrow lengths but in a single, flowing-together wave. (*Heart* 110)

Both women find, in their involvement in history, an alternative to the oppressive world of girls.

Bryher spent the years immediately after Queenwood groping for something to do. She studied hieroglyphics with Margaret Murray, read

French symbolist poetry, admired Dorothy Richardson, and longed to go to America, where "girls had jobs" (*Heart* 150–55). Depressed, even suicidal, she again writes of her experience in terms of history, again identifying with conquered peoples: "With Carthage a flame and with Troy broken there was one way out" (*Two* 122). Then, in 1918, she met Hilda Doolittle, whose poetry she admired. She consoled H. D. as she separated from her husband, Richard Aldington, and she became a "second mother" to H. D.'s daughter Perdita.[1]

In 1921 the two women travelled to America, where Bryher met and married Robert McAlmon, despite the fact that only women attracted her sexually.[2] She hoped, she explains in *The Heart to Artemis*, that she would have more freedom married than single. During the years that followed, while McAlmon and Bryher's Contact Press published many avant-garde writers, Bryher traveled, taking a crucial trip to Greece with H. D., and formed close connections to other lesbians and feminists. In 1926, Bryher divorced McAlmon and a year later she married Kenneth Macpherson, with whom she created *Close-Up*, the first journal to treat film as an art form. Eight years later, she bought *Life and Letters* from Desmond MacCarthy, renaming it *Life and Letters Today* (Guest 232). Throughout her life Bryher used her massive financial resources and her publishing connections to support what Sylvia Beach calls a "large family of intellectuals" (103).[3] Among her neediest dependents in the 1930s was Mary Butts, whose work she frequently published in *Life and Letters Today* and whose *Last Stories* she collected for posthumous publication (Hanscombe and Smyers 241). Even when generosity was dangerous, Bryher persisted, helping, during World War II, to smuggle out of Germany "dozens of Nazi victims" (Beach 103), among them Walter Benjamin (Fitch 397).

While Bryher admired her father tremendously (Barbara Guest calls her "fanatically devoted" to him [113]), mourned her mother as the source of "her sense of adventure" (Guest 249), and passionately loved many different women throughout her life, her relationship with H. D. was clearly central. It was through H. D. that she came to love Greece; it was, in fact, H. D.'s Greece she loved. She makes this explicit in her poem "Eros of the Sea," dedicated to H. D.: "For her gift of Greek." Greece for Bryher combined all the longings of her childhood—for the sea, for a lost adventurous past—and merged them with her passionate love for H. D.

Gate to the Sea, Bryher's only historical novel involving ancient Greece, is superficially a simple story about a Greek priestess's flight from Roman-occupied Poseidonia. But it tells another story as well: of Bryher's love for H. D. and, on a larger scale, of how "history" becomes, in fact, *his*: the way in which the day-to-day life of women is lost to synthesizers of the past. In all her novels Bryher shifts abruptly among multiple viewpoints, often emphasizing the misconceptions or distortions inherent in any single perspective. In *Gate to the Sea* in particular, she vividly portrays the process by which felt experience is transformed into history, highlighting the problematic relation of women to what Luce Irigaray calls "masculine" systems of representation, systems that (in Jacobus's words), "disappropriate women of their relation to themselves and to other women" (Jacobus 63).[4] As alternative she hints at a lost matriarchy and mother tongue and a laborious process of retrieval by which at least the memory of that lost landscape can be retained.

Gate to the Sea portrays the flight of a Greek high priestess, Harmonia, from Poseidonia (Paestum), where the Greek inhabitants, since the death of Alexander in 323 B.C., have been enslaved and culturally dominated by the Lucanians.[5] The book takes place during a single day, a holiday honoring Hera, the one day during the year when the slaves "speak their own language without being beaten, and worship again in temples that had formerly been their pride" (10). Harmonia's mentally unstable brother Archias, accompanied by Myro, a young girl disguised as a boy, arrives from the Italian town to which the Poseidonian exiles have fled. His task is to rescue Harmonia and to dig up the city's emblem, a carved disk, so that he can found a new city elsewhere in Italy. Passing through the "gate to the sea," they escape—barely—taking with them the aged Lykos and his wife Phila, enslaved Poseidonians who had agreed to commit suicide rather than be separated by their Lucanian master. In the process, Harmonia must come to terms with the loss of her homeland and, most painfully, her desertion of the temple to Hera. The novel is spare and apparently simple, but when read in generic and intellectual context, *Gate to the Sea* shows how women writers can rework a problematic genre and at the same time redefine their relation to their own cultural history.

This Bryher does by creating multiple—sometimes conflicting—narrative perspectives, implying that no single version is sufficient; by dramatizing the act of emplotment itself, to expose the role power plays in how stories get shaped and which particularities they leave out; and by using conflicting historical accounts as source material. Such conflicts, usually disguised by the notion of "historical probability," suggest that the very "facts" used to define an era's "difference" are themselves the products of culturally derived conceptualizations and could be construed in very different ways. By emphasizing the process by which historical discourse (as opposed to history) is made, Bryher undercuts the inevitability—the "odor of the ideal"—that would otherwise adhere to the events she describes. Such an undercutting is essential to the feminist historical novelist, for whom the recreation of the ancient past is otherwise merely the replication of her own oppression.

The novel's opening pages provide a lesson in the dangers of unitary versions of the past. *Gate to the Sea* opens from the viewpoint of the slave Lykos. Formerly a great runner, he is now immobilized by age and lameness, and we enter his mind as he lies awake at dawn agonizing over his lost dignity and prowess, and over his desire to protect and console his wife, whom he believes to be still asleep. When, abruptly, the narrated monologue shifts from his viewpoint to his wife Phila's, we recognize the limitations of Lykos's verson of his past, which circles around his concerns and his delusions and is premised on the unconsciousness and passivity of his wife, who has, in fact, "hardly slept at all" (12), and is busy planning how to obtain hemlock so that they can die together. Neither one knows the other is awake. The juxtaposition of viewpoints throughout the novel provides no startling revelations, but the series of small jolts as the narrated consciousness shifts among Harmonia, Lykos, Phila, Archias, his companion Myro, and the two Poseidonian traitors Demo and Phanion suggests the insufficiency of any single account of experience.

These shifts also suggest the role emplotment plays in giving meaning to experience. Lykos's formulation of his past is vital to his sense of self; Phila's thoughts propel her into action, as she decides to ask Harmonia for hemlock. Throughout the novel, before characters act, they reconstrue their past and their relationships, acting only after their thinking has provided a context within which their actions will have meaning. Action without such a sense of a coherent past is impossible.

The worst thing the Lucanians can do, then, is rob the Poseidonians of their ability to make sense of their past. And this is precisely what they do, by forbidding them their language. Bryher dramatizes the process through which history dispossesses the marginalized of their experience. Most painfully signifying his slavery, Lykos finds, is the loss of his language: "The very sounds that were a man's earliest memories had been taken away from him, nor might a mother hum a Greek cradle song to her child" (15). The pronouncing of foreign words for everyday things—"bread, oil, rope, fire" (16) enslaves him. The problem is intense: how survive when the very act of construing one's needs produces self-estrangement? The native language, here associated with "earliest memories" and "cradle songs," very much a "mother tongue," has been forbidden; to speak is to enter into a hostile camp—a masculine discourse—to become like the traitor Phanion, who has become "more Lucanian than his masters" (15).

The bellicose Lucanians are linked in the novel to repression of the feminine, and as such suggest a masculine discourse superimposed on an alternative culture which, if not actually matriarchal, certainly bears traces of a matriarchal past. On the one day per year on which the Poseidonians may speak their language and pronounce each other's names, the Lucanians leave to attend annual games "in honor of the god of war" (9), obviously a male deity, while the native Greeks reenact a traditional rite, probably linked to fertility, in honor of Hera and led by the high priestess. The landscape of Poseidonia—its "serpentine furrow" and "twin peaks . . . like lily stems" (115), its cave that serves as Hera's sanctuary—is unmistakably female, and Hera herself was, according to Jane Harrison, a Magna Mater—a potent earth goddess before later Greek culture married her off to Zeus ("Primitive" 75–76).

But now Harmonia discovers that the Poseidonians can scarcely pronounce the Greek words necessary to honor Hera. Denied the language that synthesizes, that evokes feeling as well as naming, the Poseidonians are forced into fragmentation, unable to identify themselves as a group or to trace their history. The slaves, Harmonia mourns, are "muttering not about liberty but bread" (66). The traitor Phanion warns her, "What you call your slavery is an episode" (62), insisting that experience irrelevant to the dominant culture is insignificant, denied the dignity of emplotment. For those whose every utterance means self-estrangement, the endowing of experience with meaning is an impossibility.

Bryher herself wrote of having felt such a linguistic alienation, which for her, too, coincided with entry into a system of sexual difference and rigid hierarchy. Entering school, she writes in *The Heart to Artemis*, she felt overwhelmed by the alien language she met there (123). The alien language was part of a system of rigidly imposed gender distinctions that labels her "masculine" ambitions inappropriate. She had at the time, she tells us, the psyche of a nine-year-old boy (122); she had wanted to be a merchant (109) or a historian (110), but at school she is faced with the laughter of others and quickly "hustled out . . . to march two by two in my first 'crocodile'" to see the celebration of George the V's accession (119). This immersion in a chain of girls typifies her new relation to history: made abruptly aware of her gender, she has been turned into a spectator of others' power.

Family circumstances reinforced Bryher's abrupt sense of marginalization. The same year she entered school, Bryher's parents had married, a brother had been born, and the family's adventurous travels ceased. Entry into school is thus simultaneously entry into a system of gender, law, and discipline; no wonder Bryher calls it a "violation of the spirit" (118). Acting out Gerda Lerner's "dialectic of women's history"—"the tension between women's actual historical experience and their exclusion from interpreting that experience" (5)—the schoolgirl Winifred is bewildered by her immersion in a discourse that defines her as other, as object, and thus estranges her from her own past.

This problem of referentiality and meaning forms the dramatic center of *Gate to the Sea*, which asks, literally, what pieces of the past do we need to carry with us in order to maintain our identity? Harmonia must decide whether to flee Poseidonia and, if she does flee, what to take with her. Bryher's novel dramatizes the moment at which the groundwork for future historical discourse is laid: the moment at which certain objects, memories, and people are retrieved, while others are lost.

These questions are raised by the return of Harmonia's brother Archias, who has been sent by the oracle at Cumae, he tells his sister, to retrieve a disk, symbol of Poseidonia, which he had buried during the sack of the city, along with the family's jewels; and to retrieve his sister, to whom he is to insist, "Loyalty is to Hera, not to a place" (41), i.e., not to the literal, but to the figurative—to the *idea* of Hera. The tasks are paradoxical: if Harmonia need not stay in Poseidonia's temple to worship Hera, why do Poseidonian exiles need the disk to found a settlement?

The answer is ambiguous, suggesting the oscillation, the "both/and vision" Rachel Blau DuPlessis links to women's identity as both "insiders" and "outsiders" in relation to culture (*Writing* 39–42). Or, as Harmonia's teacher had told her, "The road to the mysteries is not a question and its answer. It is as troubled, as unpredictable as the sea" (*Gate* 76). Harmonia leaves, carrying the statue of Hera with her, but having cut off—after great uncertainty—the ritual garlands that would have hindered its removal, thus compromising her attachment to the literal fulfillment of her religious duties. Archias successfully digs up the disk and carries it off—with the family jewels—to Salente. Unlike Aeneas, who left Creusa behind and managed to get only his father to Italy, Archias returns for his sister, affirming the role of the female, and the literal, in establishing continuity.

And along with the disk and jewels, Harmonia takes with her her mother's necklace and mirror, objects affirming her connection to a female past, her resistance to absorption into a future where her identity will be *all* idea, defined by a discourse known as history, in which the solidity of everyday objects—particularly those, like a mirror, that affirm an independent female identity—has no place. We're told of the mirror:

> Like the necklace, it had belonged to her mother, but it was an everyday possession, and the limbs of the nymph that formed the handle were dented and rubbed. It was all that was left to her of her home; she could not leave it behind. (101–2)

With these objects she is willing to sail for Salente to found a new city, which will not be Poseidonia, she thinks, but "an echo, the memory some girl kept of her home after she had followed her husband to another land" (100). Through these literal objects, then, she can keep alive a sense of connection, attenuated but real, to a lost female past. "Use the word to oppose 'necrophilia,'" writes Christa Wolf in *Cassandra*, "to name the inconspicuous, the previous everyday, the concrete" (270). This is precisely what Harmonia does, but with objects which, through the sheer force of her carrying them, will represent the past—not as metaphors, substituting for it, but as metonymical fragments, part of an uncompletable series of pieces. Poseidonia and Hera are not, finally, in Harmonia's heart; the exiles leave with a sense of loss, intent on carrying off what pieces of the past they can retain. Phila, Lykos's wife, fixes her eyes mournfully on the coastline she leaves, "trying to fix every outline in her mind, the dip, the serpentine furrow, the twin peaks that rose like lily stems" (115). And the novel concludes with Harmonia's final glimpse of "the towers and the white gateway through which they had passed to freedom" (119). These visions of a receding female landscape suggest yet again that what has been lost is an unmediated relationship to the feminine, to language, and to the past.

Through her conflicting narrative viewpoints and her use of emplotment as theme, Bryher thus questions the assumptions implicit in her chosen genre. But Bryher's choice of setting allows her also to evoke the complex resonances and implications ancient Greece has for women—because of its role in Western culture and British intellectual history, and because of its role in her own life, in her relationship with H. D. The result is a historical novel that must be read as a palimpsest, legible only with the help of other texts, which serve as clues to what has been erased.

Bryher cites as one of her epigraphs a passage from L. R. Farnell's multivolume *The Cults of the Greek States*, published between 1896 and 1909. In the passage quoted by Bryher, Farnell describes the ritual that Harmonia oversees:

> the Samian priestess at a yearly ceremony secretly made off with the idol of Hera and hid it in a lonely place in the woods by the shore, in the midst of a withy brake, where it was then re-discovered and cakes were set by its side, possibly as bridal offerings. (Farnell I: 184).

While Farnell downplays Hera's independence, emphasizing instead her marriage to Zeus, the very ceremony borrowed from Farnell by Bryher is cited by other scholars as evidence of Hera's earlier identity as an earth-goddess (Farnell 181–86). Farnell spends several pages refuting an 1893 article by Harrison in which she insists on Hera's pre-Zeus identity as evidence of a pre-Olympain gynaecocracy "that even Achaean Homer is powerless wholly to forget" (Harrison, "Primitive" 75). Harrison, a feminist, throughout her career gleefully brandished whatever evidence she could find of a Great Mother whose worship "long preceded the worship of the Father [Zeus]" (*Reminiscences* 72). The theme of her *Prolegomena to the Study of Greek Religion* was the "superposing of the official cults on the primitive chthonic nature-cults" (Stewart 31)—a superposition

anticipating the one dramatized by Bryher in the conflict between Poseidonians and Lucanians. And in *Themis*, Harrison describes Hera, in terms
that again seem to anticipate Bryher's novel, as "the turbulent native
princess, coerced, but never really subdued, by an alien conquerer," representing an indigenous, matrilinear Argive culture suppressed by Zeus's
arrival from the north (491).

In her citation of Farnell's text, then, and in her choice of setting
and plot, Bryher suggests her knowledge of the scholarly controversy
surrounding the interpretation of the very ceremony she interpolates into
her text.[6] That Harrison's article is itself a refutation of an earlier article
by Charles Waldstein ("Primitive" 72) reinforces the sense that these
controversies recede endlessly into the distance, making any resolution of
differences impossible. When Bryher insists on facts that one character
never finds out about another, when she hints at the multiple versions of
the past offered by her nonfictional sources, she is, in Irigaray's terms,
"playing with mimesis . . . so as to make 'visible' . . . what was supposed
to remain invisible: the cover-up of a possible operation of the feminine in
language" (76). She is exposing the way in which historical discourse is in
fact based on the suppression of multiplicity and uncertainty.

The focal point for the suppression is Archias, who yearns for a certainty that the text as a whole exposes as unavailable. Ironically, he is
himself a nexus of ambiguity: he may or may not be mad; he may or
may not have violated Hera's sanctuary;[7] he is accompanied by the sexually ambiguous Myro; and he finds the city's disk and his family's jewels—but not quite where he expected. All these uncertainties torment
him, and he ponders them compulsively. His sickness, he is told at Cumae,
is pride; he would rather blame himself for the fall of his city than com-
prehend the incalculable multiplicity of factors involved (48).

The apparent origin of Archias's problems is Hera's cave. This is the
cave where Archias took refuge during a thunderstorm, and thus, he
believes, invoked the wrath of Hera—subsequent cause of his madness
and the city's fall:

> He had seen a cave in front of him with no sign of life outside it or
> within, a flash of lightning had split the tree a few paces from his head,
> he had sprung as he supposed to shelter and a voice had shouted at
> him, "Ai! Fool! You have broken the sanctuary of the Goddess!" (47)

Perceived only in glimpses through Archias's chaotic mind, the cave is a
kind of textual navel: the point at which all certainty disappears. Unas-
similable into history, it remains a hint of all that history leaves out.[8]

Emblem of suppressed female power, the cave becomes a triumphant
"monster in the text," defined by Jacobus as the "repressed vacillation of
gender or the instability of identity—the ambiguity of subjectivity itself

which returns to wreak havoc on consciousness, on hierarchy, and on unitary schemes designed to repress the otherness of femininity" (5). The palimpsestic use of Farnell, with his traces of the written-over Harrison, serves, like Archias and the cave, to destabilize the terms in which the text is to be understood.

"If women are such good mimics," writes Irigaray, "it is because they are not simply resorbed in this function. *They also remain elsewhere*" (76). For Bryher that *elsewhere* is both historical and personal: the mythic past when women spoke a mother tongue and lived unalienated lives; the personal past (before 1909), where she lived a genderless, lawless life, traveling and communing, with the help of Clio, her "mistress" (*Heart* 119), with past ages; and the more recent personal past, when she traveled to Greece with H. D. and all but merged with her mind as she helped H. D. complete her visions on the wall of her hotel in Corfu—the famous "writing on the wall."[9] These elsewheres become discernible when *Gate to the Sea* is juxtaposed with H. D.'s *Palimpsest* and Bryher's poetry.

The first third of *Palimpsest* is at once roman à clef and historical novel. As roman à clef, it recreates the breakup of H. D.'s relationship with Richard Aldington; as historical novel, it tells the story of the Greek poet Hipparchia who lives, circa 75 B.C., in Rome (which has conquered Greece), and who attempts to translate Moero into Latin, to come to terms with the defeat of her homeland, and to understand her own sexuality. At the very end, the arrival of Julia Cornelia Augusta (Bryher), who loves her poetry, offers a trip to Alexandria, and will supply the intimacy for which Hipparchia yearns, resolves all three crises.

Palimpsest is dedicated to Bryher, and Bryher's *Gate to the Sea* is in some ways a response. In both works, the defeat of Greece produces linguistic and sexual alienation. In both, the question of how to preserve a lost past and still survive, how to live both within (so as not to go mad) and outside (so as not to lose one's identity) the dominant discourse is central. Archias argues "Loyalty is to Hera, not to a place." Julia/Bryher tells Hipparchia, "Greece is a spirit. Greece is not lost" (134). For both Hipparchia and Harmonia, the effort is to locate an *elsewhere*, a space within/outside patriarchal culture out of which they can write their experience without betraying it.

The "writing on the wall" suggests that for a moment they found it. That writing, a miraculously visible projection of mental images, is the product of two women's minds collaborating, on contact, briefly, with a mythic past. The images intrigued both for decades, underlying *Palimpsest*, as Deborah Kloepfer suggests (568), as well as H. D.'s *Tribute to Freud* and Bryher's *Gate to the Sea*, confirming the associations among Greece, an altered state of consciousness, an ancient past, and intimacy between women.

A similar mental mingling appears in Bryher's short novel *Manchester* to suggest intimacy beyond and resistant to language. Ernest, Bryher's persona, bitterly rejects words as inadequate (14.4: 89) and instead characterizes his feeling for Cordelia as an unmediated meeting of minds: "They met together where emotion started, where unconsciousness passed into perception" (13.2: 90). This point outside language, where emotion and perception merge, is landscape—a landscape that has been internalized even as it has been perceived: "geographical emotion," Bryher calls it in a 1937 essay ("Paris" 33).[10] In *Heart to Artemis* Bryher describes the mystically intense encounters with the past she experienced in certain places when "Clio" happened to be there (54). She took her name from a place (a Scilly island) and in *Two Selves* evokes the crucial first encounter with H. D. not by telling of it, but by describing the place where it took place: "A cottage that faced the south-blue sea" (125). Again and again landscape serves as a screen that shapes, reflects, and protects the meanings language cannot convey, for, as she writes in *Two Selves*, "If you spoke straight out your thought they called you queer and shut you up" (122).[11] Shortly after her trip to Greece with H. D., Bryher wrote a series of poems entitled "Hellenics," one of which opens:

> Your face is the flush of Eos:
> You are dawn.
> Your face is Greece
>
> Under your lifted arm
> There is lavender to kiss;
> Sea-lavender, spiced with salt. (136–37)

This description of loved woman as Greek landscape underlies Bryher's treatment of the Poseidonian coast in *Gate to the Sea* and suggests the subversive power the notion of "geographical emotion" held for her.

This link between historical fiction and lesbian desire is evident in the resemblance between Bryher's early unpublished prose poem "Eros of the Sea" and *Gate to the Sea*. Dedicated to H. D. "For her gift of Greek," "Eros of the Sea" depicts a temple, gates, and sea—all elements it shares with the much later historical novel. In the poem, however, the landscape's eroticism is more explicit; "Only the temple caught a flower of light," Bryher writes, in imagery that strikes me as unmistakably vaginal, "itself a tuft of orchard-buds, dawn-white about a calyx of dark fire" ("Eros" 7). The poem's speaker is lost, seeks the temple of Eros, and is instructed by the temple's guardian to seek the "open sea." There Eros appears, and the speaker addresses him:

"Once I was happy—once I was not afraid—in
childhood—long ago."
"There is a flower more beautiful than childhood.
Come, take it of my lips." ("Eros" 10)

Diana Collecott dates the poem around 1920 and links it to Bryher's
1918 introduction to H. D. in Cornwall. Bryher herself suggests such a
connection in *Days of Mars*, where she describes H. D. reading poetry as
a "seer prophesying from the steps of a Greek temple above a brilliant
sea" (82).

Gate to the Sea can be read, in fact, as an expression of de Lauretis's
"perverse desire," which is "sustained on fantasy scenarios that restage
the loss and recovery of a fantasmatic female body" (265). That Harmonia brings with her a mirror to recall her mother's lost self suggests that
the absent woman is a *mis-en-abime*, endlessly reproducible but inacces-
sible. Receding shoreline, dead mother, deserted temple: all suggest lost
female bodies toward whom Harmonia is paradoxically moving when she
flees seaward. And Bryher herself doubles this movement in writing historical fiction, which is itself a movement toward Clio, female figure for
a lost past.

Bryher's historical novel about ancient Greece is thus also about her
lesbianism and her relationship with H. D. In her insistence on things and
feelings and relationships that echo and evoke rather than differ from
the present, and in her portrayal of history-making as exclusion, Bryher
undercuts her book's generic identity. Her past is neither a finished, aes-
theticized object for study, like Fleishman's (14), nor has it been absorbed
into Lukacs's evolutionary flow of "inexorable necessity" (57). Bryher's
past offers above all else a chance to meddle, to remake and undo, to
merge. "To write of things," Bryher writes, was to become part of them.
It was to see *before* the beginning and *after* the end" (*Heart* 110). To
write historical novels is in fact for Bryher to collude with Clio, subvert-
ing the certainty of historical discourse, transgressing the boundaries of
historical plots, as she evokes, under erasure, a world of female power
and intimacy.

NOTES

1. Perdita Schaffner, H. D.'s daughter, used the term to me in conversation,
August 1991.

2. Memoirs have been hard on Bryher. Smoller cites Dahlberg, who blamed
Bryher's "frigidity" for McAlmon's failure. Among others accusing Bryher of
selfishness in her relationship with McAlmon are William Carlos Williams and
Kay Boyle (Smoller 42).

3. Noel Riley Fitch writes that when Bryher's father died in 1933, he left an estate of 183–280 million pounds (354).

4. Such connections with contemporary feminist theorists have been made frequently in the case of H. D. See, for example, Deborah Kelly Kloepfer's reading of H. D.'s prose in relation to Kristeva. While Bryher is far less innovative stylistically than H. D., she, like her, is intensely aware of the problems faced by a woman writing in a patriarchal culture. In her first novel, *Development*, and her autobiography *The Heart to Artemis*, she writes of the repressive schooling that squashed her own sense of self. Her view of women as outsiders, intensified no doubt by her lesbianism, leads her to an interest in how women can come to terms with their culture. Certainly the rejection, by Cixous, Irigaray, and Kristeva, of "the privilege of unity and 'sameness' as ideals of phallocentric systems of signification" and their "exploration of a 'feminine' territory in langauge (Robinson 106) have much in common with Bryher's, as well as H. D.'s, project.

5. Paestum, known for its Greek ruins, is in southwestern Italy, not far inland from the Tyrrhenian Sea. Formerly Poseidonia, it was a Greek colony until the fourth century B.C., when it fell to the neighboring Lucanians. In 273 B.C., the Romans took over and renamed it Paestum.

6. Bryher was also an enthusiastic reader of Jessie Weston, who spends most of her introduction to *From Ritual to Romance* explaining why she has accepted Jane Harrison's description of the vegetation spirits despite Ridgeway's (with Farnell, an archenemy of Harrison's) attack on it.

7. Harrison writes of an Archias in her *Prolegomena to the Study of Greek Religion* that he was cursed because he made a sacrifice which, as a male, he shouldn't have (147).

8. As a cave linked to suppressed female power it resembles the underground lair to which Apollo drives the Furies in *The Eumenides*:

> That they could treat me so!
> I, the mind of the past, to be driven under the ground
> out cast, like dirt! (164)

9. I owe this connection to H. D.'s Corfu experiences to a conversation with Margery Phelan.

10. The same term appears in Bryher's *The Heart to Artemis* (22).

11. DuPlessis suggests that H. D. used landscape similarly, as a "conventional but protected projection of private feelings into public meanings" (*H. D.* 14). For a related discussion of H. D.'s notion of "projection," see Morris.

CHAPTER 8

Ancient Rome, Gender, and British Imperialism

During the late nineteenth century, the British ruling classes found much with which to identify in the Roman Empire: its enjoyment of domestic peace and luxury, its sense of cultural superiority and national identity, and its ability to rule much of the rest of the world. Rome, according to George Landow, was more important than the Bible to the British upper and upper-middle classes, "for whom Latin was a second language and Roman history a second past" (29). The British upper classes visited Pompeii, devoured historical novels about Rome, and greatly admired the paintings of Sir Laurence Alma-Tadema, Royal Academician, who rendered the domestic life of wealthy Romans with as much intimacy and conviction as if he had lived among them.[1] "The old Romans," according to Alma-Tadema, "were human flesh and blood like ourselves, moved by the same passions and emotions" (Swanson 43). But if the Romans were moved by the same emotions, they managed to control them; Rome stood above all for the self-discipline of mature manhood.[2] Resisting, like Aeneas, the seductive women and exotic cultures luring them toward infantile self-indulgence, the good Romans did their duty, extending their empire in the name of civilization. Thus British boys, according to O. F. Christie in *Clifton School Days*, were trained "To be in all things decent, orderly, self-mastering": to be, in other words, a "Gentleman after the high Roman fashion" (qtd. in Howarth 14).

This identification between Britain and Rome increased during the course of the nineteenth century, in keeping with Britain's identity as an imperial power.[3] While Edward Bulwer-Lytton's 1834 *The Last Days of Pompeii* dismisses Rome as a colorless imitation of Greece, later writers (Macaulay, Whyte-Melville, Kingsley, Pater, G. A. Henty) find much to admire in Roman rule and military prowess, even when it comes at the expense of the Britons themselves. A. Dwight Culler points out that English neoclassical literature was not officially labeled "Augustan" until George Saintsbury's 1898 *A Short History of English Literature* (14); crucial to the "Augustan" designation was the new respect late Victorians felt for the Roman Empire and for those aspects of their own eighteenth century reminiscent of the Empire. Like Greece, of course, Rome was multifaceted. During the thousand or so years during which Rome fought Etruscans, Carthaginians, Egyptians, various European tribes, and Christianity, its government and values were transformed many times. As a cultural construct, however, "Rome" functioned with remarkable consistency in late-nineteenth-century Britain. Macaulay's "old" Roman, with his "fortitude, temperance, veracity, spirit to resist oppression, respect for legitimate authority, fidelity in the observing of contracts, disinterestedness, ardent patriotism" (186), resembles Kipling's Roman centurion, guarding Hadrian's Wall in *Puck of Pook's Hill* several centuries later.

The nineteenth-century British identification with Rome served many purposes. It blurred Britain's experience as a conquered and colonized people (with its potential for sympathy for Britain's own conquered) and glorified the notion of empire itself as rightfully earned and educative to those beneath its yoke. It defined British imperialism as the culmination of a natural, evolutionary progression, by which the extremes of British savagery and Roman decadence are alike expelled from the historical process. Most profoundly and relevantly, this image of Rome served to inculcate and reinforce what Ashis Nandy calls the colonialist "state of mind" (1). As preface to my discussion of women who re-create the Roman empire in their historical fiction, I want to explore how this image of Rome worked on the minds of young Victorian readers, by focusing on gender and maturation in two popular historical novels involving ancient Rome: George Whyte-Melville's 1863 *The Gladiators* and G. A. Henty's 1892 *Beric the Briton*.

Both *The Gladiators* and *Beric the Briton* manipulate and reinforce deeply embedded assumptions about sexual roles: the assumption that men and women are utterly different from each other; that men are individualized agents of history while women are merely the vehicles through which their heirs are embodied; that maturation means growing away from women into a male world of emotional repression and power over others. The connection between these assumptions and imperialism has recently been analyzed by Ashis Nandy. Western culture, he points out, by tending to deny any bisexual component in men, "beautifully legitimized Europe's post-medieval modes of dominance, exploitation and cruelty as natural and valued" (4). "Colonialism," he writes, ". . . produced a cultural consensus in which political and socio-economic dominance symbolized the dominance of men and masculinity over women and femininity" (4). A "hyper-masculine and oversocialized Europe," according to Nandy, which despises and links femininity, childishness, and senility, has turned the cultures it dominates into the "abode of people childlike and innocent on the one hand, and devious, effeminate, and passive-aggressive on the other" (37–38). Rome was defined, in the late nineteenth century, in precisely the terms described by Nandy: at its most successful, it symbolized male maturity battling against the primitive cultures of northern Europe and the decadent cultures of the East—both of which were associated with transgressive women.[4]

Both *The Gladiators* and *Beric the Briton* portray the conflict between Briton and Rome during the first century A.D. Both portray a heroic young Briton who is defeated in battle and transported to Rome, where he learns Roman ways and becomes more or less reconciled to the triumph of the Roman Empire. Leaving behind British primitivism, carefully skirting Roman decadence, these boys—Esca in *The Gladiators*, Beric in the novel of that name—become men, gaining, by novel's end, self-discipline, experience, authority, and Christian wives. The process is unmistakably Oedipal: as boys fighting the Roman Empire, they are—as Charles Kingsley wrote of the ancient Britons—"boys fighting against cunning men" (*Roman* 11). Defeat by the fathers thus signals integration into a community of men—a community of shared masculine values whose very existence requires its strict separation from the world of boys and, by implication, women.[5] In the process, they learn to reject any hint of either "primitivism" or "decadence"—both qualities associated throughout the novels with women and eunuchs. Having acquired the "manly virtues" of Romans (Henty, *Young* 17), these heroes might also be justified in suppressing—as the Roman Empire of course did—those peoples supposedly lacking those virtues.

This Oedipal subtext, which obviously serves to justify British as well as Roman imperialism, operates on two levels: within the texts, as Esca and Beric learn to join Rome rather than fight it; and outside the texts, in the reading process itself, which turns boys into "men," weaning them away from their childish identification with the enemies of Empire. Historical fiction has traditionally attracted young readers; Henty's novel is aimed explicitly at boys (ages nine to sixteen would be my estimate), and *The Gladiators* would appeal to a similar audience. Both these books, through their portrayal of the Roman Empire and its enemies, play on the anxieties and uncertainties of their young readers, who are offered an implicit choice between effeminacy and the narrowest possible version of male sexual identity—a version optimally suited to imperialism.[6]

Esca and Beric, insofar as they are Britons, are boys defined by their immaturity and their ties to their mothers. When *The Gladiators* opens, Esca is dreaming of Briton and of his mother. He is already a slave in Rome; he is about to be bought by Licinius, a kind, fatherlike master who is, in fact, his literal father, though neither yet knows it. His past, in which he was the son of Guenebra, a British princess, is outside the realm of the novel, accessible only through dreams. He has fought against Rome and lost; now he is the slave/son of a Roman father. Guenebra herself has died; Licinius, who loved her, discovers her dead body in a tent after one of his victorious battles. Briton is a dream, lost to reality, in which boys and their mothers fight against Roman men.

In *Beric the Briton*, pre-Romanized British culture is linked explicitly to the feminine and stigmatized for that reason. The pre-Romanized Britons, we are reminded frequently, treat men and women equally. The British tribes have even been ruled by women: Boadicea and Beric's mother Parta lead the Britons in battle early in the novel. But this female power also links the Britons to a wildness best left behind. The Romans think the British women mad as they rouse the various tribes to avenge the mistreatment of Boadicea and her daughters (78). If not mad, they are certainly less controlled than the men. After an initial victory, "Women with flowing hair performed wild dances of triumph" (105); and "cries of exultation from the women . . . rose loud and shrill" (177). In battle, while the men sensibly kill their enemies, the women "flung themselves on the spears of the assailants" (179). The very lack of control with which the Britons are faulted is formulated in terms traditionally associated with women; they are "fickle and inconstant" (116), according to Beric, in need of Roman discipline. This Beric himself learned through his stay as hostage in a Roman household—a household ruled by a fatherly Roman general.

Briton, then, is the world of boys and women. Like Aeneas, the boys, aligned with history, leave behind the past (mother Briton) for the future (father Rome, who will eventually give them wives). Guenebra dies; Boadicea, Parta, and their female colleagues kill themselves, while Beric and his followers escape into the marshes and live to be defeated yet again and enslaved by the Romans. Thus is explained and exorcised the sympathy British readers might be expected to feel for their ancestors—a sympathy already rejected in similar terms by historians Thomas Babington Macaulay and Kingsley. The early inhabitants of Great Britain, Macaulay writes in his 1849 *History of England*, were "little superior to the natives of the Sandwich Islands" (4). For Victorian Britain to identify with such people rather than with the "great civilized world" of Rome was ludicrous (9). And Kingsley, in his 1862 *The Roman and the Teuton*, calls the early Britons "great boys," without whose defeat, "Roman law, order, and discipline would have been lost" (12).

Acceptance of Roman rule means entry into a Lacanian "Law of the Father," which forbids incest with the mother and insists on the phallus as "the mark of man's difference from woman" (Homans 7). What began as a confrontation between enemies becomes instead an affirmation of shared masculinity. The site where this masculinity is most palpably demonstrated is the hero's body, which is on display throughout both novels, but most dramatically in situations of imprisonment and gladiatorial conflict.

Whyte-Melville and Henty delight in placing their heroes in the gladiatorial arena, or in other situations where a Roman crowd gazes admiringly at their near-naked bodies. Emphasizing, paradoxically, both the powerlessness of these men and their obvious strength, these displays create tremendous tension. But while the question in suspense seems to be, "Who will prevail, Roman or Briton?" the deeper question is "Is this a man?" or, more baldly, "Does this man have a phallus?" Victory in the arena is not what matters: Esca loses to the evil Flacidus and remains a slave; Beric defeats a lion, saving Ennia, a Christian girl whom it was to have killed, and remains a slave. What matters is that both men, subjected to a spectatorial gaze that threatens castration (the price for rejecting Father Rome), not only emerge unscathed, but demonstrate their phallic size and hardness.

John Berger argues in *Ways of Seeing* that Western art has tended to display female bodies for the delectation of male spectators. When a male body—Esca on the auction block or Beric in the gladiatorial arena—is displayed in the kind of helpless, erotically charged situation more common to depictions of women in Western culture, the question is raised, it seems to me, whether this is, in fact, a woman or a man. Turning them into passive recipients of the audience's gaze, these scenes threaten to eroticize—and thereby feminize—these men.

Esca and Beric manage to resist the objectifying gaze, however, and prove themselves men. Whyte-Melville and Henty emphasize the activity and size of the men, even as they stand helplessly on display, insisting on their identity as "glorious specimen[s] of manhood" (Whyte-Melville 18). The Roman general Licinius, about to buy—unknowingly—his own son as a slave, admires his physique: Esca is "a fine young man of great strength and stature, who seemed to feel painfully the indignity of his position, placed as he was a on a huge stone block, whereon his own towering height rendered him a conspicuous object in the throng" (67). And the Roman crowd admires Beric as he confronts, unarmed, the lion intended for Ennia: "Accustomed as they were to gaze at athletes, they were struck with the physique and strength of this young Briton, with the muscles standing up massive and knotted through the white skin" (266–67). Esca towers; Beric's muscles stand up. In situations that threaten to turn them into objects of others' gaze, these men's erectness signals their manhood.

The condition of the phallus is of course a crucial metaphor here. Castration punishes those who persist in Oedipal revolt (Freud 22: 129). Placed in positions in which we are more accustomed to see those without phalluses—i.e., women—Esca and Beric force us to wonder whether they have in fact paid that price. But they meet the challenge and show us that they are, in fact, men. In both cases, the evidence is enhanced by contrast: in *The Gladiators*, Mariamne, the pure Jew converted to Christianity who loves Esca, faints as she sees him defeated by Placidus; in *Beric*, Ennia, saved by Beric from the lion, faints, becoming precisely that limp and impotent object Beric is not: Beric "raised her on his shoulder, walked across the arena, passed the barrier, and, ascending the steps, walked along before the first row of spectators and handed her over to her mother" (269).

The slave auction and gladiatorial displays, far from pitting Briton against Roman, actually unite them in their shared manhood. The adversarial relation between hero and Rome is an illusion. Both Esca and Beric enter the arena trained in Roman gladiatorial techniques. As son of Licinius, Whyte-Melville's Esca is himself half-Roman. Even before his arrival in Rome, he had absorbed Roman culture from his mother Guenebra, who taught him Latin. His friend Hirpinus, recognizing Esca's prowess, says of him that he "came, saw, and conquered," linking his power to Rome's. So great is Esca's identification with Roman law and order that he attempts to prevent the assassination of the emperor Vitellius. At novel's end, Esca's filial relation to Rome becomes even more explicit. Mariamne and Esca—helpless before the conquering Roman army, which has just destroyed Jerusalem—are given into the protection of Licinius by Mariamne's uncle. Finally aware of his paternity (of which Esca remains ignorant), Licinius promises solemnly, "They are my children . . . from this day forth" (456). The literal relation of Licinius to Esca is superseded by this symbolic commitment, a move that suppresses Guenebra's maternal role while reaffirming the reconciliation of Roman and Briton.

With Henty's *Beric the Briton*, the merging of Briton and Roman becomes even more explicit: the conquered and enslaved Briton chief Beric marries the Roman Aemilia and returns to Briton with her to serve the Roman Empire as a local governor. Sanctioned by the sexual attraction supposed to exist between opposites and the evolutionary advantages of combining the two "races"—both notions surface repeatedly in the text— the Roman-Briton alliance thus appears natural, inevitable. "If we could mate all our Roman women with these fair giants, what a race we should raise!" exclaims the Roman general Petronius (185). Beric, like Esca, already incarnates such a marriage. As a Roman hostage in Britain, he received a Roman education and Roman military training, which he then imparts, with great results, to his tribe. As a prisoner in Rome, he is again trained, this time in a gladiatorial school. Rome offers invaluable training in discipline and patriotism. In terms reminiscent of Macaulay's *Lays of Ancient Rome*, Beric says of the Roman soldiers, "each was ready to give life and all he possessed in defence of his country" (70). The ideal marriage would thus combine Roman discipline and British strength.

This apparent marriage of opposites, however, overlies a wholesale expulsion of the "feminine"—identified throughout these novels with both the decadence of Rome and the savagery of Briton. Crucial to masculinity in these novels is the suppression of all that threatens sexual or ethnic boundaries; this is precisely what Roman decadence (attributed everywhere to foreign influence, but embraced particularly by Rome's unruly women) does. As early as Edward Bulwer-Lytton's 1834 *The Last Days of Pompeii*, transgressive women were associated with Roman decadence: Bulwer-Lytton's Julia, like Whyte-Melville's Valeria, is haughty, immodest, aggressive, and finally destroyed in the eruption of Vesuvius. In Henty's *Beric the Briton*, Aemilia's mother is similarly enmeshed in Roman decadence; she attends orgies and wants to marry her daughter to one of Vitellius' favorites rather than to Beric. It is Whyte-Melville's Valeria, though, who best personifies Roman decadence. A worshipper of Isis—whose cult was associated from Bulwer-Lytton on with women, decadence, and "foreigners"—she is shockingly aggressive in her pursuit of Esca. Beautiful and imperious, Valeria tries to seduce Esca, then takes advantage of Esca's imprisonment to kiss him passionately as he lies sleeping and enchained. She bravely saves his life twice, but she is doomed by her unmaidenliness: she enters an affair with a gladiator, then disguises herself as a man so she can serve in the Roman army as it beseiges Jerusalem. Demeaned and self-despising, she dies at Esca's feet.

Valeria demonstrates how little room there is in the world of the novel for women. In her unruly licentiousness she is at once womanhood at its most extreme and at its most uncharacteristic, for she is described as both typical of her sex and "unsexed"—a logical contradiction leaving little cultural space for a "good" woman. Whyte-Melville compares her finally to an Amazon who cuts off a breast in order to wage war better, but aches to nurse a child at the missing breast (410–11). No woman, he concludes, is ever entirely unsexed (95); she is thus torn apart by the contradiction between her characteristically female body and her characteristically female "thirst for amusement, incompatible with reason or self-control" (7).

If a woman cannot be unsexed, a man can: castration mimics more thoroughly the self-mutilation of the Amazon. The pervasive presence of eunuchs in *The Gladiators* reminds the reader that the alternative to "manhood" is unpleasant indeed. Spado, a fat cowardly eunuch, is one of the many "fat, slothful, weak, gluttonous, and effeminate" favorites of Rome's decadent ruler (10). He and his fellow priests of Isis are "fat, oily, smooth and sensual" (38). The repeated "fat" evokes inactivity, formlessness, self-indulgence, the female body, flaccidity . . . the opposite of phallic hardness. It also matches nineteenth-century painters' renditions of the Near East as "indolent, luxurious, erotic, and sleepily indifferent to the march of history" (Bendiner 134)—and therefore fair game for European imperialists.

Thus, both *The Gladiators* and *Beric the Briton* seem to dramatize history as the triumphant return of "natural" relations between men and women, while in fact depicting the triumph of "masculine" civilization at the expense of a "savagery" and "decadence" implicitly female—a version of male maturation with a Lacanian resonance. A young man contends with—then, having recognized the impossiblity of the task, reconciles with—Father Rome. In the process he separates from mother-dominated Briton and enters the symbolic order. The final sign of his entry is his being given, by the father, a bride.

Crucial to this expulsion of the feminine—along with eunuchs and Egyptian Isis-worshippers—is Christianity, which replaces Isis-worship with patriarchal monotheism and turns women into wholly spiritualized "bearers of the Word": transmitters of male heirs and male cultural authority (Homans 153–88). In both novels, assertive, ambitious women are destroyed; those who live on become ciphers, defined by their Christianity and ability to produce heirs. *Beric the Briton*, which opens with the war to avenge Boadicea and her daughters, displaces her entirely; she is replaced by the Romanized Beric serving the Roman Empire with a Roman wife. And despite Beric's insistence that British wives—unlike Roman—are equal to their husbands, the equality Beric grants Aemilia is equivocal to say the least. Its limits are implied both by Aemilia's voluntary submissiveness and by her cousin Pollio's comment, "I always told her she would need a masterful husband to keep her in order, and truly she is well suited" (371). If Boadicea is displaced, so, too, is Aemilia, for Beric tells her, "as my wife, you are a Briton now, and must no longer speak of the Romans as your people" (346). Esca's Mariamne is similarly defined by her innocence, docility, and Christianity. Always in these novels it is the woman who becomes a Christian first, then converts the man who loves her.[7] Charles Kingsley writes that moral development progresses faster when "woman, and the love of woman, have been restored to their rightful place in the education of man" (30). This entry of woman into history as mother/spirit coincides, however, with her expulsion as agent and power. Boadicea and Isis have been obliterated.

In the process, these novels offer their young readers a lesson in gender. Boys might favor the Carthaginians or Britons against the Romans, as Henty himself once did, but men will recognize their true allegiance is to Rome. Men who don't are not really men; the implicit choice is between imperialism and castration. Henty makes the choice clear in his introduction to *The Young Carthaginian*. "When I was a boy at school," he writes, "if I remember rightly, our sympathies were generally with the Carthaginians as against the Romans." But as he grew into adulthood, and presumably learned more about the Punic Wars and Rome itself, his sympathies shifted, as his readers' sympathies will shift after they have read his novel:

> I think that when you have read to the end you will perceive that although our sympathies may remain with Hannibal and the Carthaginians, it was nevertheless for the good of the world that Rome was the conqueror in the great struggle for empire. (v–vi)

Henty's boyish identification with rebels and losers matures into a recognition that history was right, Rome was right, and, by implication, British imperialism is right.

History, then, by subjecting boyish Britons to Roman discipline, turns them into men firmly identified with the Law of the Father—a Law dictating the strict maintenance of sexual (and ethnic) difference, a Law implictly justifying British as well as Roman imperialism. "Rome wishes you well," Beric tells his people at the end of the novel. "We form part of the Roman Empire now, that is as fixed and irrevocable as the rising and setting of the sun. To struggle against Rome is as great a folly as for an infant to wrestle with a giant" (379). Or, as Kingsley writes of the Britons' defeat in *The Roman and the Teuton*, "Therefore it was well as it was, and God was just and merciful to them and to the human race" (12).

Assimilation of these notions about Rome—Rome as father, as symbol of patriotism, discipline, and self-control—was essential to the acculturation of the British ruling classes during the late nineteenth century. Walter Ong has called the learning of Latin a "puberty rite" (131); certainly he argues convincingly that the "agonistic" element of traditional Western education—its emphasis on conflict and competition—is hopelessly entangled in cultural assumptions about the classics and masculinity (129). With its brutal insistence that young boys separate from their mothers, undergo mistreatment, and learn a new language—one taught only to men—the public school forces each young boy to live out the history of Beric the Briton, of the Teuton and the Roman.[8]

As a result, the Roman influence ran deep. Henty has a dying subaltern quote Horace's "Dulce et decorum est pro patria mori" (G. Arnold 111), a line, of course, that Wilfred Owen spits out in disgust as responsible for World War I. Rudyard Kipling's Una, in *Puck of Pook's Hill*, quotes Macaulay's *Lays of Ancient Rome* as she pretends to be Horatius defying the invading Etruscans at the Tiber bridge, and Henty's Beric tells his tribesmen the same story (25). Amid World War I, in 1916, Robert Graves narrates a poem from the point of view of Roman soldier fighting in Gaul: "The Legion is the Legion while Rome stands, / And these same men before the autumn's fall / Shall bang old Vercingetroix out of Gaul" (61).

Women writers growing up around the turn of the century did not, for the most part, have the same educational experience as their brothers, but they, too, read and loved stories about Rome—imperialist and patriarchal though they were. Kipling's Una, after all, need not, like her brother, stay in to learn Latin, but she can quote Macaulay nonetheless. Bryher loved Whyte-Melville's *The Gladiators* (*Heart* 54); Mitchison writes that as a child, she was "obsessed" with it. Bryher devoured Henty; at eight, she writes, she read *Beric the Briton* (94), at nine *Wulf the Saxon* (*Mars* 165). She especially enjoyed her sense that he was "entirely *on our side*," by which she seems to mean boyishly attracted by violence and adventure, rather than judgmental and moralistic (*Heart* 94). Bryher wrote that if she could return to any historical moment, she would choose to sit in the audience at a gladiatorial show. Mary Butts writes of her enthusiasm for the *Lays of Ancient Rome* (*Crystal* 40).

Given their childhood reading, it is not surprising that many of these women felt they needed to be boys in order to have adventures. Whyte-Melville's Valeria is an object lesson in female misbehavior. Appealing because of her courage, her activity, her desire to take control of her life, Valeria finds only unhappiness and death. Bryher suggests her ambivalent identification as she read Henty's novels: "I never felt inside his heroes but always beside them" she writes (*Heart* 95).

Women's relation to these stories was thus clearly different from men's. They too identified—but with a difference. They could not help noticing that the texts they read wrote different stories for their bodies than those their ambition desired. When, as writers, they chose Rome as their setting, they would recapitulate the stories they had read; that, after all, is what defines historical fiction as a genre. But again, there would be a difference. As in their depictions of Greece, these women resist their source-dictated plots by juxtaposing conflicting sources or ways of understanding the past (mingling history and anthropology, for example) or by focusing on details or conflicting viewpoints that resist absorption into a single plot. They also tend to focus on those moments when Rome was in conflict with another culture—Etruria, Greece, Carthage, Egypt, Briton, invading barbarians. By embracing the values of non-Roman cultures, Mitchison, Butts, and Bryher challenge the inevitability and rightness of Roman rule.

The standard tendency, of course, was to glorify Rome at the expense of its enemies, even Briton. Nineteenth-century racism made it easy to identify with Rome and despise its Semitic and African adversaries; historians at this time, according to Martin Bernal, tended to denigrate the contribut ons of "non-Aryan" (Egyptian, African, and Semitic) peoples to Western culture. Unwilling to trace European culture to any non-Aryan source, Bernal argues in *Black Athena*, Connop Thirlwall's 1835 *His-*

tory of Greece and George Grote's 1846 *History* both attacked the earlier notion that Africans, Egyptians, and Semites had had a major influence on ancient Greece (329); Bernal attributes the change to European racism and imperialism, which sought to devalue those cultures it was disempowering—and so justify the process. While Bernal's interest is in how European historians distorted Greek history, his theory has obvious implications for Rome as well: Carthaginians, Egyptians, and Jews had notable run-ins with the Roman Empire.

As in the case of Greece, however, Roman history was not monolithic even in the late nineteenth century, nor were Rome's enemies universally ignored. Egypt was rediscovered as a result of the work of Champollion (Gilbert and Gubar 2: 26). Other major scholars publishing on Egypt during the late nineteenth and early twentieth centuries included James Henry Breasted, E. A. Wallis Budge, Flinders Petrie, and Margaret Murray. As archeologists and philologists stimulated interest in Egyptian history, theorists used the Egyptian past for their own purposes. In 1877 Madame Blavatsky published *Isis Unveiled*, giving Egyptian iconography a crucial role in the quest for wisdom. In 1885–86, Sir Richard Burton defined a so-called Sotadic Zone, characterized by blurred sex roles and hermaphroditism, associated particularly with Egypt (Gilbert and Gubar 2: 26–39). In 1898 Rachel Evelyn White published an article in the *Journal of Hellenic Studies* arguing that Egyptian women under the Ptolemies had enjoyed a social, legal, and political freedom unique in the ancient world, probably due to "an old law of female kinship" (242). Egypt thus seemed to offer a world blending spiritual insight and female power. "Egypt?" a character asks in a Mary Butts story, "they knew about the soul there" ("Deosil" 46).

Cleopatra herself was the subject of controversy: in 1864, German historian Adolf Stahr published a biography vindicating Cleopatra (Hughes-Hallett 255). Several other late-nineteenth-century historians, rather than attacking her feminine cowardice, defended her flight from Actium on strategic grounds (257). Arthur Weigall's 1914 biography was sympathetic to her and respectful of her political ability (255). Egypt fascinated Butts and Mitchison enough for them to write books about Cleopatra, and several books about Egypt found their way into the library shared by Bryher and H. D., among them Breasted's *Ancient Records of Egypt* (five volumes, published 1920–23), with one volume incribed "For H. D. from Bryher Egypt 1923"; his *History of Egypt*; and various works by Budge (Smyers 17).

Bryher also had many books about Etruria, another old enemy of Rome being rethought in the early twentieth century. David Randall-MacIver, in his 1927 *The Etruscans*, traces the history of what he calls "Etruscology." Work on Etruria began with a 1616 book by Sir Thomas

Dempster and was followed in the eighteenth century by "Etrusco-mania" (102). But then, Randall-MacIver writes, reinforcing the pattern detected by Bernal, Etrusco-mania was replaced by its Greek equivalent; "even our best art critics of to-day," he writes, "are strongly pro-Hellenic in their bias" and as a result insist on the imitativeness of Etruscan culture (103). There is a tendency, he complains, to see the Romans as bringing the "blessings of an incomparable civilization by dint of ceaseless effort" to barbarians (*Italy* 10), when in fact the Etruscans were far more civilized than their conquerors (*Etruscans* 38). Randall-MacIver's work influenced D. H. Lawrence (Vickery 93), who in 1927 traveled to Etruria and wrote *Etruscan Places*, an enraptured account of what he saw there. Lawrence emphatically reverses the standard valuation of Etruscan versus Roman art. Mommsen, Lawrence complains, pays little attention to the Etruscans because the "Prussian in him was enthralled by the Prussian in the all-conquering Rome" (*Etruscan* 31). Contrasting the straightforward physicality of Etruria with the desire for "empire and dominion" of Rome (44), Lawrence detects in Etruscan art the "natural beauty of proportion of the phallic consciousness" (40). Etrurian religion, according to Lawrence, posits an animate universe filled with vitality (83), which he contrasts favorably with Rome's "decadent" mythology (101).

Both Randall-MacIver and Lawrence link Etruria and Egypt; the Etruscans were "touched with the distant glamour of Egypt" according to Randall-MacIver (*Etruscans* 138), and Lawrence sees parallels between Etruscan and Egyptian art (40). Clearly they shared a sense that Roman hegemony had been taken for granted for too long; their attempt to rehabilitate Rome's enemies was in part an effort to challenge the way Rome had been written about by nineteenth-century scholars. Certainly Lawrence in particular was intent on challenging the preeminence of a Rome whose greatness was defined by its ability to conquer and control "barbarians."

If Rome's ability to conquer and rule had long been admired, its decadence and fall had been despised. Bulwer-Lytton's *The Last Days of Pompeii* and Kingsley's *Hypatia* contrast decadent Rome with the energetic rise of Christianity. For Bulwer-Lytton, Rome is incapable of anything noble, an "unnatural and bloated civilization" (75), while Kingsley calls the empire a "dying idiot" (xii). Obviously the last days of the Roman Empire will call forth different responses than the early days of the Republic or the rule of Augustus Caesar.[9] And in fact the proud parallel between British and Roman Empires could turn easily to uneasy fear: if Rome could rise and fall, so, obviously, could Britain. In the 1890s a fear of degeneracy took hold of Great Britain, manifesting itself in the Boy Scouts, invasion novels, eugenics and racism, and antifeminism. Jeffrey Weeks points out that many feared a decline resembling that of

Gibbon's Rome and saw corrupted youth as a major threat (107). Kingsley's praise of the Goth's body "untainted by hereditary effeminacy" (xii) resonated in a Britain shocked by Oscar Wilde, its losses in the Boer War (Weeks 125) and feminism (162).[10] Thus, while the negative depiction of predecadent Rome was a tool of social change in the early twentieth century, the negative depiction of decadent Rome served to reinforce British fears of degeneracy—and thus to reinforce racism, homophobia, anti-feminism, and imperialism.

Stock figures of this drama of decadence are the Old Roman (schooled in Stoicism, uncomfortable with the excesses he sees foisted upon Rome by corrupt emperors); the sexually transgressive young woman, exemplified by Bulwer-Lytton's Julia, with her "handsome but . . . bold and unmaidenly countenance" (134); the non-Roman young man, physically impressive and pure; and the Christian maiden. The drama enacted by these figures obviously serves to warn young people against the transgressive sexuality that leads to degeneracy. But what happens when women writers turn to this time period? To a large extent they recapitulate familiar plot elements and these stock figures. But again, with a difference. While for Bulwer-Lytton and Whyte-Melville Isis-worship is financially and sexually corrupt, for Mitchison it is a spiritual refuge for suffering women. While for Bulwer-Lytton and Kingsley and Whyte-Melville Roman rule is undermined by the transgression of sexual boundaries (by effeminate men and masculine women), for Bentley and Bryher it is undermined by excessively polarized notions of masculinity and femininity.

While Roman decadence haunted Britain during the early part of the twentieth century, a different Roman threat rose to prominence during the 1920s: fascism. Mussolini and his followers, taking the *fasces* as their symbol, aligned themselves with the power of imperial Rome. In the minds of many, modern and ancient Rome became conflated, and the close identification so many Britons had felt with Rome at the start of the century dissolved. Mitchison's *Blood of the Martyrs*, Butts's *Scenes from the Life of Cleopatra*, and Bentley's *Freedom, Farewell!* were all written during the 1930s, at a time when anyone thinking of Rome would think also of Mussolini. Both Mitchison and Bentley wrote in conscious protest of fascism; Bentley uses a passage from Mommsen as her epigraph to underline the parallel:

> The history of past centuries . . . is instructive because the observation of earlier forms of culture reveals the organic conditions of civilization generally—the fundamental forces everywhere alike, and the manner of their combination different. . . . In this sense the history of Caesar and of Roman imperialism is in truth a more bitter censure of modern autocracy than could be written by the hand of man.

Bentley's critique of Caesar's unprincipled quest for power is thus a response to fascism as much as a working out of the relationship between gender and Rome. But it is *also* about gender, as I will show, unlike Mitchison's *Blood of the Martyrs*, which seems to set aside gender as a concern, so pressing is the need to depict a community of anti-imperialists.

Butts's *Scenes from the Life of Cleopatra* is perhaps the anomaly here, for it glorifies Caesar and a mystical understanding of leadership at the very moment when fascism was doing the same. Butts's attitude resembles Lawrence's, and both could be attacked for admiring those who, by tapping into some mysterious energy source in the universe, come to be more than human. Both, however, depict leaders more in tune with natural forces than Mussolini aspired to be. For Lawrence, Italian fascism resembled the Roman imperialism he despised, not the Etruscan culture Rome defeated (*Etruscan* 56, 141). And if Butts's admiration for pure power seems amoral and even protofascist, her choice of a woman as subject makes a difference. For fascism was insistent in its polarizing of sexual roles, and dynamic leadership was clearly the domain of the male. "One can hardly fail to be impressed in Rome by the sense of unmitigated masculinity," Virginia Woolf writes of Mussolini's Italy in *A Room of One's Own* (106).

The Roman Empire, so admired at the start of the twentieth century, was, by the 1930s, well on its way to being Britain's enemy. But if women writers could feel themselves in harmony with their culture in criticizing Roman imperialism, they remained uniquely aware of gender as a critical issue in understanding both its appeal and its flaws. Rome—like Greece—had been seen as a kind of play dramatizing universal human issues: a context in which to explore government, religion, ethics. What Mitchison, Butts, Bentley, and Bryher explore in their historical novels about Rome is the extent to which this apparently universal drama was in fact played out in wholly male terms.

NOTES

1. The excavation of Pompeii triggered extensive use of Roman settings by historical novelists and painters. While Pompeii had been excavated since 1689, it was only since the defeat of Napoleon that interest in the site spread to Great Britain. With the publication, in 1817 and 1819, of Sir William Gell's two volumes of *Pompeiana*, British interest in Pompeii skyrocketed (Lloyd-Jones, *Classical* 47). Painters as well as novelists toured the site and studied Gell. Among those influenced were Frederick Leighton, Albert Moore, Edward Poynter, Edward Armitage, and Alma-Tadema, who became known as a painter of "Victorians in togas" (Swanson 18).

2. The Roman gentleman served as boarding school ideal; the boys were to grow into "gentlemen after the high Roman fashion, making a fine art, almost a religion, of stoicism" (Christie, qtd. in Howarth 14). The boarding school system itself was engineered to reinforce that stoicism, as Walter Ong has pointed out. Separating boys from their mothers, disciplining them brutally, and teaching them Latin and Greek—a "father" as opposed to a "mother" tongue—these schools socialized middle- and upper-class boys into a rigidly defined notion of masculinity based on violence, competition, and male bonding (129–32).

3. Patrick Brantlinger cites 1850 as the date from which British imperialist ideology dates (14).

4. This dismissal of Eastern, non-Aryan cultures was a specifically nineteenth-century phenomenon; Martin Bernal argues that European racism and belief in progress, which combined to justify nineteenth-century imperialism, caused historians to devalue older, non-Aryan civilizations: "Racism and 'progress,'" he writes, "could thus come together in the condemnation of Egyptian/African stagnation and praise of Greek-European dynamism and change" (190).

5. The Oedipus complex, of course, involves a boy's desire for his mother and rivalry with his father. Freud writes, however, that the normal boy, threatened by castration as the punishment for his subversive desires, gives up both desire and rivalry: "Under the impression of the danger of losing his penis, the Oedipus complex is abandoned, repressed and, in the most normal cases, entirely destroyed, and a severe super-ego is set up as its heir" (22: 129).

6. Elizabeth Segel writes that it was not until the second half of the nineteenth century that any distinction appeared between children's literature aimed at boys and children's literature aimed at girls. Significantly, this move to define boys' interests in contrast to girls' arose at the same time as the spread of imperialist ideology, which depends, as Nandy points out, on rigid gender distinctions.

7. Victoria, in Charles Kingsley's *Hypatia*, fits this pattern also; she is Christian, and converts the man who loves and marries her.

8. Ong distinguishes between the *patrius sermo*—a father language associated with power and public life—and the *matria lingua*, or mother tongue (36n, 37n). See also Gilbert and Gubar 1: 252.

9. Linda Dowling points out that "decadence" itself was the creation of historians intent on seeing a "Providential" pattern and meaning in Rome's history. In 1896, J. B. Bury argued that decadence did not cause the fall of Rome and that no analogy was possible between the rise and fall of Rome and that of Great Britain (Dowling, "Roman" 603).

10. Wilde, flaunting the transvaluation of Roman decadence embraced by late-nineteenth-century aesthetes, wore a "Neronian coiffure" (Dowling, "Nero" 2).

CHAPTER 9

Hostage to History:
Naomi Mitchison and Rome

Wanting power, Naomi Mitchison writes in *The Moral Basis of Politics*, is "my own besetting and class sin" (338). Given that preoccupation, it can come as no surprise that Mitchison wrote again and again about Rome. For Mitchison, and others of her class and age, Rome *was* power—the Rome, that is, of Macaulay's *Lays*, memorized by generations of English schoolchildren. "One always has to learn the Lays as soon as one goes to school," Mitchison writes, explaining her interest in Rome; she quotes from them:

> Thine, Roman, is the pilum:
>   Roman, the sword is thine,
> The even trench, the bristling mound,
>   The legion's ordered line;
> And thine the wheels of triumph,
>   Which with their laurelled train
> Move slowly up the shouting streets
>   To Jove's eternal fane.
>
> (Mitchison, *When* 315)

The passage evokes Roman military might and discipline, and also narrative power: the ability to define the story that will be told. For the ultimate sign of Roman power is the "triumph," the parade through Rome to honor victorious generals by displaying their booty and victims. Like a dramatized history book, the triumph turns the past into a coherent story whose end gives it meaning. This double power of Rome—to conquer and to narrate—fascinated Mitchison throughout her career.

As a child, Mitchison tells of acting out sexually charged dramas of bondage and slavery with her friends; as an adult, she wrote her first novel about the capture and enslavement of a Gaul captured by Rome. Rome recurs as setting in so many of her novels and short stories because it allows her to explore her simultaneous attraction to and recoil from the exercise of power. The result, I will argue, is to defuse power, to rob it of its erotic appeal. Late-nineteenth-century male-authored fictions of Rome—by Kingsley, Whyte-Melville, Henty, and Kipling—depicted Roman imperialism as a happy ending to a fairy tale, in which the conquered Britons merge their energy with Roman self-control and live happily ever after. The merging often takes literal form in the marriage of Roman and Briton, channeling all of the reader's romantic voyeurism into a desire for this marriage to take place. Mitchison's fictions of Rome—particularly *The Conquered*, my focus here—refuse to satisfy this desire, exposing rather than exploiting the way erotic energy has in the past served to reinforce oppressive plots.

Mitchison turned to Rome in her first novel, *The Conquered* (1923), in *The Blood of the Martyrs* (1939), and in a number of her short stories. Whenever Mitchison depicts Rome, she depicts its interactions with the vanquished and victimized; in *The Conquered*, for example, she aligns her narrative with Meromic, a conquered Gaul, and in *The Blood of the Martyrs* her central character is Beric, a Briton raised in Rome. Through her fiction, Mitchison explores what the conquering process means to the defeated, depicting the ambivalence of men who covet the power of Rome while still feeling loyal to their past identity as defiant fighters against it. Central to Mitchison's depiction of these men is the notion of the "hostage": someone who is imprisoned but well treated by an enemy power and thus prone to the "hostage syndrome," the emotional attachment hostages sometimes develop to their captors. The word *hostage* has a suggestive etymology, as Elaine Scarry has pointed out:

> the protective, healing, expansive acts implicit in "host" and "hostel" and "hospitable" and "hospital" all converge back in "hospes," which in turn moves back to the root "host" meaning house, shelter or refuge; but once back at "hos," its generosity can be undone by an alternative movement forward into "hostis," the source of "hostility" and "hostage" and "host" . . . the host of the eucharist, the sacrificial victim. (45)

The apparently contradictory terms *hostile* and *host* come together neatly in hostage—and sum up the theme to which Mitchison repeatedly returns in her fiction. Hostages, of course, are taken from their homes and imprisoned by their enemies. But they are also entertained and protected by their enemies, whose own interests lie in preserving them for future bargaining power. This protection turns hostages against themselves, for they feel themselves at home with their not-so-hostile hosts. Thus Meromic and Beric both come to love their masters and to experience their hostility to Rome as disloyalty to their hosts.

This hostage syndrome is replayed by Mitchison over and over in her collection of stories for children entitled *The Hostages*. The title story, the "first story I ever wrote" (36), is typical. It tells of the relationship between three young Etruscan hostages and the kind Roman family that cares for them. The narrator is finally ransomed by his father, but the youngest of the three, Elxsente, is invited to stay with the Romans as their son. The narrator urges him to refuse: "Think of your City, Elxsente! Don't put yourself into the hands of the enemy!" But the boy replies, "Would it be very wrong to stay? I think I'd like to stay" (53).[1] And he does. What happens to the psyche, Mitchison asks repeatedly, when the powerless love—and shift their loyalties to—the empowered? How can and why should they resist the temptation? But who do they become when they succumb?

On a larger scale, the hostage suggests the position of any colonized territory—Rome's Briton or Britain's Ireland—rebellious but also hostage to its absorption into the colonizer's institutions, values, and "improvements."[2] Colonizing nations like Rome see themselves as hosts, in a sense, offering "protective, healing, expansive acts" through administration, education, and building projects that serve the colonized even as they subjugate them. A defeated Briton offered the privileges of a Roman education, Roman government, and Roman military training is thus liable to identify himself with his host even as he feels himself held hostage. Privilege and imprisonment are inextricably tangled.

Finally, the contradictory terms associated with the word *hostage* also sum up Mitchison's ambivalent relation to power and history. If, as storyteller, Mitchison is an effective host, welcoming her readers into a story she controls as narrator, she is also her story's hostage, imprisoned by previous narratives that disempower her as a woman and leave her little leeway to reinvent the past. In depicting hostages Mitchison is thus also depicting herself, a rebellious woman enmeshed in British life, hostage to her desire for power and cultural authority.

The hostage, then, is a nexus of "conflicting loyalties," "one of the main modern problems," according to Mitchison ("On Writing" 114). Certainly as a female writer of historical fiction it is one of her main problems. As a writer, she aspires to the power of male historians to shape the past, even as she recognizes that power insistently marginalizes women. Attracted by the power of Rome, she tries nonetheless to resist complicity in its subjection of others, a complicity she knows entails her own subjugation as woman and Briton. These complex associations underlie the obsessive concern with "conflicting loyalties" and hostages—both literal and figurative—in her fiction.

Mitchison's choice of Rome as subject was thus determined by her fascination with power and her recognition that women in particular bore an ambivalent relation to it.[3] The epigraph for *The Conquered* suggests such a connection: "Victrix causa diis placuit sed victa puellis" (The victorious cause is pleasing to the gods, but the conquered cause to girls). The suggestion is that as a woman, Mitchison could not help but read the defeat of Gaul (and of Briton) differently from her male contemporaries. Certainly she read it consciously as one whose sympathies were with the vanquished: "Not unnaturally," she writes, "one always used to take sides with the barbarians against Rome" (*When* 316). But the barbarians, too, are attracted by power. What surfaces again and again in all her writing about Rome—and most intensely in *The Conquered*—is the self-alienation wrought on the individual psyche by conquest and colonialism, a self-alienation dramatized by her own narrative ambivalence.

Mitchison's narrative ambivalence is evident in the way she reproduces the plots and themes of her childhood reading even as she parodies them. For she, like the hostage, is in love with her captors; her childhood obsession with *The Gladiators* (*All* 35–37) can only be explained by her love for simple, erotically charged plots of conquest and marriage. But she is not simply imprisoned by these plots. In *The Conquered*, at least, several strategies enable her to resist the pull of these plots toward a happy ending of marriage, military triumph, and progress. Meromic's quasi-incestuous relationship with his sister, his homoerotically charged relationship with his master, and his totemistic connection to wolves— taken so seriously by Mitchison's narrator that he literally becomes a wolf at novel's end—all enable him to rewrite Whyte-Melville's and Henty's story of identification with a paternal Rome. Even where Mitchison seems to borrow most explicitly from her sources—in her story "Romantic Event" (dedicated to Whyte-Melville's Esca) and her novel *The Blood of the Martyrs* (whose hero is named after Henty's Beric)—she is able to parody and undercut the stories of Rome she has inherited.

What were those inherited stories of Rome? Most obviously, Rome for Mitchison was an entity imposed on an unwilling schoolgirl by those more powerful than herself. "My period was the First Century B.C.," Mitchison wrote in 1935 of her first novel-writing experience, "—Caesar's Gallic Wars, about which I remembered only the little which had been driven into my reluctant head at school while learning Latin" ("Writing" 645). The comment depicts Latin—and its avatar Julius Caesar—as a discipline forced on a rebellious girl whose forgetfulness is her only weapon. Serving as *patrius sermo*, in Walter Ong's terms, Latin absorbs students into stories of conquering heroes—Aeneas and Julius Caesar—who stand for masculinity, self-control, and success in opposition to the barbarians to the west, who let their women run wild, and the decadents to the east, who succumb to effeminacy. This, at least, is the scenario implicit in Bulwer-Lytton's *Last Days of Pompeii* and Kingsley's *Hypatia*, mentioned as influences in Mitchison's *When the Bough Breaks* (316); in Henty's *Beric the Briton*; and in Whyte-Melville's *The Gladiators*, Macaulay's *Lays of*

Ancient Rome, and Kipling's *Puck of Pook's Hill,* her source for the Roman soldiers in *The Conquered* ("Writing" 646).[4] From all these writers, Mitchison got a sense of nondecadent Rome as the masculine opponent of the wild, untamed, female-dominated indigenous peoples of Gaul, Britain, and Ireland. Unlike Greece, Rome—whether Republican or Imperial—offered a monolithically masculine image to Mitchison; it was, she writes in her 1934 *The Home and a Changing Civilization,* the "most typically patriarchal society that we know" (19).

These, then, are the texts holding Mitchison hostage, limiting the power she can conceivably give her female characters, defining the conflicts her male characters will face. All tell essentially Oedipal stories, suggesting that the successful man moves from early loyalty to a barbarian motherland toward mature allegiance to the victorious patriarchal culture. Just as Aeneas leaves behind Creusa and Julius Caesar leaves Cleopatra, Henty's Beric shifts his allegiance from his dead mother to his Roman wife. But even as Mitchison recapitulates this Oedipal plot, she complicates it. Her hostages resist the shift of allegiance to Father Rome. Roman power tempts them, causes them agonies of ambivalence, but finally finds them unwilling to identify fully with their hosts. They resist marriage, heterosexuality, and "success," opting, finally, out of history itself. Success itself is robbed of its appeal, as Mitchison explores the sexual politics of imprisonment and torture, aligning her narrative with victim rather than onlooker and thus de-eroticizing the slave market and gladiatorial arena.

Mitchison's most direct response to her predecessors—specifically, to Whyte-Melville—comes in the story "Romantic Event," which bears the epigraph "In loving memory of Esca and The Gladiators." It tells the story of a Roman general who buys a handsome Briton slave, Bleddyn, from a brutal master. Just as Whyte-Melville's Esca turns out to be his master Licinius's son, Bleddyn is revealed—through a tattoo on his chest—to be the general's own son. But Mitchison's treatment of this discovery differs from Whyte-Melville's. While Esca never discovers that Licinius is, in fact, his father, he admires him and puts himself under his protection, at novel's end, just as if they were father and son. Bleddyn, however, is faced with the truth in a melodramatic scene of discovery, and his response to Roman paternity is less enthusiastic. He is first enraged, then grief-stricken by the discovery. "Then it was you—you!—who did that to my mother!" he berates his father (*Delicate* 310). Despite his initial anger, he yields to his new father's embrace, but Mitchison describes the yielding as an insidious seduction rather than a happy ending:

> The tide of comfort and bewitchment was rising through him in a trembling warmth. He knew it for the magic of the other name, the other per-

son that he was becoming. The arm across his shoulders was tight and
trembling a little. He turned in it very quickly, slipped round so that he
faced the General. He was rather taller, but he dropped his head into the
hollow of the older man's shoulder; he felt both arms holding him now,
completing the circle. He accepted the magic, whispering: "Father."
(312–13)

Bleddyn's initial grief suggests his loyalty to and identification with his
mother and her victimization; quickly, however, he forgets the injury
done his mother, choosing to identify himself instead with his father and
his father's power. This is precisely the process Whyte-Melville depicts so
admiringly in *The Gladiators*. Mitchison, however, manages to make
Bleddyn's shift in allegiance—from pre-Oedipal immersion in his mother
to post-Oedipal identification with his father—seem abrupt and unmoti-
vated. Those arms holding him suggest imprisonment as much as protection; the wave of "comfort," "bewitchment," and "magic" that move
him towards his father evoke self-surrender rather than discipline and
shared manhood.

Mitchison is also, of course, parodying Whyte-Melville's melodramatic brand of historical fiction. The title, "Romantic Event," however,
implies that the conflation of "Rome" and "romance" is no accident;
successful empires thrive on stories with happy endings. For those who
align themselves with the Romans, history retains its "odor of the ideal";
it is a "romance," a linear progression toward triumph epitomized by
Macaulay's stanza:

> And thine the wheels of triumph,
>   Which with their laurelled train
> Move slowly up the shouting streets
>   To Jove's eternal fane.

(Mitchison, *When* 315)

The "triumph" is literally the parade of booty and captured slaves with
which Rome honored its victorious generals, but it also makes vivid the
way the losers are caught up in the story told by the victors, their defeat
made to seem historically inevitable, natural, for the best. "Gaul is a
province," the Gallic leader Vercingetorix learns in another of Mitchison's
stories, "happy, and prosperous: under a Roman governor" (*When* 86).
This absorption of Gaul—or any other conquered territory—into Rome's
romance is precisely what Mitchison's *The Conquered* works to undercut.

The Conquered tells the story of Meromic, from northern Gaul,
whose people are repeatedly defeated by the Romans. The son of Kormiac
the Wolf, Meromic is, in the tradition of such novels, strong, brave, and

loving. His tribe is defeated early in the novel, his sister kills herself, and he is enslaved by the Romans. After much suffering, he is rescued by Titus Barrus, a Roman leader who treats him kindly and respectfully. Meromic swears to serve Titus faithfully, despite the fact that the Romans are fighting his own people. As a result of this oath and his deep attachment to Titus, Meromic's loyalties are constantly pulled in conflicting directions, and the novel's plot consists mainly of his agonizingly shifting loyalties, until the execution of Vercingetorix triggers his final flight from Titus and Rome. In *The Conquered* Mitchison, rejecting the amnesia that was her first defense against history, explores Meromic's conflicting loyalties and finally creates a space in which he can resist the physical and mental pressures that threaten to absorb him into Roman ways.

Predictably, Meromic's Gaul is associated with strong women. Described as a "mother in chains" (181), Gaul is full of "strong, full-breasted Gallic women," who can "run beside a horse, . . . swim against a foaming current, . . . [or] stand in [a] doorway with a spear, threatening the soldiers" (260).[5] Of these, the strongest is Meromic's sister Fiommar, who seems in the novel's opening pages to be its protagonist. "Free and fair and upright, a picture of the Celtic genius" (13), she dominates until the defeat of the Veneti by the Romans. Then, she kills herself, unwilling to survive the defeat of her tribe. With Fiommar's death, women are virtually effaced from the novel; those few who turn up are domesticated cliches.

Unlike his sister, Meromic survives and surrenders to the Romans, Fiommar having told him, "But you're a man: life may hold something for you still; and besides, you're the last of us left, the only hope for the name of the Wolf to go on" (80–81). Men are supposed to survive and marry into the new world order, just as Aeneas married Lavinia in order to found Rome. And Rome, of course, is the place for men—at least the Old Rome is, represented by Stoic values and best evoked by Macaulay's *Lays* and Kipling's centurion Parnesius. Thus Titus, the Roman Mitchison says derives from Kipling, is taught by his grandfather to "disapprove of scent and pretty clothes and Greek singers and frivolous poetry." He is "full of the early Roman virtues" (27): self-disciplined, eager both to obey and command, enamored of work, order, and war, regardless of personal pleasure and "feminine" comforts.

While thus far the sexual politics of *The Conquered* seem quite traditional, reinscribing the losing battle of female barbarians against male Rome, suggesting Mitchison is in fact hostage to past accounts of imperial Rome, she does take sufficient control of her narrative to undercut her apparently familiar plot. Meromic does not forget his motherland, align himself definitively with Rome, and marry a Roman. Meromic's quasi-incestuous relationship to his sister, his ambivalent relationship to his master, his refusal to marry, and his final opting out of history altogether all work against the "odor of the ideal" that would otherwise attach to the story of Rome's triumphant absorption of its enemies.

Brother-sister relationships play a vital role in many of Mitchison's works; in *The Conquered*, Meromic's relationship with his sister is clearly eroticized, hinting at a sexuality beyond the control of patriarchy. If Meromic can find sexual gratification within his family, he need not outgrow his initial attachment to the mother (here figured by the sister, since there is no mother depicted); he need not align himself with Rome, or, in Lacanian terms, the Law of the Father. The relationship between brother and sister is erotically charged; Meromic likes to play with Fiommar's hair and Fiommar dislikes the fiance her father has chosen for her because he is not as handsome as her brother. Brother and sister spend the first day depicted by the novel on an island where they fish and play, aware their freedom is threatened by both Fiommar's upcoming marriage and the Roman invaders. Fantasizing about a future together on their island, where he will be king and she queen (68), the two are resisting entry into their respective plots of marriage and war—plots that will lead, inevitably, one to death and the other to Rome.

The hint of incest is reinforced by the role the book played in Mitchison's relationship with her own brother, Jack Haldane. The opening of *The Conquered*, she later wrote, was about her and her brother (*You May* 162). In fact, it grew out of an incestuous moment they shared in the Auvergne, which Mitchison visited in the course of her research for *The Conquered* (*You May* 62).[6] The book's dedication to her brother and its conclusion with a poem by him reinforce the connection. Much as Bryher's Greece in *Gate to the Sea* is a palimpsest evoking both an erased matriarchal past and her relationship with H. D., Mitchison's ancient Gaul evokes both a fantasized alternative to patriarchally defined sexuality and an actual, recent relationship with her brother.

The island scene is a moment of resistance—doubly transgressive because of its evocation of incest and its use of personal, contemporary material in an historical context. But it is also an expression of the author's own conflicting loyalties. If men oppress Mitchison, she can either revolt against them or join them and attempt to share in their power. Incest is thus "sleeping with the enemy," but also an act of defiance against the rules of patriarchy. Eager for adventure and achievement, Mitchison wrote historical fiction in part as a way of getting access to the power conferred by masculinity. Incest is one form her ambivalent love of power takes, allowing her simultaneously to identify with and subvert her brother's autonomy.

Another locus of resistance is Meromic's ambivalent relationship with Titus. Titus is the Roman father-figure who—in a traditional version of the Rome-Gaul interaction—would oversee Meromic's absorption into Roman life and supervise his marriage. But in fact the relationship is so tortured and sexually charged that it too, like the hint of incest, serves to resist absorption into an Oedipal master narrative. Rescued from a cruel overseer by Titus, Meromic swears loyalty to him, and repeatedly keeps that oath even when fighting his own people on Rome's behalf. He is in love with Titus—in love with Titus's power and mastery and generosity. He tells his fellow-slave Lerrys:

> Can't you see, Lerrys? There's half of me aching to get off, to be fighting on my own side, the side I ought to be on; and there's the other half—oh God, Lerrys, I'd give my life for him, I would truly; he's all I've got, he's wife and child and home and everything. (199)

While Meromic is too much in love with Titus to leave him, he is too loyal a Gaul to remain faithful to him. Repeatedly during the novel Meromic leaves Titus to help his fellow Gauls, yet always returns. Sometimes he seems to lose track of his intentions entirely, as when he tries to help a dying Gallic friend but gets lost and finds himself among Romans again—the "woods are so thick and the path twisted," he explains (167), the landscape clearly a projection of his own dreamlike confusion. Even as he fights for Rome, he wants Vercingetorix to win, despite the Romans' "trade and peace and prosperity, good roads and good laws" (221–22). At Vercingetorix's defeat, his self-hatred intensifies, and when the captured Gaul Caltrane calls him a traitor, he leaves Titus to rejoin the Gauls once again, "the wolf side coming up, untamed after all this time" (244). For this loyalty to his motherland, Meromic pays a price: the Romans, once again victorious, chop off his right hand. From the helplessness that ensues, Meromic is once again rescued by Titus, whom he leaves yet again for Gaul, at novel's end.

Meromic's wildly inconsistent actions are explained by his deep attachment to his master, an attachment that echoes that between Esca and Licinius in *The Gladiators*, but again with a difference. Looking at the two books together illuminates the way in which Mitchison's novel questions even as it reinscribes the earlier text. Meromic, like Whyte-Melville's Esca, is an impressive figure—strong, loyal, intelligent. But unlike Esca, he remains powerless throughout the novel. His identification with his homeland persists, through his dreams and the intervention of a Druid storyteller with magical powers. Though both are under the care of fatherlike Romans at novels' ends, Meromic flees, unlike Whyte-Melville's Esca, who will marry his Christian Mariamne under the paternal eye of his Roman father Licinius. Significantly, Meromic refuses to marry, partly because he seems uninterested in women, but more importantly because children are a link to the future, an acquiescence to history. Any children would be "little lone wolves with no pack and no hunting" (307). By rejecting marriage and reproduction, he refuses complicity in the merging of Gaul and Rome. His homoerotic attachment to Titus, like his incestuous relationship to his sister, serves to reject the Oedipal trajectory he is expected to follow, and which Esca followed before him. That his right hand is chopped off with painful vividness may suggest that he has paid the traditional price for his revolt.

Unlike Whyte-Melville's Esca, Meromic resists assimilation. His relationship to Titus keeps him in Italy yet precludes rather than fosters the marriage that might signal his integration into Roman life. And after the triumph in which Vercingetorix is humiliatingly displayed then killed, even that relationship is powerless to hold him. As a weapon against Rome and history, Meromic has his Druidic roots, manifested by the periodic reappearance of the magical storyteller, and his totemic relationship to the wolf. As in *The Corn King and the Spring Queen*, magic and totemism are validated as alternatives to the choices offered by historical reality. Living peacefully in the home of Titus, Meromic hears of Caesar's triumph and the execution of Vercingetorix. He leaves in the night, persuaded by the sound of wolves and the mysterious appearance of a Druidic storyteller to head north, toward Gaul. The footprints he leaves, however, indicate that he has literally become the wolf that was his people's totem. At novel's end, Meromic hears a wolf howling and thinks, "little of a wolf he had shown himself, to wear the Roman dress and play with the Roman children!" (314). He joins the storyteller, who appears outside his window inviting him to accompany him to Gaul, and in the morning, "on the paths and under the bushes there were tracks of wolves, and one wolf that went lame of the right fore-foot; the tracks went north" (315). The lame right forefoot, of course, suggests that Meromic has become his totem. As a wolf, he has finally freed himself from Rome.

Mitchison's use of totemism thus reinforces her anti-Oedipal plot; if history moves men from pre- to post-Oedipal relations to their parents, totemism allows them to step out of the procession altogether, to leap back in time into a pre-Oedipal return to the maternal, to nature, to immersion of self in world. In realistic terms, of course, Meromic has presumably died at the moment he becomes a wolf. The body is hostage to the world even when the soul escapes. Mitchison's totemistic ending to *The Conquered*, like the island fantasy with which it opens, serves to undercut the inevitability and romance of history, to insist on the alternative endings imagined by its victims. It provides no easy consolation, however; the bloody, lame right pawprint Meromic leaves behind him suggests his body is still defined by his history as much as by his magical transformation. This entrapment of the body in history fascinates Mitchison, who recognized that while she could imagine herself male, her body still inscribed her as female, with consequences she could not ignore.

Meromic abandons life-in-history after he hears of Vercingetorix's appearance in Caesar's triumph, the ultimate demonstration of the body held hostage. Vercingetorix, frail after years of captivity, made to parade through Rome in the very clothes that once signified his power, is now an expression of Rome's power. Mitchison writes again and again about physical domination—the process by which slaves, captives, and torture victims are turned into bodily statements of their enemies' power. The body, in a sense, is made to testify against itself; it becomes the tool and voice of the master or victor. In writing of her interest in Roman history, Mitchison moves quickly from her identification with the ancient Britons to their enslavement, to their torture:

> But it's the Northerner, one's possible ancestor, who is really thrilling: "Where ride Massilia's triremes, Heavy with fair-haired slaves." And that makes one interested in the Roman idea of slavery.
>
> There are all the obvious horrors to begin with, the lamprey pond and the whips and the chains. And the more one reads the nastier it looks. (*When* 316–17)

The sadistic overseer is a staple of her novels and short stories. Like the triumph, the scene of torture forces the body to speak in the voice of another, as an expression of the torturer's power. The slave market display, when the dealer arranges his wares to their best advantage, works similarly.

Mitchison's interest in physical domination is not, needless to say, unique. Here, too, Whyte-Melville provides a model. But just as Mitchison provides a new twist on the Briton-son/Roman-father relationship, she undercuts the drama of the slave market. When, in *The Gladiators*, Whyte-Melville describes Esca on display at a slave-market, he is given tremendous, erotically charged power. His master-to-be Licinius responds:

> His attention was, however, especially arrested by the appearance of one of the conquered, a fine young man of great strength and stature, who seemed to feel painfully the indignity of his position, placed as he was on a huge stone block, whereon his own towering height rendered him a conspicuous object in the throng. . . . There was something in his face, and the expression of his large blue eyes, that roused a painful thrill in the Roman general's breast. He felt a strange and undefinable attraction towards the captive. (67)

While Esca is embarrassed, he seems nonetheless to rise above the situation, literally and figuratively. Despite being the object of Licinius's gaze, he manages to play a relatively active role; it is Licinius's attention that is "arrested," while Esca rouses and attracts. Esca's own feeling of humiliation is even eroticized by the tension between his obvious power and his imprisonment. The reader feels, with Licinius, a "painful thrill" that objectifies Esca even as it grants him the power to arouse.

Mitchison, on the other hand, emphasizes the slave's own discomfort and the sordidness of his situation in an effort to de-eroticize and problematize the gaze. In *The Conquered*, she describes the slave dealer's arrangement of his slaves so as to bring the best possible price and Meromic's almost involuntary resistance to his role; "every bone and muscle seemed to parody" the pose, the slave dealer thinks exasperatedly. When gags and chains finally get the slaves properly arranged, Meromic hates "being stared at with no clothes on, by all and sundry" (96). Throughout the time he is on display, the narrative returns almost obsessively to Meromic's gaze, which seems to be fighting against his objectification. At first he looks back at the crowd (97), then he "eyed his prospective master sideways like a shy horse" (98), and finally "fixed his eyes on the ground, resolved not to be aware of what was passing, to be pure mind squeezing itself out of the unwanted body" (98). When, in her short story "Quintus Getting Well," Mitchison is describing a situation virtually identical to that in *The Gladiators*—a Roman suddenly attracted by a barbarian slave—Mitchison emphasizes the slave's powerlessness in very unerotic terms. Quintus, a young Roman invalid, is drawn to a slave from Gaul on display at the slave market. While physically riveting, just like Esca, the slave is helpless and uncomfortable:

> He had bright blue eyes that he kept on blinking because of the sun, and matted yellowish hair that came down on to his neck, and he shifted about constantly with his feet and turned his head about, but could not get into any patch of shade. (*Hostages* 105)

Displayed at the slave market and in the gladiatorial arena, the victims of Roman imperialism face the inescapable gaze of others as part of the disciplining process. Mitchison's narrative serves to undercut the reader's pleasure in looking.

The Conquered was Mitchison's first novel. She returned to Rome as setting in a later novel as well, *The Blood of the Martyrs*. Here once again she tells the story of a conquered man—this time a Briton named Beric—raised by Romans. Like Meromic, Beric feels obligated to a paternal master who treats him more like a son than the former hostage he really is. But he also remains faithful to his identity as a Briton. Complicating matters, though, is the fact that *The Blood of the Martyrs* is set later, in a decadent Rome witnessing the birth of Christianity. Beric resists absorption into Rome just as Meromic did, but his resistance is made considerably easier—by the despicable actions of those Romans in power, and by the solidarity of the Christians, who offer a more tempting alternative to Rome than any offered Meromic.

In *The Blood of the Martyrs* Mitchison tells how twenty or so inhabitants of Rome, from a wide range of backgrounds, all come to be Christians. Primarily, they share a sense of disempowerment; all have been treated like "dirt," dehumanized by someone with power over them. The power of early Christianity is precisely its insistence on treating everyone like a person. But it also gains power from its mythic paradigm: premised on a sacrifice that is infinitely repeatable (in that it can be imitated by others), Christianity offers an escape from history in much the same way as Meromic's totemism. Paradoxically, however, Mitchison superimposes her socialism on Christianity, suggesting that the Christian myth offers a means of transforming history as well as escaping it. Her name for this potential transformation is the "Kingdom," which she evokes in her introduction as what "we all want in our hearts," presumably a world of justice and equality.[7] Feeling the pressure of rising fascism, Mitchison can, by fitting socialism into a Christian paradigm, imagine its inevitable triumph as the result of its adherents' martyrdom. If people lack the power to be host in the hospitable sense, she seems to be saying, they can at least be host in the eucharistic sense.

Just as *The Conquered* responds to Whyte-Melville's *The Gladiators*, *The Blood of the Martyrs* reworks another male-authored story of Roman power, G. A. Henty's *Beric the Briton*. Both novels depict the adventures of a Romanized Briton named Beric amid a Rome rapidly dividing into two hostile factions: the old aristocrats with the traditional Roman virtues, and the decadent emperor Nero and his hangers-on. A spiritual vacuum fuels the rise of Christianity, especially among women and the downtrodden. Both novels describe the burning of Rome and the persecution of Christians that followed. Henty's Beric, however, rescues the Roman Christian Ennia from the lions, marries her sister Aemilia (with the approval of her old-fashioned Roman father), and after the death of Nero becomes a Roman governor in Briton, and a Christian, neatly following an Oedipal trajectory from mother-Briton to reconciliation with father-Rome.

Mitchison's Beric fares less well, at least in practical terms. Raised almost as a son by Crispus, an old-fashioned Roman, Beric becomes a Christian after he is humiliated by Crispus's decadent daughter Flavia. Unlike his older brother Clinog, who has become a successful Roman administrator, Beric rejects complicity in Roman imperialism and slavery, and is finally executed, along with his Christian friends, after a failed attempt to kill Tigellinus, Nero's underling. Like Henty's Beric and Whyte-Melville's Esca, Mitchison's Beric has a loving relationship with a fatherlike Roman, but unlike them he rejects cooperation with Rome, refusing, in his words, to "use chain-gangs of Britons who *have* revolted to make roads for the legions!" (*Blood* 270).

To join Rome, Beric realizes, is to be complicit in a longstanding history of exploitation and cruelty, a point even the old Roman Scaevinus recognizes by novel's end. As his friends contemplate the senseless brutality of Nero's Rome, Scaevinus insists that Rome's most admired qualities—its administration, its justice, its building projects—have always involved the economic and social exploitation of others. Another aristocrat, Balbus, mouths the standard justification for Roman imperialism: "We had to step in because the rest of the world was decadent. . . . All those Greeks and Easterns squabbling! That was what made the Empire." "That was what we said," Scaevinus replies (382). But the truth was that from its earliest days, according to Scaevinus (sounding a lot like Marx), Rome was intent on expanding its empire to generate more wealth for itself:

> It was in the great years of the Republic that we got our first million-aires, making money out of organised trade and usury, not out of anything they took or made in the old ways: men using money not as something to exchange with but as pure power. (384)

Like Meromic, Beric rejects the practical success offered by Rome in favor of alignment with a mythic paradigm. This time, though, the myth is Christianity rather than totemism; because Mitchison sees a potential for social transformation in the myth, in faith that a Kingdom of justice is near, Beric's sacrifice seems paradoxically triumphant. The Britons fought the Romans and lost and were forgotten, according to Beric. "But we shan't be. No one's going to be able to get rid of the Kingdom" (434). The power of the Kingdom grows out of the Christians' ability to suffer well. The problem of those who suffer, of course, is that they lack power. They suffer, die, and are forgotten, as Beric suggests. But Christianity offers a suffering that is also a triumph. Even in dying, the martyrs spread their message. Mitchison is less interested in the promise of an afterlife than in the power of death to communicate and inspire social change. The martyrs die as witnesses to their faith and thus inspire it in others. And the logical effect should be social revolution. Paul explains, "We believe in the value of the individual human being, his right to be bought by the blood, his right to choose for himself, his right to be in brotherhood. We cannot give consent, even formal consent, to any principle which denies this" (335).

Paul argues for the value of the individual human being, and martyrdom is available to both women and men. But even among these early Christians the prominent roles belong to men. Mitchison's only major female character is Lalage, a deacon of the Christian group with which Beric gets involved, in fact the person who actually converts him. She offers a hint of how a more sexually flexible Christianity might have evolved, for her earliest exposure to religion has been through Isis-worship. Lalage emphasizes the Frazerian parallels between Christ and other dying and reborn gods, a category into which she puts not only Isis, but also Cleopatra, who

> was too great a queen ever to love, but she had sons by the men who loved her, who were to rule all over the world. For, although she had no mercy on the rich or the strong, yet always she was compassionate as Isis herself, to the people. And so it was, in the end, that she had Rome against her, Rome which means naked power, Rome with the sword and the whip. She fought Rome for the thing which we all want, for the golden age of peace and joy and compassion, when the common people shall at last be free. (100–101)[8]

Cleopatra kills herself, according to the priestess of Isis, to avoid being in Augustus Caesar's triumph. In making that sacrifice she escapes the powerlessness of Vercingetorix and instead becomes yet another ruler who dies for his or her people—one of Frazer's dying and reborn gods, a scapegoat anticipating Christ. Both Cleopatra and Isis put women at the center of the religious experience, and, most important, make female sexuality a part of the sacred. Lalage is a potentially disruptive character because of the way she connects sacrifice, sacrament, and sexuality. Nancy Jay has argued that sacrifice is a process by which men purify society of a corruption borne of women's bodies (28). Lalage's admiration for Cleopatra and Isis undermines this process, as does her effort to make her own sexuality part of her gift to others. Like female characters in works by Mitchison from "Lovely Mantinea" to *We Have Been Warned*, Lalage offers herself sexually as part of her program for social change. While suffering is easily sacralized, however, female sexuality is not, and Lalage is rebuked for her generosity. Her potential to subvert the emergent patriarchical nature of Christianity dissipates as she disappears into prison and dies with the other martyrs.

The novel does end with a female character, but one who definitely rejects the disruptive power of Lalage. Eunice, the baker of the bread that serves as host during the Christians' "love feasts," is about to offer three visitors a piece of cake. If, because of her powerlessness, she is hostage to Roman power, she has discovered in Christianity the power to turn her homely hospitality into a powerful act that sacralizes the suffering she cannot prevent. "I'll cut one of my cakes for them, she thought, I can't really afford to, I suppose, but there, what's the use of saving up these days. And maybe I can make them a hot drink, too" (499). So ends *The Blood of the Martyrs*, with an image of domestic service that seems all too familiarly feminine.

In this novel, we see the limits of Mitchison's power to imagine a transformative role for historical fiction. The totemism of *The Corn King and the Spring Queen* and *The Conquered* was essentially premythic, in that it was enacted through ritual for which there was no coherent explanation or set of stories. With *The Blood of the Martyrs*, however, Mitchison is presenting a carefully articulated mythic paradigm as the model for universal salvation. We do get a warning—as we see Paul composing his epistles—that advice applicable to one religious community should not be read as absolute truth. But the very notion that there is a kingdom "we all want in our hearts" has a terrible power to synthesize and thus to marginalize those who want only with a difference—the fate, in this novel, of the Jews, described as viewing "the rest of the world lumped together as so much dirt" (367). The depiction of martyrdom also glamorizes torture and suffering in a disturbing way. Mitchison makes much of the Christians' abilities to die well, thus serving as witnesses to their faith. But such a distinction between those who withstand torture nobly and those who crack under the pressure is fallacious, as Elaine Scarry points out, and vindicates the premises by which torturers defend their activities.

Throughout Mitchison's work, magic and ritual and myth are a refuge against defeat. Tarrik recognizes his own ritual role as Corn King in the story of Kleomones, the king who dies for his people, and their story, which anticipates Christ's, transforms the world's imagination. Mythic paradigm thus outlives any single historical victory. Meromic's transformation into a wolf rescues him from personal defeat in a similar way. According to Francis Hart, this movement from historical defeat to mythic triumph is typical of Scottish literature; Scottish writers, he argues, see history as a "record of betrayal and defeat," with history finally "less real than myth," as characters must return to an "archetypal self" to regain lost power (188). The pattern is certainly evident in Mitchison, though she herself became involved in Scottish nationalism and literature in the 1930s, well after her writing of both *The Conquered* and *The Corn King and the Spring Queen*. In fact, the use of myth as a refuge from history is typical of many works written out of an acute consciousness of defeat and exclusion.

The Blood of the Martyrs is thus in some ways a logical outcome of Mitchison's examination of the "conquered." If, as historical novelist, she cannot undo the past and describe the victories of those with whom she sympathizes, she can, as mythmaker, describe their defeats as victories, auguring a future of apocalyptic social change. There are two problems with such a use of myth. First, rather than instigating social change, myth is likely, in Angela Carter's words, by dealing "in false universals, to dull the pain of particular circumstances" (5); it provides solace by fitting suffering into a universal (and seemingly inevitable) pattern, when only an examination of historical particularities can motivate social change. Second, once mythic sacrifice is seen as sacred, it is hard to limit the uses to which it may be put. Most frequently, as Jay points out, it has been used to legitimize male succession at the expense of women's bodies:

> Sacrifice can expiate, get rid of, the consequences of having been born of woman (along with countless other dangers) and at the same time integrate the pure and eternal patrilineage. Sacrificially constituted descent, incorporating women's mortal children into an "eternal" (enduring through generations) kin group, in which membership is recognized by participation in sacrificial ritual, not merely by birth, enables a patrilineal group to transcend mortality in the same process in which it transcends birth. In this sense, sacrifice is doubly a remedy for having been born of woman. (40)

Mitchison's hostages—Meromic, Beric, and the others—highlight the psychic toll political domination takes on its victims and, to the extent that they undercut earlier versions of the same story, create a readerly unease with happy endings. When, in *The Blood of the Martyrs*, on the other hand, Mitchison allows a single story to dominate, subjugating Lalage's sexuality to her sacrificial plot, turning victims to martyrs, and hostages to eucharistic hosts, she reinforces the power of old patterns to contain the human imagination.

NOTES

1. In "Cottia Went to Bibracte," a young Roman wife cares lovingly for two Haeduan children, and in "Quintus Getting Well," a Roman boy is cured of invalidism by his love for a Gallic slave, whom he finally returns to his own people.

2. Mitchison's stated aim in writing *The Conquered* was to inspire sympathy with the Irish. Mitchison herself explains her choice of subject in her 1935 article "Writing Historical Novels":

> Why then, had I got to choose this period? Because my mind was all stirred up with the troubles in Ireland in my own year of grace—1921— and the injustices committed by the Black and Tan troops during the British military occupation. . . . So it was that Gaul presented itself to me, plastic materials for my parallel with Ireland. (645)

In *You May Well Ask*, she writes that Great Britain's role in Ireland parallels Caesar's in Gaul (183).

3. Mitchison's role as honorary member of an African tribe in Botswana suggests her sympathy for and identification with former colonies (see *Return to the Fairy Hill*).

4. For Bulwer-Lytton, Rome is inseparable from its decadence; the only noble sentiments in the novel are expressed by Greeks. But Bulwer-Lytton's depiction of Roman decadence as driven by out-of-control women and Egyptians fits

the overall pattern I am suggesting. See Rana Kabbani's *Europe's Myths of Orient* for a discussion of this link between the East, sexuality, and female misbehavior (14–36). "The West is social stability," she writes of Shakespeare's *Antony and Cleopatra*, "the East pleasure, unrestricted by social dictates" (21).

5. A 1936 poem suggests that for Mitchison the image of ancient Briton as Rome's adversary is inseparable from its strong women; she writes that Colchester is where the "strong sons of Cymbeline" and Boadicea were defeated by the Romans ("Thinking" 1386).

6. Jill Benton, in her biography of Mitchison, writes that her brother Jack Haldane was her major love, and suggests this is the explanation for the recurring incest theme in her work (12).

7. In 1935 Mitchison wrote an article entitled "Cloud Cuckoo Borough" suggesting the Soviet Union was such a place.

8. These are ideas Mitchison develops in her 1972 *Cleopatra's People*; here too Cleopatra resembles Isis and is trying to inaugurate a "Golden Age" (70).

CHAPTER 10

When Mana Meets Woman: Mary Butts's Cleopatra

When Mary Butts wrote *Scenes from the Life of Cleopatra* in 1935, she was on well-trodden ground. As Lucy Hughes-Hallett has pointed out, the figure of Cleopatra has been reconstrued countless times since her death in 30 B.C. Generally reviled, sometimes patronized, and rarely admired, she has consistently been the means by which a culture conveys its attitudes toward female sexuality and power, usually by putting her on the less privileged side of a series of dichotomies: Rome versus Egypt; self-control versus self-indulgence; mind versus body; conqueror versus conquered; energy versus indolence; male versus female.

Such dichotomies do not bode well for women interested in power and cultural authority—women, in other words, like Mary Butts. In *Scenes from the Life of Cleopatra*, Butts explores the polarities underlying her culture's understanding of Cleopatra. Arguing that standard explanations of Cleopatra's behavior are insufficient, she suggests that *mana*—that all-pervasive energy so vital in her other novels and in her depiction of Alexander the Great—is the crucial, overlooked element. This energy emanating from the universe is above all a resolver of contradictions, for it charges matter with spirituality, thus bypassing Western dualism. But Butts does not merely write *about* mana. She allows its fluidity and intangibility to pervade her narrative and characters. Dramatizing the battle between Rome and Cleopatra as a confrontation between a monovalent, authoritarian, phallogocentric rhetoric and the destabilizing discourse of her own mana-driven narrative, Butts posits a new version of woman-with-power, one that rejects dichotomies. Insisting instead on the power of the immaterial and divine to resolve contradictions and shape human character, Butts depicts a queen who can wield power while remaining autonomous, maternal, and sexual.

Before examining Butts's text, however, I want to look more closely at the cultural tradition within which she was writing, a tradition that has remained remarkably stable since Octavian became Augustus Caesar and found in Cleopatra a convenient way of justifying his war against Marc Antony.[1] "The records of her reign are actually very few," Butts's narrator points out. "Octavian saw to that—forced by his own acts to destroy as well as defame the memory of her and of Antony" (179). Most subtly and effectively, Octavian sponsored Virgil's *Aeneid*, in which Aeneas must repeatedly resist the chaos and danger offered by women in order to found the Roman Empire. Tempted by Dido to abandon his effort and stay with her in Carthage, he defines his particular version of heroism by resisting the wiles of a woman. Success requires self-control, which requires the control of women, who are themselves linked to fire, storm, and social disorder—represented in the *Aeneid* not only by Dido, but by the Trojan women so desperate to stop traveling that they try to burn Aeneas's fleet. Most historical accounts of the struggle for power after the assassination of Julius Caesar portray the Marc Antony/Octavius competition in similar terms: in defeating Antony, Octavius wins a war against chaos (Egypt and Cleopatra), not against his fellow Romans. The very notion of empire thus comes to be justified as the containment of disorder. Subdued colonies—whether "primitive" northern Europe or "decadent" Asia and northern Africa—are associated with the same qualities as women.

Egyptian culture to Rome, of course, was not "primitive," but frighteningly old. If primitive cultures are "feminine" because they are wild, then older cultures—named "Asiatic" by Plutarch—are "feminine" because they are sensual, self-indulgent, over-elaborated, dishonest. Plutarch writes of Marc Antony, for example, that he adopted the Asiatic style of rhetoric, which had "much in common with Antony's own mode of life, which was boastful, insolent, and full of empty bravado and misguided aspirations" (*Makers* 272). Cleopatra, like Asia, mirrors Antony's worst qualities and releases his inhibitions. Plutarch writes that she "excited to the point of madness many passions which had hitherto lain concealed, or at least dormant, and . . . stifled or corrupted all those redeeming qualities in him which were still capable of resisting temptation" (292). After the brief respite of his marriage to Octavia and sojourn in Rome, when, like Aeneas before Dido, he is "torn between his reason and his love for the Egyptian queen" (298), Antony goes down to destruction, having sacrificed his military ability, his self-control, and even his courage to Cleopatra.

Thus in the popular imagination, Cleopatra is everything that Rome is not. Woman and foreigner, she is the quintessential Other: childish, sexually insatiable, hedonistic, cowardly, scheming, at once deadly and irresistible to men. Butts explicitly declares her book an alternative to this standard version of Cleopatra. Chaucer, she notes, was sympathetic in *The Legend of Good Women* (283). But from then on, with the exception of Arthur Weigall's *Life and Times of Marc Antony*, Cleopatra has been universally portrayed as a "crowned courtesan" participating in "nameless orgies" (280).[2]

This image of Cleopatra as a decadent devotee of sensuality is reinforced, Butts complains, by the nineteenth-century Academy painting "which shows a large black gipsy-woman, half-naked, lolling with an air of insincere despair between crouching slaves; a small snake held firmly to a melon of a breast" (*Cleopatra* 285), and by the Russian Ballet's *Cléopatre* (282). Given Butts's long friendship with Jean Cocteau, who designed ballets for Diaghilev's company, it is not surprising she knew the plot, about a lover Cleopatra lures away from a slave girl, then has executed after a single night of love (Sokolova 74). This plot, with its attribution to Cleopatra of a sexuality not only voracious but also murderous, is, Butts suggests, a way of explaining the absence from the historical record of any known lovers other than Julius Caesar and Marc Antony. Unable to believe Cleopatra might have been both ambitious and sexually discriminating, historians assume she had a series of lovers who left so little evidence of their existence that they must have been "exterminated" (Butts, *Cleopatra* 282). Butts's appendix, with its litany of past injustices, makes clear the task Butts has set herself: to right the record, to fill the void created by the inability of men—"historians or not"—to imagine "an active woman, alone, enjoying the use of power" (282).

The decadent Cleopatra resembles a number of sexually dangerous females haunting the Western literary imagination during the late nineteenth and early twentieth centuries. Citing Walter Pater's Mona Lisa, "older than the rocks among which she sits," Rider Haggard's She, and other femmes fatales, Sandra Gilbert and Susan Gubar argue that the late Victorian fascination with such women reflected not only male anxiety before female ambition but "a series of other key cultural changes, including the feared 'recessional' of the British empire, the intensified development of such fields as anthropology and embryology, and the rise of a host of alternative theologies" (2: 7). I would argue also that Queen Victoria herself, sitting on the throne so imposingly and for so long a time, offered a disconcerting image of female power. Granted, she used her power only to reinforce patriarchal notions of gender and empire. But her very presence on a throne conjoined womanhood and power in a way that might well discomfit a culture obsessed with dichotomous sex roles, a point made also by Adrienne Munich, who suggests that when Queen Victoria joined maternity and monarchy, a "boundary in the cultural imagination was transgressed" (265).

Growing up in the final years of Victoria's reign, Butts was eager for knowledge and literary achievement. She was also bitterly aware of the limitations gender placed on her life and education. Her mother warned her against becoming a "Bluestocking" (*Crystal* 115) because "men did not like women who 'knew things'" (122). But she also recognized the way her culture masked the contradictory demands it made on women, whose "sexual functions, at one and the same time, too disgraceful to be mentioned," were "yet the be-all and end-all of her existence" (180). Their only power dwelt in the display of ignorance; knowledge—whether of their own bodies or of the world—rendered them at once corrupt and powerless. In Cleopatra, Butts must have found a kindred spirit, one whose desire for knowledge and power had been mistaken (as had her own by her mother) for sexual insatiability. Butts's fascination with Cleopatra—and with Cleopatra's divine self Isis—grew out of that ambition and anger. Cleopatra-as-Isis offered her an alternative queen, one that brought together all the qualities her culture struggled to keep apart.

Isis, of course, was demonized almost as thoroughly as Cleopatra during the nineteenth century. Associated with the lower classes and especially with unruly women, its priests are corrupt in *The Last Days of Pompeii* and licentious would-be rapists in *The Gladiators*. Theodor Mommsen, by the end of the nineteenth century Rome's most authoritative historian, writes, "a wager might be laid, that the more loose any woman was, the more piously she worshipped Isis" (446). But there was a countertrend in the interpretation of Isis. Madame Blavatsky's 1886 *Isis Unveiled* repeatedly compares Isis to the Virgin Mary, as does Frazer in *The Golden Bough*, who contrasts the spirituality of rites in honor of Isis with "the bloody and licentious rites of other Oriental goddesses" (6: 118). Frances Swiney, in her 1909 *The Bar of Isis*, evokes a maternal yet virginal Isis in arguing for the sanctity of the "gravid womb" (17).[3] And for Naomi Mitchison, in *The Corn King and the Spring Queen*, Isis is a crucial image of female nurturing and sexuality. Both fertility goddess and virgin, Isis is a good bridger of oppositions. In fact, she is associated in many descriptions of her power with the fusion of opposites. Simultaneously loving wife and autonomous ruler, she is symbolized by multicolored robes, "for her power is concerned with matter which becomes everything and receives everything, light and darkness, day and night, fire and water, life and death" (Plutarch, qtd. in Hughes-Hallett 81).

Butts herself uses Isis in several nonhistorical short stories to suggest the way the supernatural impinges on daily life. In "Mappa Mundi," for example, Butts's narrator writes of Paris as superimposed on a deeper reality: "One aspect of a central fire, or the womb of Isis, eternally fertile, eternally bringing forth" (*From* 223). This "central fire" resembles mana—a source out of which spiritual energy flows. Butts links this spiritual energy to the female body by associating it insistently with the womb, or "matrix," both words that turn up repeatedly in "Mappa Mundi." The matrix is a kind of tunnel into all time and history, all good and all evil. Through Isis, then, Butts connects mana to timelessness, the embracing of contradictions, and the womb. The notion of myth that was emerging in the Taverner stories—a myth aligned with women and *jouissance* against Eliot's "mythical method"—evolves in Butts's later work into an explicitly female power manifest only as an infinitely receding line of uncertainties. Isis, with her veils and mystery, is, for Butts, the unknowable. "Do not pretend to yourself that you have seen her eyes," she writes. "Still less her smile. Least of all, perhaps, do not ask what she is smiling about" (*From* 219). Butts calls on these attributes of the goddess in her characterization of Cleopatra.

Power fascinated Butts; she had already examined its manifestations in *The Macedonian*, her novel about Alexander the Great, of which *Scenes from the Life of Cleopatra* is in some ways a continuation. Cleopatra is, of course, the descendant of Alexander's friend Ptolemy, a Macedonian like him, ruling in the city Alexander himself founded. The book is structured much like *The Macedonian*, consisting of scenes defined less by external event than by the workings of invisible forces. The sentence structure is similarly oblique, separating relative pronoun from referent, forcing the reader to forge connections implied but never made explicit. But most significant (and underlying all these other parallels) is the role of mana in defining the great and shaping the course of human history—and in evading the dichotomies that work so much to Cleopatra's disadvantage.

Butts defines *mana* in her preface to *The Macedonian* as "the sheer force that lies behind the manifestations of life" (xi). Alexander experiences the presence of this energy as "something that shaped equally the Universe and an acorn, and It called him friend" (65). Those suited to power, in other words, are befriended by mana. Julius Caesar alludes to this—and to *The Macedonian*—when he comments, "I won't have it that we're in the grip of something that has the last laugh at us. Not laugh. At least I hold that they meant something when certain of the Hellenes claimed an invisible Friend" (54). Julius Caesar is a novice at divinity, however, compared to Cleopatra, whom he recognizes as an avatar of Isis: "To her subjects a creature who was a physical incarnation of the Deity, Our Lady of Earth and Heaven, Mother of men and Gods. Not 'Herself,' of course, but Her representative, an idea of Her made flesh, a being endowed with Her mana" (67–68).

It is Cleopatra herself who is most articulate on the subject of godhead. She explains to Julius Caesar that there are certain moments, when she is dressed in the robes of Isis, when she feels it most strongly. She feels herself given "to the air and the light and the earth":

> Then it is that I come out of myself, and Something—call it the Goddess—becomes me and I That. That which was August in time had departed: that which is eternally August entered. When it has done that, my body is as though it had been in a different state, as though it were impregnated with a life that is not the common run of the blood. I

move, distinct, elated, but not with myself. I do not want—I am—
power. I am filled to the lips though I do not speak. I have seen the
things of which our actions are the translations. (125)

These moments of contact with mana are also moments of bodily dissolution, conflating time and space in terms suggesting Kristeva's notion of
"monumental" time. Even more exactly than Scylla's vertiginous
moments, they recapitulate divine events of the past—moments of resurrection suggestive of an "anterior or concomitant maternal cult" (191).
Thus Charmian, Cleopatra's Egyptian waiting woman, explains that they
have come to Rome "So that what they [Cleopatra, Caesar, and Caesar-
ion] are can go on happening till it is perfected. It is Isis and Osiris and
Horus all over again, ready to happen to the world, if only the world will
let it" (128). Each manifestation of power is thus a repetition of an earlier
version: a reinsertion of the same mana into the universe, and simultaneously a movement into "woman's time."

Along with mana, Butts sees the toleration of contradiction as a
defining characteristic of the great. For her, Julius Caesar is, in this sense,
almost as great as Cleopatra, and his epileptic seizures are moments of
mana-contact similar to hers. While Cleopatra's complexity seems to be
hers by birth, however, Caesar's is the product of experience—an experience she portrays in one of her last stories, "A Roman," written during
the same years she was writing *Scenes from the Life of Cleopatra*. The
story is strongly reminiscent of Joseph Conrad's *Heart of Darkness*, as
though Butts wanted to explore Marlow's implied comparison between
Roman and British imperialism. In the story, Caesar and a Roman centurion named Florus talk to pass the time before the tide will turn and
enable them to leave Britain for Rome. Caesar is Marlow, Florus his
audience. In answer to Florus's question as to why he has sided with the
People and the Assembly against the Senate, Caesar tells a story from
his youth about an encounter with evil. Fleeing Rome, where Sulla sought
his death, he was caught by pirates.[4] There he had his first experience of
men outside the law, men who wanted not community but "excitement
and risk and killing and oblivion and the dream of revenge. A sort of
cheap ecstasy" (*Last* 56). They live a "parody of our lives, who have
passed under the yoke, the great arch we call the Law" (57).

These violent and crude pirates free him on receiving his ransom, and
he returns with soldiers to wipe them out and crucify their leaders. The
story concludes with a moment of religious revelation in which Caesar and
the crucified pirate seem one. While the pirates are the "final opposite
statement of mankind" (62), what emerges is the interdependency of order
and disorder, community and chaos. Community defines itself through the
suppression of that which disrupts it; the act of crucifying the pirate leaders is an essential act of societal self-assertion. This is something the pirates

recognize themselves, for their ecstatic violence requires a Law to be outside. They, too, have a "mythology of their own" (56).

Most disturbing of all, the sacral power of violence and sacrifice, shared by Caesar and the pirates, brings them irrevocably close. Sacrifice, according to Harrison, is a kind of bridge between one's own mana and that outside (*Themis* 137); in crucifying the pirates, Caesar has not distanced himself from the horror of their misbehavior, but shared a sacramental moment with them. If Caesar is Marlow to the pirates' Kurtz, the two commune far more intimately than in *Heart of Darkness*, with Marlow/Caesar's values far more deeply challenged. Work, self-restraint, duty—the concepts that keep Marlow from succumbing to "darkness"— refer to behaviors Marlow finds self-defining and self-evident. For Butts, they are themselves shot through with the very violence they pretend to control. For Caesar to do his duty he must himself become a godlike figure prepared to die as the pirates have. For Caesar to rule, he must, in a sense, become Kurtz, employing the very powers Conrad's Marlow finds so horrifying. While *Heart of Darkness* emphasizes epistemological and moral complexity, there are assumptions it backs off from questioning. Marianna Torgovnick describes Conrad's "ritualized enactments of violence and death" as "flirtations with boundary dissolution":

> they both test and affirm men's need to maintain separation, difference, and control as attributes of masculinity. They become simulacra of, but also charms against, the loss of self inscribed in the fullest erotic experience. (151)

Butts's "ritualized enactments of violence and death," on the other hand, genuinely dissolve boundaries, suggesting that crime and redemption are messily intertwined. Caesar's wisdom results from the recognition that without the pirates' criminality and pain, his identity and power are gone; that their death prefigures his own; that the same sacral force feeds both rule and misrule.

Caesar makes the connection to "A Roman" explicit in *Scenes from the Life of Cleopatra*. As his son is being born, he experiences his own death and rebirth, and thinks to himself that never before has he felt so conquered—except by the pirates "hanging on their crosses." "It's from that little adventure and that moment of submission," he says, "that I trace my life" (80). Anticipating Christ, recapitulating Osiris and, more recently, the pirates, Caesar is both crucifier and crucified. The result of this insight is Caesar's unusual ability to embrace contradictions. "What has happened to the man who rides the double horse of the soul, and in two directions at once?" Pompey wonders, as he contemplates Caesar. He is referring, of course, to Plato's *Phaedrus*, which characterizes the soul as a chariot drawn by two horses, one reason, the other passion (19):

> Life is shown to us, projected, in pairs, contradictions. It is all choice
> between this and that, twin-opposites. A man who has resolved even one
> opposite has gone outside life as it is presented to us, with its before and
> after, its true and false, its dark and light, its acceptance and refusal, its
> here and there. (19)

Caesar, in embracing opposites, has gone outside ordinary life, immersing
himself in mana, which acknowledges no polarities at all.

Butts's depiction of sacred force actually shares more with Lawrence
than Conrad, perhaps because both were enthusiastic readers of Jane Harrison. In *Etruscan Places*, Lawrence detects in Etruscan art a preanthropomorphic "cosmic religion" (101) based on an underlying "vitality"
in nature (83) that sounds a lot like Butts's mana. Those who are strong
enough to absorb the most vitality become gods, and thus become Pharoah,
Tarquin, Alexander, Caesar, or Napoleon (84). This Etruscan religion,
according to Lawrence, resembles Egypt's, and both are in stark contrast to
"Latin-Roman mechanism and suppression" (62). Lawrence also points
out that many Etruscans were pirates; certainly the insight Caesar gains
from Butts's pirates echoes what Lawrence learns from the Etruscans.

Lawrence's Rome *resists* nature (110); his Etruria is one with it. For
Etruscans everything is interconnected: "The blood-stream is one, and
unbroken, yet storming with oppositions and contradictions" (104).
Lawrence's Etruscans don't flirt with "boundary dissolution," to borrow Torgovnick's terms; they live it. So, too, do Butts's mana-laden leaders. To fully experience mana means to lose the self entirely in the flow of
energy, to merge inside and out, self and world, mind and body, past
and present. As Cleopatra gives birth to his son, Caesar has such a mystical experience:

> Caesar was overwhelmed in Caesar, whose control of Caesar had been
> the being of Caesar. Caesar was lost in Caesar and reborn of Caesar—
> self and not-self, subject and object whirling in some spiritual fusion, dis-
> solved into their ultimate particles and setting to partners like a system
> of planets; and it was the instant of death and the reassembling of a new
> Caesar, new as the new-born man-offspring of his thin loins. (87–88)

Caesar's self, best known for a sentence epitomizing the subject-object
split—"I came; I saw; I conquered"—is dissolved in a syntactically chaotic
sea of contradictions. As his son is born, he slips into an epileptic seizure
which reenacts the sacrifice of Frazer's dying god (as well as the pirates'
death) and thus suffuses him with mana.

Caesar's understanding of his own divinity is minimal and somewhat uncomfortable. Cleopatra's godhead, on the other hand, is more
self-confident, her understanding of its meaning more profound. The
result of this deeper understanding is her laughter. Because she is so

intensely conscious of her dual role as woman and as goddess, she can live neither life with total conviction. Everything she does is infused with laughter, the only way to signify that her actions, like her words, cannot possibly convey the whole story. Her life resembles Irigaray's notion of mimicry: "to play with mimesis," Irigaray writes, "is . . . to try to record the place of her [woman's] exploitation by discourse, without allowing herself to be simply reduced to it" (76). A world based on language and logic offers Cleopatra no alternative mode of self-expression, so she speaks the language of everyone else—with a laugh. Her every action has two meanings at once, not because she is dishonest, but because she is two. Often depicted as scheming, Cleopatra is at once consciously manipulating Marc Antony and moved by him, and she recognizes her own doubleness: "I am a woman given a double thread. Which will break, and breaking, strain the other till it breaks? Or hold firm, so that the other is useless? Which is going to save me, my love or my imitation of it?" (246–47). Cleopatra is immersed in feeling and detached from it— straight and parodic at the same time. Historians would have treated her more gently had her motives and feelings been simpler—a point she recognizes and mourns. "Oh, it sticks, my women, it sticks in my throat— what men will say of me" (248). Cleopatra is, of course, right to worry. The laughter at the core of her character infuriates because it challenges the meanings that others have attached to the world without providing any discernible alternative. Butts's narrator writes that her laughter "has done her no good with historians" (186).

Butts's Cleopatra resembles Riding's Cressida in her terrifying tendency to "make 'visible' . . . what was supposed to remain invisible: the cover-up of a possible operation of the feminine in language" (Irigaray 76). Like Cressida, she is a "monster in the text," a reminder that if she cannot be reduced to the terms offered by "masculine logic," neither can we. Like Cressida, she must be comfortably categorized as sexually monstrous, since that, at least, is a familiar form of monstrosity. Charmian anticipates the process: "Oh, she will have enduring fame, but of pride and insolence and lust. What Roman can endure to see a woman stand up against them?" (244). And Caesar, watching Cleopatra being misunderstood, worries that she will be "Made to suffer. Brought to shame by force of traduction" (76).

Butts's depiction of Cleopatra runs the risk of reinforcing that traduction if she does not somehow replicate the fluid and ineffable quality of her being. Cleopatra's motives and sense of self are defined by her relation to mana. As in *The Macedonian*, Butts must suffuse her narrative with a sense of that intangible energy.

Butts does this, first of all, by emphasizing the discontinuities and inconsistencies in her narrative. Every scene is slanted through the perspective of someone, its version of reality obviously incomplete and self-serving. There is no "Cleopatra": we see her only indirectly, through the perceptions of those around her. Several times, with no transition, Butts replaces narrative with letters supposedly written by Iras, Charmian, and Marc Antony.

These narrative breaks are reinforced by geographical, chronological, and cultural gaps. We enter the novel through the eyes of an unknown fisherman laying nets in Lake Mareotis as Nearchos, Alexander the Great's admiral, approaches. The novel then leaps several hundred years to join Pompey in Rome, as he thinks about Egypt, then moves geographically to Pompey's arrival and death in Egpyt. Then we move to Julius Caeasar in Rome. Next, back in Egypt, we join Cleopatra and her waiting women, Iras and Charmian. In each case the emphasis is on gaps—chronological between the first Lagid Ptolemy and his last offspring Cleopatra; cultural between Romans and Egyptians.

These cultural gaps are highlighted by the incompatible ways different characters understand what's happening. Pompey, for example, identifies with the West against "the witless flow of blind being, the planless politics of the barbarian or of eastern man" (14). The Egyptians see Rome as hopelessly provincial and clumsy. Iras, Cleopatra's friend and waiting woman, writes to her brother from Rome of her "exile among barbarians" (91). While the Romans see Cleopatra as Egyptian, the Egyptians plot to kill her because she is Greek, and she sees herself as "a Hellene against barbarians" (180). The roles of cultural identity, self-interest, and passion in shaping perception are laid bare.

Along with emphasizing conflicting viewpoints, Butts employs what Ian Watt, writing of Conrad, calls "delayed decoding" to emphasize the laboriousness and inadequacy of perception (175). Pompey's wife Cornelia watches her husband's murder and decapitation without fully processing the phenomena; his body is a fallen tower, then "she could see that something was being done to the tower where it lay, something small and round taken off it and held up for everyone to see.... A head? That was the round thing, capped with silver and running scarlet, that Pothinos the eunuch had in his hands" (45).[5] Cornelia's physical distance and emotional resistance make it hard for her to fit these visual details into a meaningful pattern.

Cleopatra's waiting woman Charmian writes in similarly bewildered language of Rome, where her vocabulary does not suffice to describe the topography or people. Hills become "ups and downs" (128); trees in winter "strip and box one another" (127). Charmian's writing sounds like an awkward translation—one that insists on the difficulty of transposing experience from one language to another. If perception is so defined by language and culture, the novel implies, any single version of history can hardly aspire to Truth.

As in *The Macedonian*, Butts's very syntax insists on gaps and elisions, offering frequent fragments, and sentences like "It was almost the first time she had left Alexandria, who had been reared in a palace complete in itself as a small city and ideally healthy"; or "She was not seventeen, in whose veins ran not one drop of eastern blood" (61).

In addition, Butts challenges Rome's assumption that logical, unambiguous language can refer to and contain reality. Cicero, for her, epitomizes the Western use of language: stringing words together in logical form under the pretense of saying something about the world, but really in order to gain power. Butts's Cicero is a repellent figure, his enemy Catiline's widow the only true friend of the visiting Egyptian women.[6] "From her I learned her husband's side of the story," Iras writes, "that Cicero has seen shall not go down as history" (109). Cicero's rhetoric is authoritarian, violent, claiming the sanction of absolute truth—"agonistic," to use Walter Ong's term.

Cicero, called by Mommsen "creator of the modern classical Latin prose," excised from his language any words of foreign, obsolete, or lowly provenance (Mommsen 455–56). Similarly, Butts's Romans excise from history any but the authorized version of their past. "Of course they fake their pedigrees from Troy" (95), Iras says contemptuously, and complains to her brother:

> Listen to Caesar and the rest of their orators, pointing my words and rounding my sentences. It is only now and then that I babble as I used, when it delighted you. Now all the time I hear words, weighted and sharpened, carved into great sentences; and my ear catches the sound; while my mind is being used. (100)

The Romans' carved sentences with their "sharp" words suggest weaponry; Iras, on the other hand, was accustomed to "babble" for the sake of delight. The contrast is between a Lacanian symbolic, where language is an act of separation and self-definition and a Kristevan semiotic, where language is a nonreferential expression of intimacy. The Asiatic rhetoric Plutarch calls "boastful, insolent, and full of empty bravado" is for Iras and Cleopatra language as play.

The novel also refuses the closure of death. It concludes with Antony and Cleopatra at Pelusium ruminating over their past actions and their relationship, turning their lives into the stuff of symbols to such an extent they seem almost to bypass death. "But what he remembered for ever," the book concludes of Marc Antony, "as if his gilt corselet had been stripped off him, was her breast against his. As though the touch of her body had turned its gold to air" (278). The moment is at once sensual (her breast against his) and disembodied (her body turns the gold to air); at once fleeting (he uses the past perfect to describe the memory) and eternal (he will remember it forever). The paradox lingers; the book, like their lives, like history itself, feels unfinished. Butts rejects what Christa Wolf calls "necrophilia"—the love of plot which is really a love of death.

William Plomer accused Butts's work of having an "excess of manner over matter" (269). The comment recalls Plutarch's criticism of Asiatic rhetoric as "boastful, insolent, and full of empty bravado and misguided aspirations" (272). But the manner, of course, is precisely the point. Bryher writes of Butts's "sense of the perfect world before history happened" ("Recognition" 161) and argues that her work conveys a uniquely accurate sense of the years 1910–1930 (163). I would argue that Butts's work is best understood in the context of women's efforts during this time period to make room in Western culture for the very concept of a female maker of history. By locating the power to rule in mana, which is experienced in out-of-body flashes, Butts makes the gender of its wielders completely irrelevant and drowns all those mind-body dichotomies in a flow of contradiction-embracing spiritual energy.

NOTES

1. Lucy Hughes-Hallett's *Cleopatra* provides an excellent overview of how depictions of Cleopatra have changed over time. Like Butts, she emphasizes the role of Octavian's propaganda in defining our view of Cleopatra. But she attributes the longevity of this image to Cleopatra's role as "she-who-must-be-renounced," or "Woman epitomized." Hughes-Hallett goes on to quote Lacan: "On the one hand, woman becomes, or is produced, precisely what man is not, that is sexual difference: on the other as what he has to renounce, that is *jouissance*" (63). This formulation is useful in understanding both the cultural context within which Butts was writing and the transformative potential Cleopatra offers her.

2. Weigall's Cleopatra is notably more sympathetic than most, a view Weigall is careful to justify by arguing, "we must doff our modern conception of right and wrong" (vi). In fact, rather than doffing contemporary morality, Weigall embraces his contemporaries' sentimental view of motherhood and women, and their racism. He defends Cleopatra as motivated above all by maternity: "Can this tender, ingenuous, smiling mother of Caesar's beloved son be the Siren of Egypt?" (12). His "little Queen" is "essentially feminine—highly strung, and liable to rapid changes from joy to despair" (425). And he repeatedly insists on her Greek—as opposed to Egyptian or African—identity (19, 22, 25, 45, 171). Weigall's view of Cleopatra, in other words, if less judgmental than most, is still intensely patronizing in its treatment of women and power.

3. Swiney blames men for the "degeneracy" so widely bemoaned at the time, because they ignore the "bar of Isis" by having sex with their wives during pregnancy and lactation (9–17). And in *The Awakening of Women* she uses the success of England's "Great White Queen" to prove that as humans evolve, mental rather than physical power is what matters, as a result of which women have

the same—if not a superior—right to power as men (41). Isis and Queen Victoria alike, for Swiney, thus represent female autonomy and power.

4. In fact, Caesar was captured by pirates when he left Rome to study rhetoric in Rhodes, in 75–74 B.C.: "as he had promised them while awaiting the arrival of his ransom, he secured their subsequent crucifixion" (*Encyclopedia Britannia* 574). The experience was not, however, the cause of his siding with the *popularis* against the *optimates*: he had already done so long before.

5. There is another echo here of Conrad's *Heart of Darkness*, in which Marlow struggles to make sense of the balls decorating Kurtz's hut—balls which turn out to be shrunken heads.

6. In an early short story, "Angele au Couvent," Butts's schoolgirl narrator, sounding a lot like Butts herself when she boarded at St. Leonard's School, prays to God, "Make my Cicero translate right" (*Speed* 129).

CHAPTER 11

Phyllis Bentley:
Historical Fiction as Equivocation

Born in 1894, Phyllis Bentley comes from the same generation as Bryher, Mitchison, and Butts, all of whom wrote of the painful conflict they felt between their literary ambition and their role as dutiful Victorian daughters. All wanted to distinguish themselves somehow, yet felt their parents and/or their society did not quite approve of women who distinguished themselves. In her autobiography, Bentley identifies herself explicitly with that generation of the 1890s and characterizes their collective experience as "transition." Despite the social upheaval of twentieth-century England, she felt bound by the Victorian conventions amid which her mother had been raised—conventions she trailed "like restrictive ribbons of seaweed" (*O Dreams* 12).

Bentley is, in many ways, a more old-fashioned novelist than the others discussed in this book; certainly she doesn't do anything recognizably modernist. She does not use myth to undercut history, as do Mitchison, Bryher, and Butts, nor does she experiment with style and narrative method, as do Butts and Riding. She lacks the sexual explicitness of Mitchison and Renault. She wrote minutely detailed regional and historical novels and saw herself as a follower in Charlotte Brontë's footsteps— the Charlotte Brontë of *Shirley*. Above all an observer and transmitter of detail, Bentley lived a conventional life and wrote apparently minor novels well within the conventions of her chosen genre. Her one historical novel with a non-British setting, her 1936 *Freedom, Farewell!*, is at first glance a standard account of Julius Caesar's rise and fall. But Bentley's realism is not just the submissive care of the miniaturist. Her emphasis on detail and the literal in *Freedom, Farewell!* allows her to explore the way history is made at the expense of women's bodies.

Crucial to an understanding of Bentley's novels is Margaret Homans's account of the way nineteenth-century women writers dealt with the conflict they felt between feminine self-submission and literary ambition. Like her fellow Yorkshire writers Elizabeth Gaskell and Charlotte Brontë, Bentley sought to write and to serve at the same time. By writing regional and historical novels, by embracing "realism" as her aesthetic, Bentley was "bearing the word," to use Homans's term, selflessly conveying data, and thus reconciling literary ambition with the traditional female role of transmission. Homans has analyzed this juggling of roles in the work of Gaskell and Brontë, among others; Bentley, in her *The English Regional Novel*, actually names Brontë's *Shirley* as her model. What distinguishes *Shirley* and the genre it inaugurates is precisely its avoidance of romance in favor of realism. Bentley quotes its opening lines: "Calm your expectations," Brontë writes, ". . . something real, cool, and solid lies before you; something as unromantic as Monday morning" (Bentley, *English* 17). Homans suggests that a woman seeking to write while remaining "feminine" could do so by avoiding imagination and invention. The apparent transcription of reality, or of male versions of that reality, replicated the female role within Victorian ideology—that of conveying an heir from father to world—and was thus relatively acceptable.

Bentley's life and career exemplify the ambivalent self-alienation that Fetterley describes as "immasculation": a yearning for recognition under the terms of the status quo, i.e., acceptance as writer and scholar in a patriarchal culture; and at the same time a dim sense that such a recognition alienated her from her own experience as a woman. Bentley's immasculation emerges from a welter of experiences: her childhood reading and daydreams; the "Code" inculcated in her by her education; the sudden freedom offered by World War I, followed by the domestic retrenchment that followed it. All pushed her toward identifying her female role with service to others, while at the same time teaching her to despise that role as feminine—and therefore marginal, unimportant. *Freedom, Farewell!*, her only novel not set in Yorkshire and therefore most dependent on historical source material, is for that reason her most ambitious—in that it tackles the "male" realm of Rome and ancient history— and her most fascinatingly ambivalent. The writing of historical fiction at once consummates Bentley's desire for identification with male power and disciplines that desire, reminding her of her inevitably secondary relation to that power—limited as she is by her gender to the role of wife or transcriber.

Bentley grew up, she writes, "something of a tomboy" (*O Dreams* 30). An early and voracious reader, she read the books recommended by her three older brothers: Kipling, Conan Doyle, Dickens, and Scott. A business partner of her father's "gave my brothers regularly the Henty and Hocking novels which I too devoured" (44). "All this fiction . . ." she writes, "poured into my mind stories and characters which furnished my daydreams" (43). Reading about adventurous boys and young men is itself an equivocal experience for the young girl; while identification with the male hero may seem to offer a positive role model, Elizabeth Segel points out that this would involve "such a strong consciousness of inappropriateness that it would render boys' books little more than escapist fantasy for most girls, not much use in expanding the possibilities of their own lives" (177).

Escapist fantasies are indeed what Bentley indulged in. She calls them daydreams, and they play a vital role in the lives of Marjorie (the ambitious scholar-heroine of *Environment*), of Laura (*Sleep in Peace*), and of her own self as portrayed in *O Dreams, O Destinations*. All three women discover in these fantasies a potent alternative to the daily life in which they are taken for granted and dominated by their families. The daydreams often mingle ambitious and erotic plots: the daydream-self bravely overcomes some form of tyranny and in the process wins the passionate love of a man.[1] Bentley describes them as following "the usual Cinderella lines: the little girl, despised and rejected, who was eventually recognised as the most beautiful and charming little girl in the world" (*O Dreams* 35), but in fact her heroines are generally more active than Cinderella, being "bold as lions in defence of the right" (36). Borrowing energy and action from boys' adventure stories, these dream-heroines abandon adventure to marry young, their husbands Rochester-like figures of brooding handsomeness. While in her earliest childhood, Bentley may well have found reinforcement for her ambition in her brothers' books, she also learned that the proper closure for her stories was marriage, not heroic triumph.

The daydreams, which mobilized her dangerously powerful imagination, Bentley always regarded with shame—perhaps due to their flagrant unreality, or due to their tinge of sexuality. One is reminded of Southey's famous warning to Charlotte Brontë: "The day dreams in which you habitually indulge are likely to induce a distempered state of mind. . . . Literature cannot be the business of a woman's life, and it ought not to be" (Gaskell 173). While in conflict with the fulfillment of her daily duties, however, the daydreams served also to sublimate sexual desire. During her adolescence, Bentley writes in *O Dreams, O Destinations*, "any stirrings of sex (rare at this period) I experienced were satisfied by vague daydream, usually in some strongly plotted historical story" (63). The strong plot and the discipline provided by historical accuracy serve to keep any disruptive impulses in check. Her reading, in other words, by providing ready-made plots, disciplined and defused her desire.

That the lover of Bentley's daydreams resembles Brontë's Rochester is no accident. The stern Rochester with the tender heart is the quintessential father-figure, a product of Brontë's—and Bentley's—ambivalent relation to patriarchal culture, which is similarly oppressive yet fascinating. As Homans points out, Jane Eyre chooses Rochester over Mother Nature, recognizing that too complete an identification with Nature would mean to "stop writing and speaking intelligibly within the symbolic order"

(85). As a novelist, Brontë's "main allegiance is to the father's symbol making" rather than to the literal, preverbal presence of the mother, which to her signifies silence or death (94). By strongly plotting her day-dreams and providing them with the closure of marriage to a dominating male, Bentley subdues her impulse to reject or rival male power, while pursuing a kind of love affair with male culture.

Some years later, when Bentley wrote her first novel, *Environment*, she aimed at writing a novel so realistic as to be unplotted. Her publishers objected to the lack of closure, and suggested she settle her heroine definitively in either a career or marriage. Bentley agreeably supplied a desirable young man and married her scholarly and ambitious young heroine to him (*O Dreams* 124). In her writing, as in her inner life, plot—conventionally conceived and often historically derived—has the final say, serving to discipline her rebellious attention to detail.

Bentley's education, like her reading and daydreaming, was equivocal in its impact. While she did brilliantly in school, attending Cheltenham Ladies College, then taking her B.A. from the University of London in 1914, Bentley absorbed most lastingly from her education a belief in a "code" of "Duty," "Honour," and "Responsibility" (*O Dreams* 77–78) that seemed to forbid the independent pursuit of her own goals. While the opening of education to women allowed them to gain knowledge, a sense of purpose and community, and fostered self-respect, it did not always foster ambition. During the last quarter of the nineteenth century, boarding schools for young women—such as Cheltenham Ladies College—opened on a large scale. Run by women of powerful personality, these schools nonetheless faced pressure to prove that educated women were still respectable, feminine women (Vicinus 134). The result was an emphasis on service to others rather than personal ambition (Dyhouse 73–74). Certainly this was the message absorbed by Bentley, who writes that her education produced women "admirably fitted for the tasks the British Empire then imposed on them" (*O Dreams* 79). Bentley left Cheltenham determined to be a "good daughter to my parents," which meant being less interested in books, "more feminine, more sociable, more daughterly" (81). She remained a good daughter until her mother's death, having spent twenty-three years juggling the care of her aging, demanding widowed mother with a career as writer, librarian, and lecturer.

World War I offered Bentley the opportunity to move to London and work for a living, but the liberation it offered was paid for by the postwar reaction, when it was the "duty of all women to clear out" (*O Dreams* 106). While feeling women had the right to work, Bentley herself cleared out and returned to Yorkshire to be with her parents. Encouragement from publishers and her success as a lecturer gave Bentley the confidence necessary to keep writing, but throughout her life she seems to have recognized and admired the courage of less conventional women without being able to emulate it herself. Even her autobiography, published in 1962 at the end of a long and prolific career, is apologetic and equivocal, hinting at but deferring her anger at the way her culture's notion of female identity had limited her life.

Despite her sense that they condemn her to minor roles, Bentley is in love with male plots and male culture, and so exiles whatever angry, articulate women she creates to the margins of her stories. Like Gilbert and Gubar's Victorian woman writer, Bentley creates her madwomen but puts them in the attic—aligning her narrative with the forces of exclusion. Judith Tennant, of *Environment*, is Bentley's most fully realized madwoman in the attic. Marjorie Johnson, the novel's brilliant and ambitous but repressed heroine, is impressed by Judith's intelligence and wide reading; ugly but "clever," Judith was raised by a feminist aunt. This aunt, "a tall, untidy woman in a weird, loose-fitting purple garment," is herself a doctor and a writer (107). Judith tells Marjorie of "innumerable theories, books, and ideas which the girl had never heard of before, and taught her to think for herself by presenting to her an absolutely different view of life from any she had previously encountered" (83). Judith is also permanently enraged. Her "wickedly bright eyes" are full of "sparkling malice" (79); she is mean to Marjorie and to her stepsister, and on several occasions she curses indiscriminately at people on the street. Marjorie, however, impressed by her intellect, is persuaded to run off with her to Boulogne, where Judith intends to pursue a career as a medium.

The spiritualism, intellectualism, the pioneering professionalism of her aunt, even her thinness, boniness, and spectacles link Judith to the stereotypical late-nineteenth-century feminist. Once in France, however, Marjorie discovers that Judith is not just bright and ambitious; she is insane. Not only did she steal the money that financed their trip; she proceeds to throw her purse out a train window and hurl invective at everyone she passes.

Marjorie's effort to do a "mad, wicked, outrageous, blatantly unconventional thing" (90)—her effort to defy circumstances and act out her desires—is thus linked to feminism through Judith and her aunt, and it is a disaster. Judith, she decides, is "degeneracy disguised as unconventionalism" (106). *Degeneracy* was a loaded term in early-twentieth-century England, where the decay of the race worried imperialists—a decay to which inappropriate activities by women were believed to be a major contributor. Judith's later institutionalization serves as a powerful warning against feminine self-assertion. Bentley's apparent sympathies are with Marjorie's effort to accomodate herself to her world, though Judith's uncompromising rage might well be an inscription of her own (not fully articulated) anger and feminism.

In Bentley's later work, she remains Marjorie-like in her submission to convention, but her insistently realist aesthetic becomes also an attempt to unsettle, to be "feminine" with a vengeance. This aesthetic is most completely explained in *Sleep in Peace*, a 1938 novel about a young girl, Laura Armistead, who gives up her initial dream of art study in London in order to stay with her Yorkshire family, but does manage to become a successful artist. In this semiautobiographical *Kunstlerroman*, Laura rejects any kind of patterning or conventionality in her art. Scolded by an art teacher for a "too childish insistence on petty realism in detail," Laura insists, "It's life itself I want to render." Life, she argues, is continuity; given that continuity, any effort to make things fit into a self-contained pattern is a lie. "There may be an immense pattern, perhaps," she thinks, "but it's so immense that the shape of its curves is hardly visible: it is a lie to pretend that the pattern can easily be seen, and everything fitted neatly into it" (253).

Such an insistent approach to detail would seem to threaten traditional ways of seeing the world, certainly of seeing history. Scholarly detachment and analysis depend on leaving out *some* information and on separating the present from the past, the historian from her object of study. In the same novel, Laura's friend Grace Hinchliffe becomes a historian, with unconventional teaching methods that get her into trouble with her male supervisors precisely because they encourage identification and involvement rather than objectivity. History, Grace insists, echoing Laura on life's continuity, reaches into the present. Teaching history at a boys' school, Grace has the children act out a scene from *Ivanhoe*. Her aim, she says, is "to make history seem a continuous living story, stretching into their own times." A male teacher rebukes her: "That sort of thing is all very well for girls' schools. . . . But at Henshawe I think you had better keep to the curriculum." Grace's reply is made more urgent by the fact that World War I is raging around them as they speak: "Their lives may depend on my way of teaching history" (333). Later in the novel Laura pokes her head in the door as Grace is lecturing on the teaching of history and hears only a single phrase: "*the continuity of human experience*" (537).

The disturbing implications of Grace's teaching methods become clear when one of Grace's students is quizzed by a critical male instructor. Asked the date of the First Crusade, he answers, "The Crusades were supposed to be for the recovery of Jerusalem" (332). The answer horrifies the male teacher, because the student has avoided dating the Crusades, then explained them in terms of pretense, implying the actual motive was more self-serving. Finally, the fact that this boy is dressed as a woman—in costume as Scott's Rebecca—suggests a female mocking of male versions of history.

Bentley's own historical fiction does not question the importance of standard historical formulations to such an extent. But her choice of the regional and historical novel as her genre parallels Laura's photographic realism, with its odd mixture of submission and revolt. Like Laura, her aim is fidelity to detail—"detailed faithfulness to reality," Bentley calls it in *The English Regional Novel* (45). Putting fidelity to external objects before self-expression, this aim is a symptom of their submissiveness. But for both, attention to detail is also a way of making people see how things *really* are, of disrupting the process of historical interpretation by which the myriad details of experience are digested and condensed into a single plot.

Homans suggests that even "bearers of the word" have disruptive potential when they depict certain aspects of experience: those that highlight the relation between the literal and the figurative. Following Lacan, Homans argues that language and culture, based on figuration, require distance from the literal, most specifically, from the mother (2). Women, however, because of their early identification with their mothers, will have a different, less totally repressed relation to the literal than men. When they depict childbirth, translation, or textual transmission, she argues, the process by which figuration takes place—through detachment from and repression of the female body—will surface. Bentley's *Freedom, Farewell!*, as a historical novel, is one big act of textual transmission. But it also focuses at crucial moments on the female body. Through her depiction of rape, pregnancy, childbirth, and silencing, Bentley suggests the price women pay for male metaphor-making.

Like Mitchison in *Cloud Cuckoo Land*, Bentley seems, in *Freedom Farewell*, to replicate the exclusion of women from power. And the women don't mind; their romantic passion for their men makes them acquiescent. Julia, Julius Caesar's daughter, adores her father and Pompey, the man she marries; Porcia's love for her husband Brutus is so obsessive it gets on his nerves; and Servilia, Julius Caesar's lifelong mistress, loves him despite his high-handed treatment of her. While there are glimmers of feminism in Bentley's autobiography—"I felt fiercely," she writes there, "that women should have the right to work . . . for only so could they become independent" (107)—in *Freedom Farewell*, her women love the hand that holds them back.

Bentley's relation to male cultural authority, in other words, is deeply ambivalent. Her female characters want to get involved in political action, but neither she nor they question the cultural paradigms—romantic love, the idealization of the Roman Republic—that sanction their exclusion. Bentley shares Macaulay's mid-nineteenth-century admiration for the

Romans as slayers of tyrants and opponents of autocracy. But if she, like the Victorians and her male contemporaries, idealizes the Roman Republic, Bentley differs on the reasons behind its collapse. While Bulwer-Lytton, Kingsley, and G. A. Henty attributed Rome's fall to decadence, and associated decadence with insufficient manliness, Bentley blames—at least in part—Rome's mistreatment and marginalization of women.[2]

Bentley's critique of Roman sexual politics comes through most clearly in her portrayal of pregnancy and childbirth. Homans has written of the woman writer's use of maternity as a way of working through her relation to language. In the "founding texts of our culture," according to Homans, "the death or absence of the mother sorrowfully but fortunately makes possible the construction of language and of culture" (2), for in allowing herself to become literal, she becomes an object to be despised and rejected by her androcentric culture (153–61). The nineteenth-century ideology of motherhood, by devaluing the female body as a passive conduit between father and son, recapitulated this exclusion of women from culture (153–61). For the woman writer eager for access to male cultural authority, then, maternity would mean silence, marginalization. It is to this ideology that Homans traces Charlotte Brontë's negative treatment of childbearing, which, she argues, involve literalization: something within the woman becomes externalized (93). Like Brontë in so many other ways—her Yorkshire roots, her fantasy-life, her limited experience, her domestic obligations—Bentley also seems to share this horror of childbearing. In a scene that leaps out at the reader for its intensity and incongruity, Bentley's Laura, in *Sleep in Peace*, visits her sister, who has just given birth to a son and expresses her disgust: "The whole business of sex, conception and child-bearing, seemed to her revolting; she could hardly control herself sufficiently to sit in Gwen's room" (240).

If revolting, "the whole business of sex, conception and child bearing" nonetheless fascinated Bentley enough to become a central concern in *Freedom, Farewell!*. It makes sense that in this novel about her own nation's cultural patrimony, Bentley should be particularly interested in the problematic relation between woman and culture. Through her portrayal of woman as childbearer, she depicts the compulsive figure-making of men at the expense of women. Conventional though the novel is in its use of sources and in its judgment of Caesar as corrupted by his quest for power, in its treatment of literal and figurative, of male linguistic power and female silence, it is complex and ambiguous enough to be disturbing.

In *Freedom, Farewell!*, the best of Rome, and the best impulses of Julius Caesar, are symbolized by a mother and child. At the start of the novel Caesar is fleeing the proscription of Sulla. Lost in the mountains on a rainy night, he catches his first glimpse of Servilia, who later becomes his mistress:

> The glimpse of the young mother with her child against her breast had touched the fund of hope and tenderness in his heart and set it flowing; it was a picture so truly natural, so right, so essentially Roman. Rome was great, Rome was noble, Rome did not lack the virtue needed to rule the world, he felt, while Rome could produce such matrons, with soul so lofty and eyes so clear. (23)

Caesar sounds like a late-Victorian gentleman, sentimentalizing motherhood and empire. But while he is apparently at his purest here, still young and idealistic, in fact he has just bribed some soldiers to let him escape—an act he sees as natural and inevitable until Servilia mourns the pervasive corruption that made it both necessary and possible. The idealism that seems to predate his fall is in fact already a product of it. Turning Servilia into a trope for Rome, he elides her personhood, her disturbing existence as flesh. The picture of mother and child he calls "natural" is in fact its opposite: what Caesar admires is not the natural mother, but mother-as-metaphor. "If in the symbolic order language is constituted as desire for a chain of substitutes for the mother," Homans writes, "a translation of her literal body into figures, then we can see this law at work in the denial of her material priority and the replacement of it by powerless figurative substitutes" (160). Seeking Servilia's husband, Caesar finds Servilia instead, but instantly turns her body into soul, and then into Rome, a male-dominated city-state struggling to rule the world.

The memory of this scene recurs throughout the novel, a symbol of the moral purity Caesar sacrifices through a series of self-serving choices: his sexual submission to the Bithynian king Nicomedes in order to gain his military support; his relentless manipulation of others to gain power. His corruption is most vividly dramatized, however, through his rape of Servilia, which recapitulates that primal moment. Meeting her some years after their encounter in the mountains, Caesar desires her, but she, though obviously attracted, resists. Inwardly debating whether to overcome her scruples gradually, through love, or instantly, by force, he chooses the latter course, again making her the "silent ground of representation" (Homans 161) for his own desire.

As Caesar lies dying on the floor of the Senate at the novel's close, he again reads Servilia as a metaphor for Rome, and recognizes this decision to rape her rather than wait as decisive: "He had used her as he had used Rome, taking by force what was only of value when it was freely offered" (473). Even as he recognizes his mistake, Servilia remains the page on which he writes his own story. Ironically, however, the metaphor takes its revenge. His idealized matron is also the mother of Brutus—that same Brutus who helps stab him to death on the Senate floor.

Bentley powerfully portrays the price women pay for male metaphor-making—a price paid not only in rape, but also in childbirth and miscarriage, events she emphasizes through juxtaposition, elision, and repetition. Immediately after Caesar's first encounter with Servilia, the scene shifts to Rome, where Pompey, under pressure from Sulla, has divorced Antistia, whom he loves, to marry Aemilia. Aemilia is so recently divorced that she is carrying her ex-husband's child. Midway through the celebration, having just heard that Antistia's mother has committed suicide, Aemilia shrieks, then miscarries and dies:

> Suddenly a loud hoarse moan broke violently on the air. Horribly startled, Pompey looked down at the girl on his breast, from whose pale and distorted lips the distressful sound was still issuing; her eyes were closed, her cheeks like wax; her hands beat the air convulsively. (35)

Caesar's famous seizures are notably absent from Bentley's novels; it is women whose seizures fascinate her, for they bear the weight of suffering and rage.[3] Aemilia seems to be expressing Antistia's pain as much as her own. She cannot express it articulately, however; as pregnant woman she is aligned with the literal and thus excluded from the symbolic order. The fact that her eruption takes place at a wedding banquet underlines the contrast between a society intent on making meanings out of experience and the literal, bodily experiences undergone by women. One is reminded of Nancy Jay's argument that sacrificial ritual—including rituals of communion such as a wedding—work to purify patrilinearity from the taint of women's bodies. In any case the wedding guests can respond only with horror and incomprehension as Aemilia turns into a grotesque, moaning object.

Aemilia's outburst is about as explicit an expression as women's rage gets in the novel. Caesar's daughter Julia, lively and charming though she is, miscarries and dies in childbirth. When, during her miscarriage, she asks for her husband, Pompey, her grandmother tells her, "You must be a Roman wife and bear your trouble alone; we cannot send for him" (255). Her death, in her second pregnancy, is entirely elided; we learn of it only after the fact, through a conversation between a heartbroken Pompey and his slave Demetrius. The death gains power through the elision, and its impact on Pompey is tremendous, but the effect is also to underline the irrelevance of women's suffering to history. Pompey himself quickly moves from sorrow to possessiveness, thinking that as a result of her death, "Now I shall never know whose she was most, mine or Caesar's" (277). Her body when alive, the comment suggests, served only as the ground on which he planned to write his own story.

Mitchison emphasizes the link between Rome's self-image and the triumph; Rome exults in its power to tell the story of its victories. Bentley, too, seems to see Rome as a personification of the act of figuration. When Romans are defeated, it is because, in their eagerness to translate the world into their own story, they have misread its text. Julia's death is followed by two abrupt scene-shifts: to Julius Caesar in Briton and Crassus in Syria. Both scenes depict an alien landscape, impenetrable to Roman eyes. Caesar dislikes the cold British mist, which cloaks hills and trees, "so that everything is less or more than it looks." "This Britain is an accursed place," Caesar thinks (277). The description of Syria two pages later opens similarly: "The landscape was highly disagreeable to Roman eyes" (279). Like the British mist, the Syrian sun makes the landscape monotonal, impossible to read. The literal refuses to be comprehended in terms of the symbolic.

Betrayed by their Arab guide Ariamnes—as impossible to read as the landscape—the Romans, led by Crassus, are badly defeated, and both Crassus and his son beheaded. The chapter concludes: "The head of Crassus was sent to the Court of Parthia and tumbled about the floor at a triumphal banquet, its mouth filled with molten gold" (293). Like Brutus's stabbing of Caesar, the banished literal is returning here: the land itself, regarded by the Romans merely as the ground for their victories, is taking its revenge. So, too, are the Parthians, who turn the wealthy Crassus into a literal moneybag.

As in Mitchison's *Cloud Cuckoo Land*, Bentley's women speak only through their suffering and their silence. As Caesar tells Servilia when she attempts to argue with him, "You are a mere woman, I am the head of the Roman state—what I say is law" (454). The silence resonates powerfully, however, at the end of the novel. There, Caesar at his death at least begins to recognize what history elides: "He understood all Servilia's silences now, all in his life and hers that was too piteous, too tragic for her to say" (473). These silences are dramatized by Porcia's death. Daughter of the iron-willed Cato and wife of Caesar's assassin Brutus, Porcia, "When she heard of her husband's death, snatched some burning charcoal from the brazier; holding it close against her mouth she stifled herself with the fumes, and so died" (509).[4] These are the last lines of the novel proper; the final image of stifling—silencing and choking—leaves us listening for some faint echo of women's voices, even as we know we won't hear them. We hear instead, in the novel's epilogue, the meaningless babble of the now impotent Senate confirming the decrees of Augustus Caesar, emperor.

In the late nineteenth century, the Roman Empire had been much admired; by the 1930s, however, imperialism was under fire, and Bentley's critical view of Augustus is less surprising than it would have been fifty years earlier. What gives the novel its power is the link Bentley forges between sexual and national politics: the interdependency of autocracy, male sexuality, and the male valuation of the figurative. We are left with Servilia's silence and Porcia's stifling, in contrast to the mechanical talk of the male senators: language itself becomes an act of submission, silence the only weapon against tyranny.

Ironically, Bentley herself exemplifies the silencing she depicts. Over and over, reading Bentley's autobiography, one is reminded of her character Marjorie's fierce desire to tell her grandfather what she really feels about his "tyranny" in *Environment*, a desire she stifles as she goes "meekly" behind the counter of his grocery store:

> She wanted furiously to tell her grandfather just what she thought of him and his tyranny; she wanted to defy him and continue to do her lessons; she wanted to do something of a heroic nature; but custom and upbringing were too strong, and she went meekly behind the counter. (41)

Bentley herself used the apparently safe, conventional form of the historical novel to disguise her own anger. She recognizes the power of historical context to disguise and defuse in her autobiography, where she writes of her adolescent use of "strongly plotted" historical daydreams to satisfy her sexual yearnings (63). In the case of *Freedom, Farewell!*, the disguise was too effective; her novel was misread as an effort to cash in on the success of Robert Graves's *I Claudius*, its contemporary relevance ignored (*O Dreams* 204). She herself, like her Roman women, were read only in relation to male achievement, her silences misunderstood.

NOTES

1. In *Sleep in Peace*, Laura's first daydream is of saving others from the sea, then being praised by a man (113). She then generates others, using "events of history, and incidents she read in books," generally constructing a plot in which a girl "like Laura but not Laura" escapes "a lion, perhaps, a kingly tyrant, savages with spears" (113).

2. Her reinterpretation of Rome's fall was facilitated by the work of Theodor Mommsen, whom she quotes in her epigraph to *Freedom, Farewell!*. Mommsen, Linda Dowling points out, had moved away from the moralistic view of Roman collapse promulgated by Kingsley and Thomas Arnold and in fact questioned the very existence of Roman decadence as an historical phenomenon ("Roman" 580, 596). Relying less on well-known literary sources and more on inscriptions and nonliterary texts, Mommsen, according to Dowling, "subverted the idea of historical plot" (595). Certainly he complicated the "Providentialist" plots then prevalent (580).

3. Another notable absence is any mention of the slave revolt led by Spartacus, dramatized in James Leslie Mitchell's 1933 novel. Bentley mentions a slave revolt put down by Crassus—with some help from Pompey—but that is all the attention the event receives. Slavery as an institution receives little attention in *Freedom, Farewell!*, nor does Bentley question Roman attitudes toward the East; her Asians are stereotypically devious and immoral.

4. Plutarch describes one version of Porcia's death in remarkably similar terms: "she contrived to snatch up some live coals from the fire and swallowed them, keeping her mouth closed, and so suffocated herself and died" (*Makers* 269).

CHAPTER 12

Bryher the Graeco-Phoenician and Rome

In *The Heart to Artemis*, Bryher tells of a visit, with Robert McAlmon (her husband at the time), to a Paris nightclub. The proprietor, who prided himself on providing for his customers' needs, offered for her pleasure first a man, then a woman, then hashish, all of which she turned down. She saw that he thought her terribly depraved to desire a pleasure even he couldn't supply. And, she says, "the fellow was right, I had my vices. I longed for danger, to sail around the Horn and to explore the inmost recesses of the human mind" (222). The story has long fascinated me because of its equation of travel and psychological analysis—the stuff of historical fiction—with vice. Bryher is notably reticent about her lesbianism in *The Heart to Artemis*; in retelling this incident, she seems to displace onto her activity as historical novelist her enjoyment of forbidden pleasures.

How could the writing of historical fiction about Rome be an act of transgressive sexuality? As I suggested in relation to *Gate to the Sea*, in taking up historical fiction where G. A. Henty left off, Bryher enacts a kind of narrative cross-dressing merely by telling her stories. Much as Mitchison was fascinated by Mithraism and Renault by Platonism (because to enter those worlds imaginatively they had to become "male"), Bryher, narrating her two novels about Rome, becomes a masquer of masculinity. In the process, she creates characters and plots that marginalize and subvert a Roman hegemony linked to rigid sexual dichotomies.

Bryher's *The Coin of Carthage* (1963) is set during the defeat of Carthage by Rome in the Punic Wars, and *Roman Wall* (1954) depicts the beginning of the end of the Roman Empire, as barbarian tribes destroy a Roman stronghold in Switzerland. Both novels are thus set on the edges of crumbling empires—in spaces and moments of geographical, temporal, and cultural betweenness. Both novels focus not on "historical" events, but on private acts of friendship between men. And both novels are dominated not by Romans—depicted as rigid, obsessed with control and empire—but by flexible, nurturing Greek traders. Finally, in both novels there is a fascination with small concrete objects and sensations: a narrative fetishism that responds to the loss of a homeland by lavishing attention on an object that can evoke it. For both novels depict men yearning for what de Lauretis calls a "fantasmatic female body"—figured in one as Greece, the other as an actual woman—and regaining that body only in the form of metonymic substitutes that assuage but cannot undo their loss. All these characteristics suggest that for Bryher, history and geography are a palette with which she can depict subversively subtle shades of gender and sexuality.

Bryher explores the freedom offered by moments of betweenness in her 1925 story "South," where the narrator comments on the collapse of Victorian England: "It was interesting to watch an empire scatter in a million fragments before one's mind. It was not altogether a pessmistic spectacle. Scattered seeds might mean a better fruit." The entire story is set on a boat in transit between Britain and Africa, where the passengers are "suspended upon this instant between old conditions, new conditions, as two days are cut apart utterly by sleep" (29). Bryher's own writing activity is a kind of going "south," in which the Greek traders through whom she mainly tells her story mirror her own sense of being at once outsider and everywhere—a blurrer of boundaries, a crosser of seas.

At the opposite extreme from these Greeks are the Romans. Like Mitchison, Butts, and especially H. D., Bryher assumes the standard Roman is strait-laced, disciplined—a human version of the "Roman wall" so often cited as representing Roman achievement. H. D.'s *Palimpsest*, her autobiographical novel dedicated to and transparently about (in part) Bryher, provides a clearcut view of the way H. D. and Bryher must have construed Rome. "I'm sick heartily of Romans," H. D.'s Hipparchia tells Marius Decius, her Roman lover in *Palimpsest* (9). They are wine pressers, she says repeatedly, stamping on conquered civilizations, their feet wine-stained (4). Marius, on the other hand, Roman that he is, brags that "Rome . . . builds rock upon the ruins of a decadent civilization" (4). In his eyes Rome is self-confident, militaristic, male, a necessary complement to Greece's femininity: "Could Greece live, queen, insolent but near extinction, without the heavy drone again to fertilise her?" Marius asks Hipparchia (19).

Hipparchia is H. D.'s persona in *Palimpsest*; Bryher is depicted as Julia Cornelia Augusta, daughter of a Roman scholar. She is not as Roman as her name would indicate, however. On the contrary, she is quickly aligned with Rome's traditional enemies: she is, according to Hipparchia, "Graeco-Phoenician" (123), a "half-Asiatic child-Hera" (123), resembling the Greek poet Moero, whom Hipparchia is translating (124). And Julia herself declares that she and her father—despite their Roman names—are fascinated by Greek culture and history. "I write history," she tells Hipparchia. "My father and I are completing certain records on the Macedonian conquest" (126). If Rome is gendered as male and Greece as female, Julia, at once "Graeco-Phoenician" and "Roman," is multiply gendered.

In fact, the Graeco-Phoenician combination is highly significant. It is enacted literally in *The Coin of Carthage* through the relationship between the Greek trader Dasius and the Carthaginian sea captain Mago, who cohabit in Carthage for the two happiest years of Dasius's life. "Graeco-Phoenician" also immediately links Bryher to two cultures defeated by Rome—Greece and Carthage—two cultures with which Bryher did, in fact, identify. Perhaps because of Bryher's childhood visit to Tunis, Carthage is one of the places that symbolize for her a lost past—lost because associated with her own childhood, when she felt closest to having the boy's life she so longed for, and lost because so little documentation of it remains. As she points out in her introduction to *The Coin of Carthage*, the details of the Punic War are lost, for the Romans destroyed the libraries when they sacked Carthage (ix). As novelist, she aligns herself with those lost details, much as she aligns herself with the suppressed Greek culture—suppressed again by Roman occupiers—in *Gate to the Sea*. People "could not plunder her of Carthage," Bryher writes in *Development* (187). Limited by her role as "girl," she cannot go to sea, but she can retain her imaginative freedom, which defines her as "boy"; and her name for that freedom is Carthage.

In the *early* nineteenth century, many besides Bryher saw Carthage, a model of ancient trade and naval dominance, as a kind of British alter-ego.[1] "Many Victorians," Martin Bernal writes, "had a positive feeling towards the Phoenicians as sober cloth merchants who did a little bit of slaving on the side and spread civilization while making a tidy profit" (350). In 1889, G. F. Rawlinson, in his admiring *History of Phoenicia*, called the Phoenicians "the people who of all Antiquity had the most in common with England and the English" (Bernal 350).

But with the rise of anti-Semitism during the nineteenth century, Bernal argues that the Phoenicians were increasingly linked to the Jews and rejected as racially other (337). Gladstone in old age argued that the Phoenicians, whom he admired, were not Semites, an argument made necessary by increasing anti-Semitism (Bernal 351). The French had long disliked Phoenicia for the qualities it associated with its rival Britain, and its racial theorists gave it added grounds throughout the nineteenth century. Michelet, in his 1830 *Histoire romaine*, writes that the Punic Wars were fought "to settle which of the two races, the Indo-Germanic or the Semitic, was to rule the world" (qtd. in Bernal 341). According to Bernal, "By the late nineteenth century, the deserved destruction of the city [of Carthage] was a platitude" (359).

Bryher's consistent sense of identification with Carthage was thus not typical of her time, but suggests on her part a particular affinity for traders, sea-voyagers, those associated with a more southern climate and darker skin, for ethnic outsiders. This affinity may have been connected to her admiration for her father, a tremendously successful merchant who was probably, according to Barbara Guest, Jewish (112–23). At any rate, it was an identification Bryher shared with Sigmund Freud, whose attachment to the Carthaginian general Hannibal grew as European anti-Semitism increased (Gay 20). Bryher, too, was especially fond of Hannibal, an affection that began at the age of nine, when her parents gave her G. A. Henty's *The Young Carthaginian*: "It fired my imagination because I was just the same age as Hannibal when he had sworn his famous oath to fight Rome" (*Coin* x).

Hannibal and Carthage offered Bryher an alternative to the repressive Victorian environment around her—an alternative, in particular, to repressive gender and sexual roles. As a child, she wanted to be a cabin boy like Hannibal and a merchant like her father (*Heart* 109): "if I wanted to be happy when I grew up I had to become a cabin boy and run away from the inexplicable taboos of Victorian life" (17). Unlike Matthew Arnold, who contrasts the Hellenism of Greece with the Hebraism of the Semites, Bryher sees in both the Semitic Carthaginians and the Greeks an identification that allows her to bypass gender and lay claim to the adventure of which she had always dreamed.[2]

Bryher's identity as "Graeco-Phoenician" at times overlaps with her nostalgia for southern and Middle Eastern lands as well—a nostalgia redolent of typically European attitudes toward the South and the Orient.[3] In *The Days of Mars* she writes of the "Near East" of her childhood as the fulfillment of desire (59); in adulthood she wanted to learn Persian to revive her lost sense of freedom (55) and identified with Sir Richard Burton (67). I would argue, however, that Bryher's Greco-Phoenician allegiance is neither nostalgia nor exoticism, but an effort to evoke a world where neither gender nor sexuality need be conceived in binary terms. Marjorie Garber has pointed out the association in the European mind of Arabia and Persia with cross-dressing and homoeroticism (Garber, *Vested* 304–52). For Bryher, a Middle East conceived as "transvestic, pan-sexual . . . a place of liminality and change" (Garber 337) offered an alluring opportunity to complicate gender.

If the "Phoenician" part of her identity links Bryher to one defeated enemy of Rome, the "Graeco" links her to another. In both *The Coin of Carthage* and *Roman Wall* the most prominent and sympathetic figures are Greek traders who, despite the loss of their homeland to Rome, finally dominate the story. Again one is reminded of *Palimpsest*, where Hipparchia decides against translating Sappho into Latin. She will leave the poem in Greek, she decides, and "The Greek words, inset in her manuscript, would work terrific damage" (100). The palimpsestic method uses history's underwriting to challenge the dominant story; Bryher's drifting Greeks, inset in her novels, seem to escape definition by their location, allegiance, or even gender, thus challenging the story of Roman imperial triumphs that would otherwise appear to be all history has to tell us.

These drifting Greeks are most extensively depicted in *The Coin of Carthage*, which tells the story of a series of nurturing relationships, primarily between men. Zonas, a Greek trader in Italy who has been robbed and beaten while trying to sell bridles to the invading Carthaginians, is rescued by a boy, Bassus, and helped by another Greek trader, Dasius.[4] Zonas and Dasius, the novel's two main characters, as traders and Greeks are by definition defeated, homeless, crossers of national boundaries. "Neither city wants us as citizens," Zonas and Dasius agree, and so reject both Rome and Carthage (51). "You have been crossing from side to side, you Greek," Dasius tells Zonas, "since you were born" (142).

The allegiances that determine their actions are shaped by personal, not national loyalty, as a series of nurturings take over what would seem at first to be an adventure story. Bassus rescues and tends Zonas, just as Zonas rescues and tends Karus, a young Roman soldier; Mago, a Carthaginian sailor, rescues and tends Dasius, just as Dasius rescues and tends Orbius, another Roman soldier who is also Karus's beloved. These men are unaccountably tender with each other, whether their relationships are sexual or merely protective. The seamless continuity of these male-male relationships, as they shade from nurturing into homosexuality, is striking. Eve Sedgwick points out that such seamlessness is uncharacteristic of modern men, who sharply distinguish between patriarchically oriented male bonding (whose practitioners are often homophobic) and homosexuality (4). Bryher makes no such distinction, in part because she is depicting a different era, when such seamlessness was more common, but also, perhaps, because she is encoding her notion of female community, where "an intelligible continuum of aims, emotions, and valuations links lesbianism with the other forms of women's attention to women" (Sedgwick 2). Her male characters, in other words, care for one another in ways that shade imperceptibly from social to sexual, evoking a continuum more characteristic—in the twentieth century at least—of women's than men's behavior.

The Greeks who have been "crossing from side to side" since they were born, having lost their homeland, reveal the connection among liminality, geographical emotion—as a melding to times, places, or other people—and the role of the detail in triggering and memorializing that emotion. Because they have lost contact with their past—i.e., their homes—the past can become real to them only in pieces, as flashes of sensory experience. When Zonas, for example, remembers his birthplace,

Formiae, the memories are triggered by certain smells or words, and the impact is literal, physical: he begins "stepping over acorns as if they were cobbles" (192). The cobbles, metonymic replacements for Formiae, resemble Harmonia's effort to preserve the past when she leaves Poseidonia by taking with her a collection of objects. And of course, yet again, one thinks of Christa Wolf's valuing of the "previous everyday."

One thinks also of Bryher's own desire for Carthage to reemerge with a similar physical immediacy. In *Development* Bryher contrasts her early enthusiasm for history with the boredom she felt in museums; she wants details, she insists. She wants to reexperience the immediacy, the multiplicity of the past; of a visit to Tunis, she writes, for example, "She wanted the war elephants to sway over the rough stones" (*Development* 51). At twelve, she imagined a history of Sicily that would include not just "history," but also the details history leaves out: "All the life of the time, the customs, the armour, especially the trade would be depicted, the tiny details she missed in the longest history, all that she wanted to know and was told she was 'too young to understand'" (59).

The "tiny details" often feel unhistorical because they don't typify an epoch, in Lukacs's sense. Cobblestones underfoot or a lizard sunning itself on a rock could date from the fourth century B.C., or today. But if generically counterproductive, these details are essential to her aim, which is not to analyze or reconceptualize the past, but to identify with it, to enter it, even to meld it to her mind. These details erupt magically into consciousness at those moments Bryher describes in her autobiography, when "Clio was there," when the past arose with the immediacy and intensity she calls "geographical emotion." The ultimate example of such a moment, of course, was her experience with H. D. on Corfu. This yearning for detail can thus be read as a yearning for reentry into the lost, more complexly gendered past of "Carthage"—understood as both personal past and historical moment. But it can also be read as a fetishized recovery of a lost "home" that is not only Greece, but the female body itself. Figuring her own desire as male—to convey desire for the "fantasmatic female body" in culturally convincing terms—and dramatizing that recovery through the emergence of metonymic substitutes, Bryher enacts a process of "loss and recovery of the female body" that resembles Teresa de Lauretis's description of lesbian fetishism (265).

The "coin" of Carthage, in fact, is itself a fetish, substituting for Hannibal himself, who gave Zonas the coin at a grand parade, when Zonas rushed out to save his straying donkey from the elephants. The coin, the narrator tells us, is a "symbol of victory, of the fact that in this harsh, uncertain world, some men shone above their fellows not through power but through understanding" (239). Unlike the coin of safe passage Zonas was given at the start of the novel, a coin that does nothing but endanger him, Hannibal's coin serves no purpose, except to suggest an allegiance to nurturing, inconsistency, and identity with the defeated. As in *Gate to the Sea*, Greece in *The Coin of Carthage* is the ultimate homeland, its loss a given from the start. Carthage will also be lost, but it serves in the meantime as an alternative to Rome's relentless march toward empire. What's left, finally, is the coin: a concrete object produced by yet resistant to history, like Harmonia's mirror a metonymic link to a lost past.

In *Roman Wall*, Rome's enemy is not Carthage but the barbarian tribes invading from the north. Bryher portrays the Alemanni, "strong, healthy, stupid" (42), penetrating the outskirts of the Roman Empire, their success due to Roman complacency, corruption, and rigidity. In Virgil's *Aeneid*, the wall symbolizes order, civic growth and pride, peace. For Bryher, however, it is inseparable from blindness and inflexibility. As in *The Coin of Carthage*, however, the novel finally subverts its ostensible subject, as the narrative focus shifts from Romans to the Greek trader Demetrius, and from the present battle to a past romance. As in *The Coin of Carthage*, relationships based on friendship and nurturing—Demetrius and his old friend Thallus, Demetrius and Julia, a young Roman woman—prevail over political allegiances, and boundary-crossers succeed where partisans fail.

The quintessential Roman is Marcus, a Roman soldier whom Julia finally agrees to marry at novel's end. "If we keep the laws," Marcus tells Julia of Roman government, "they are a wall around us that no enemy can pierce" (59). Julia herself is anxious to preserve Roman order even among the wild hills of Switzerland. She is a compulsive house cleaner and watches carefully over her ward Veria's virtue and upbringing, wanting to pass on to her the "majesty of Rome" (60). She worships Apollo the lawgiver in preference to the "wailing and the incense of the East" (61), presumably allusions to Isis-worship. It's precisely this sense of order, however, that nearly kills Julia and her brother Valerius. For even when they realize their outpost is surrounded by the Alemanni, Julia and her brother Valerius will not leave until a command comes from the Roman commander, who, they are perfectly aware, has forgotten they exist. The fall of Aventicum enacts this self-destructive rigidity: the Roman army is crushed beneath the weight of the collapsed Treasury building.

In contrast to this rigidity stands Demetrius, strikingly similar to Zonas, the Greek trader of *The Coin of Carthage*. Both put trade above ethnic, national, or religious loyalties. "The essential rule in trading," Demetrius thinks, "was never to anger another man's gods" (140). As a result, they are often outside the law, but also more humane and better able to survive than their more law-abiding but narrow-minded contemporaries. Demetrius quotes Heracleitus, explicitly arguing that "everything moves" (158) and suggesting that it's important "not to forget, but to be aware that no moment was ever the same as its fellow" (176). "Life is fluidity and change," Demetrius tells his friend Thallus. "The barbarians move, and you and your fellows in the Treasury watch our misery with a marble indifference" (195).

Similar to *The Coin of Carthage* in its culturally transitional setting, its Greek protagonist, and its emphasis on personal relationships even amid crucial historical developments, *Roman Wall* differs in placing an actual woman at its center. The book is in fact constructed around a "fantasmatic female body," making the loss of that body an even more explicit theme than either *The Coin of Carthage* or *Gate to the Sea*. Julia's brother Valerius is stationed in Helvetia (Switzerland) because many years before he had had an affair with his commanding officer's wife, Fabula. The affair is dramatized in the novel only through Valerius's fragmented memories; now long past, it continues, however, to dominate Valerius's life. Yet Fabula herself is a shadowy figure, her name of course suggesting her link to fiction and story. Valerius's greatest happiness, he says, was the moment when he dove into the water as Fabula approached—a moment characterized by incomplete movement, by anticipation, by mental and physical projection. Such a moment moves perception inward, placing the most meaningful realization in the mind rather than in any consummatory action.

Fabula herself is unfixable. Her eyes are described as "oceanic," oscillating between "wave-blue" and "rivergreen" (184). When Demetrius first sees her, he thinks her a goddess: "The body was that of a youth, the skin hardly bronzed, and not lined, yet I knew that I was in the presence of something ancient and timeless, a flower, if you will, from the youth of the world" (197). Demetrius says of her, she's "a fable, the flower that sends us wandering, and looking for something we can never find" (198). "Perhaps the world is a fable," Valerius finally concludes (219), as he decides that while he cannot regain that lost moment, he can at least give happiness to Veria, who is not Fabula, but at least "would let him dream in peace" (218). The novel ends with an echo of *Gate to the Sea*, with movement away from one life toward another:

> "Perhaps the world is a fable," he said. Then, because she looked up at him in bewilderment, he added gently, "The pass is open; and, if the gods will, we shall reach Ceresio and end our lives there together." (219)

Fabula is not just a femme fatale haunting Valerius's imagination, but a hint of an alternative past, a palimpsestic reminder of lost intimacy. She is a moment in the past that refuses to stay there, an erasure that refuses to stay erased. As an image in Valerius's mind she determines his present and future even though in physical terms she has been left far behind. Roman walls are vulnerable not only because of their rigidity; the very history that records their defeat can be subverted, when movement and memory provide alternative stories. Like Cressida and Cleopatra, Fabula suggests Irigaray's "disruptive excess," her very name suggesting her role of "jamming the theoretical machinery itself, of suspending its pretension to the production of a truth and of a meaning that are excessively univocal" (78).

Also like Cressida and Cleopatra, Fabula complicates gender and sexuality, but differently: both "youth" and "goddess," she confounds gender categories as much as the young woman Valerius does marry—Veria—who is "neither boy nor girl but a bit of moving landscape" (26). And she evokes homo- as much as heterosexual desire: Fabula's flowerlike quality and her "oceanic" green-blue eyes link her to H. D, whom Bryher describes in *The Days of Mars*: "her eyes would be a clear blue that when the light caught them turned to the green that is only visible when waves wash over sands" (163). As I suggested, de Lauretis's description of a lesbian fetishism seems relevant: both novels depict the loss of a female body, figured in one as Greece, in the other as Fabula, with H. D. hovering over both. In both novels, Bryher's narrative cross-dressing can be read as an effort, through a fetishized masculinity, to simultaneously control the loss and adopt the masculine role that most effectively signifies desire for the female body (243). Both depict a recovery of that body: through objects like the coin in *The Coin of Carthage* and the saucer Julia takes with her in *Roman Wall*, through memory, and through Veria herself, whom Valerius marries, in *Roman Wall*. De Lauretis insists such fetishism is not a flight to a pre-Oedipal mother, as Freud suggested to H. D., but a restaging of the "subject's own loss and recovery of the female body"—not regression, in other words, but successful restaging of "perverse desire" (265).

Bryher's novels are thus far more complicated than the male-authored works she admired and the adventures she yearned to experience. The desire for adventure that Bryher expresses repeatedly in her autobiographical writing and poetry, her focus on male wanderers, and her admiration for G. A. Henty's boyish heroes might seem to suggest that she is identifying with a traditional male norm that devalues female experience. She even dedicated *The Coin of Carthage* to Henty. She herself felt that she was a boy with a girl's body; like Mitchison and Renault, she felt being a boy offered more excitement and privilege than being a girl. But she is not simply reincribing Henty-like plots merging masculinity and empire.[5]

Despite her admiration for Henty, when Bryher writes her own adventure stories, she does so with a difference. As mediated by her own experiences and reading, her boy-heroes become permanent outsiders, struggling not to lead the "right" side to victory, but to survive and carry some meaning intact into the life thrust on them by history. Henty himself writes of having felt sympathy for the Carthaginians when, in his boyhood, he read of their defeat by Rome. Perhaps he felt some identity with them, for as a Briton, he too could feel defeated by Rome. But in *Beric the Briton*, he makes it clear that Roman victory was for the best: the Beric who has absorbed Roman education and discipline and been converted to Christianity by his Roman wife makes a far better leader than the early Beric, follower of Boadicea, warrior against the occupiers. In the case of Carthage, too, Henty is willing to be reconciled with history:

> When I was a boy at school, if I remember rightly, our sympathies were generally with the Carthaginians as against the Romans. Why they were so, except that one generally sympathizes with the unfortunate, I do not quite know. . . .
>
> I think that when you have read to the end you will perceive that although our sympathies may remain with Hannibal and the Carthaginians, it was nevertheless for the good of the world that Rome was the conqueror in the great struggle for empire. At the time the war began Carthage was already corrupt to the core, and although she might have enslaved many nations she could never have civilized them. . . . Carthage . . . was from the first a cruel mistress to the people she conquered. (v–vi)

Henty has come to recognize this truth through his research, he suggests (v); the process of writing historical fiction is a kind of maturation, curing him of boyish notions. For Bryher, however, historical fiction is an act of transgression, a rejection of the very notion of "maturity," with its implication of adjustment to the status quo. As a childhood reader she felt herself one of the "dear lads" to whom Henty addressed his novels (v), yet she never did outgrow her identification with Carthage. Indeed, a Carthage "corrupt to the core" is for her a properly transgressive setting for the encoding of lesbian desire.

Writing historical fiction is, for Bryher, the adventure she dreamed of as a child, an adventure available only to boys; "Oh to be a boy and have the world. . . . roughness and adventure, these formed her desire," Bryher writes of her persona in *Development* (139). Adventure for Bryher is thus charged with an oppositional aura, a sense of the forbidden that surfaces in her implication that "sailing around the Horn" is a vice comparable to sensual self-indulgence. From an early age she wrote poems yearning for adventure, poems that make her sound like a young Conrad wanting to see the blank spots on the map. But when Bryher does this kind of imagining, she also turns herself into a boy. This double fantasy distinguishes her adventure-dreams from any sense of national destiny; her success is premised on successful disguise, on a permanently ambivalent relation to her fellow-adventurers.

In her 1921 prose poem "Extract," Bryher writes:

> It is no use pretending; I hate it all, all of it. I want Tyre, Carthage, Athens; I want the age that has never been known in the world.

All that her world allows to exist, the speaker hates; Tyre, Carthage, and Athens are equated with an unknown age—not the past in which they surely existed. In a somewhat later adventure poem (1924), "Out of Boyhood," the use of a male persona suggests the interrelationship between geography and gender:

> Can I be what my own heart wills
> Between firs and the white surf?
> "Much to find in a new land."
>
> ("Three Songs" 78)

Bryher's historical fiction reenacts the loss and rediscovery of that "new land" even as she recreates the old.

NOTES

1. Bernal points out the rest of Europe did not share Britain's enthusiasm for the Phoenicians. French dislike, for example, culminated in Flaubert's novel *Salaambo*, about third-century B.C. Carthage.

2. Carthage is alluded to sympathetically in Arnold's "Scholar-Gipsy," reflecting the mid-nineteenth-century British tendency to identify with Carthage. But unlike Bryher, who tends to merge Carthage and Greece, Arnold contrasts them: his scholar-gipsy is compared to a serious Carthaginian trader who flees contact with a "merry Greek coaster" (*Poems* 232–50).

3. Paul Fussell discusses the pervasively inviting meaning "south" held for writers between World War I and II (131); prominent among those lured southward was Norman Douglas, author of *South Wind*, and good friend of Bryher.

4. Bryher seems to choose her Greek characters' names from the *Greek Anthology*; Archias, Moero, and Zonas are all there; Bryher's translation of "Nine Epigrams of Zonas" appeared in *The Nation*, February 22, 1919: 615.

5. Elizabeth Segel writes that during the late nineteenth century many novels aimed at boys depicted the "good bad boy" whose mixture of energy and inventiveness—if sometimes mischievously employed—was also invaluable when harnessed in service of "commerce and empire" (173, 179).

CHAPTER 13

"I am his fulfilment":
Claiming the Paternal Inheritance

Mary Butts was talking about her father when she wrote, "I am his fulfilment." She was the one who understood his values and wanted to carry them into the future. She was the one who valued literature, the arts, and especially the classical past. Like many before her, however, she found the estate entailed, destined for a male heir. Her predicament resembles Bryher, who so admired her merchant-father; and Mitchison, who admired her scientist-father. On a less literal level, it is shared by all the writers I discuss here. All laid claim to a cultural inheritance inextricably linked to the patriarchy it defined and undergirded—an inheritance claiming universality but unmistakably gendered as male.

To retell that past is thus in many ways to identify oneself with the masculine subject. The historical novelist's dependence on sources and "historical probability" aligns her with a preexisting and intrinsically masculine discourse—whether because all logical, referential language is phallocentric, as French feminists suggest, or because historical discourse, with its tendency to value public action at the expense of female experience, is particularly male-oriented. Women writers eager for cultural authority were obviously drawn to the rewriting of the past for that reason: because it offered an opportunity to identify with male freedom and power.

Equally important, however, is the extent to which Mitchison, Butts, Riding, Renault, Bentley, and Bryher complicate even as they recapitulate the past. Their novels provide some insight into the way fairly ordinary women, bombarded with accounts of the human past, could still escape total definition by them. Faced with certain experiences simply because they were female—Bryher's, Butts's, Renault's, Bentley's, and Mitchison's schooling comes immediately to mind—they knew that gender mattered. Bringing that knowledge to their reading of a supposedly gender-neutral historical discourse, they managed to expose the way in which these accounts were, in fact, inflected by gender. This is the cultural work achieved by these writers, and it is not insignificant.

These are not, of course, major novelists. Riding and Butts are the only two who were stylistically innovative; their eccentricities are fascinating, purposeful, and worth more attention than they have received. Mitchison, Bentley, Bryher, and Renault fall more into the category of good storytellers. Mitchison's writing is downright clumsy at times, while Bentley's radiates timidity. Most also suffer from cultural blind-spots; they are not beyond the occasional ethnic or racial stereotype. But limited though these novels may be, all offer insight into how women can resist texts that would otherwise force them into a position of self-alienation and self-denigration, how they can inherit their culture's past without disowning the way their own experiences have been inflected by gender.

Their strategies, of course, are varied. Renault and Bryher write primarily of men, often narrating from a male persona's viewpoint, but use that narrative cross-dressing to challenge gender boundaries rather than to align themselves with the male subject. Both depict boyish girls (Renault's Axiothea, Hippolyta, and Eurydike; Bryher's Myro and Veria) and nurturing men (Renault's Bagoas; Bryher's Greek traders), emphasizing the ways these paradoxically gendered bodies disrupt certainty and closure. Their admiration for stereotypically male action is always undercut—by a bodily fetishism in Renault, which challenges stable notions of bodily integrity and biological sex; and by a narrative fetishism in Bryher, a focus on physical immediacy and detail at the expense of plot and historical probabilty.

Bryher's Fabula, underminer of a history construed as objective, authoritative, and true, links Bryher to Riding and Butts; all three writers create female characters who personify Irigaray's notion of disruptive excess. Fabula, like Riding's Cressida, and Butts's Cleopatra, is disruptive because she is incalculable, refusing to be construed in terms of an "economy of the Same" (Irigaray 74). Male discourse, according to Irigaray, defines women only as variant males and thus obliterates their difference; Fabula, Cressida, and Cleopatra, however, remain maddeningly elusive, suggesting that despite the power of male discourse to structure the world, it remains vulnerable to the ambiguities and desires it seeks to banish. Bryher, Riding, and Butts all discuss historical transmission, another way of underlining the way power shapes discourse. The "correct" story is the one told by the winner. Thus Riding and Butts explicitly discuss the distorted versions male writers have produced of their subjects, while Bryher centers her plot, in *Gate to the Sea*, around Harmonia's decision about what to preserve from her past life.

Both Butts and Mitchison were heavily influenced by Frazer's *The Golden Bough*. Both embrace myth and ritual as weapons against a history that, from a feminist perspective, seems to tell only of defeat. By construing human experience as a series of repetitions of primordial events, myth allows Mitchison to imagine alternatives to that defeat: each recurring cycle presents an opportunity to open up the past, to replay it with a difference this time. And both Mitchison and Butts are enamored of magic, which gives tremendous power to those who lacked it in purely historical terms. Angela Carter in *The Sadeian Woman* argues that myth is counter-productive for feminists; stories about "hypothetical great goddesses," she suggests, encourage women to feel at one with a "great creating nature," but in practical terms only encourage self-deception (9). Carter is certainly right that myth, by dehistoricizing, may discourage social activism; turning past defeats into a timeless pattern, it makes those defeats seem inevitable, and offers a sense of coherence or belonging as a solace. But Mitchison and Butts don't just embrace myth; they juxtapose it with alternative ways of understanding the past. Most directly, in *The Corn King and the Spring Queen*, myth is not a solace, but a way of challenging the primacy of plot and closure in construing the past. Mitchison uses magic and totemism, much as Butts uses mana, to evoke a world where the individualism and objectivity so prized by historical discourse are helpless against the powers of nature and women. This notion of a "great creating nature" may offer a hope that in "real life" is unavailable, but in challenging the boundaries that define "real life," it does important work. What we define as "realistic" has a great deal to do with our assumptions about what life ought to be like. Those groups most unhappy with the status quo may well be those most likely to seek alternatives to literary realism.

Phyllis Bentley, of course, is the exception here. She is not stylistically experimental, as are Butts and Riding; she does not employ myth, as do Mitchison and Butts; nor does she depict gender-bending characters, as do Renault and Bryher. The least modernist of these writers, Bentley nonetheless shares with them an intense awareness of women's marginalization and silencing.

Mitchison, Riding, Butts, Bentley, Bryher, and Renault were steeped in male-authored texts and pressured by a genre defined by its ability to match—at least partially—its readers' assumptions about the past. But as women conscious of the way gender had shaped their own lives, they clearly felt uncomfortable about the way history treated and depicted women. This tension between reinscription and resistance offers a particularly intense paradigm of the relationship between all writers and their cultures. Stephen Greenblatt points out that while art often "reinforces the dominant beliefs and social structures of its culture," it can also question those structures: "The ability of artists to assemble and shape the forces of their culture in novel ways so that elements powerfully interact that rarely have commerce with one another in the general economy has the potential to unsettle this affirmative relation" (231). All six of these twentieth-century women writers used this process of juxtaposition, emphasis, and selection to unsettle their culture's sense of the past and to claim their cultural inheritance.

WORKS CITED

Ackerman, Robert Allen. "Frazer on Myth and Ritual." *Journal of the History of Ideas* 36 (1975): 115–34.

———. *J. G. Frazer: His Life and Work*. Cambridge: Cambridge UP, 1987.

———. "Jane Ellen Harrison: The Early Work." *Greek, Roman, and Byzantine Studies* 13 (1972): 209–30.

Annan, Noel. *Leslie Stephen: The Godless Victorian*. New York: Random House, 1984.

Apter, Emily. *Feminizing the Fetish: Psychoanalysis and Narrative Obsession in Turn-of-the-Century France*. Ithaca: Cornell UP, 1991.

———. Introduction. *Fetishism as Cultural Discourse*. Ed. Emily Apter and William Pietz. Ithaca: Cornell UP, 1993.

Arnold, Guy. *Held Fast for England: G. A. Henty, Imperialist Boys' Writer*. London: Hamish Hamilton, 1980.

Arnold, Matthew. *The Complete Poems*. Ed. Kenneth Allott. 2nd ed. Miriam Allott. London: Longman, 1979.

———. *On the Classical Tradition*. Ed. R. H. Super. Ann Arbor: U of Michigan P, 1960.

Ash, Russell. *Sir Lawrence Alma-Tadema*. New York: Abrams, 1990.

Bachofen, J.J. *Myth, Religion, and Mother Right: Selected Writings of J. J. Bachofen*. Trans. Ralph Manheim. Princeton: Princeton UP, 1967.

Beach, Sylvia. *Shakespeare and Company*. New York: Harcourt, Brace and World. 1959.

Bendiner, Kenneth. *An Introduction to Victorian Painting*. New Haven: Yale UP, 1985.

Benstock, Shari. *Women of the Left Bank: Paris, 1900–1940*. Austin: U of Texas P, 1986.

Bentley, Phyllis. *The English Regional Novel*. New York: Haskell House, 1966.

———. *Environment*. London: Sidgwick and Jackson, 1922.

———. *Freedom, Farewell!* London: Victor Gollancz, 1936.

———. *"O Dreams, O Destinations": An Autobiography*. New York: Macmillan, 1962.

———. *Sleep in Peace*. New York: Macmillan, 1938.

Benton, Jill. *Naomi Mitchison: A Biography*. London: Pandora, 1990.

Bernal, Martin. *The Fabrication of Ancient Greece 1785–1985*. Vol. 1 of *Black Athena: The Afroasiatic Roots of Classical Civilization*. New Brunswick: Rutgers UP, 1987.

Berger, John. *Ways of Seeing*. London: BBC and Penguin, 1972.

Blaser, Robin. "'Here Lies the Woodpecker Who Was Zeus.'" Christopher Wagstaff 159–223.

Blavatsky, H. P. *Isis Unveiled: A Master-Key to the Mysteries of Ancient and Modern Science and Theology.* Pasadena: Theosophical UP, 1972.

Brantlinger, Patrick. *Rule of Darkness: British Literature and Imperialism 1830–1914.* Ithaca: Cornell UP, 1988.

Broe, Mary Lynn, and Angela Ingram, eds. *Women's Writing in Exile.* Chapel Hill: U of North Carolina P, 1989.

Bryher (Annie Winifred Ellerman). *The Coin of Carthage.* New York: Harcourt, Brace and World, 1963.

———. *The Days of Mars: A Memoir 1940–1946.* London: Calder and Boyars, 1972.

———. *Development.* New York: Macmillan, 1920.

———. "Eros of the Sea." *H. D. Newsletter* 3 (1990): 7–10.

———. "Extract." *Contact* 3 (1921): 12.

———. *Gate to the Sea.* New York: Pantheon, 1958.

———. *The Heart to Artemis.* New York: Harcourt, Brace and World, 1962.

———. "Hellenics." *Poetry* 17 (December 1920): 136–37.

———. "Manchester." *Life and Letters To-day* 13 (December 1935): 89–112; 14 (Spring 1936): 94–114; 14 (Summmer 1936): 74–98.

———. "Paris, 1900." *Life and Letters To-day* 16 (Summer 1937): 33–44.

———. "Recognition not Farewell." *Life and Letters To-day* 17 (Autumn 1937): 159–64.

———. *Roman Wall.* New York: Pantheon, 1954.

———. "South." *Contact Collection of Contemporary Writers.* Paris: Contact, n.d. [1925]. 11–29.

———. "Three Songs: Out of Boyhood, Gulls, Thessalian." *Poetry* 25 (November 1924): 78–79.

———. *Two Selves.* Paris: Contact, nd.

Bulwer-Lytton, Edward. *The Last Days of Pompeii.* (1834). London: Routledge, n.d.

Butler, Judith. *Gender Trouble: Feminism and the Subversion of Identity.* New York: Routledge, 1990.

Butts, Mary. *Armed with Madness.* London: Wishart, 1928.

———. *Ashe of Rings.* Paris: Contact, 1925.

———. *The Crystal Cabinet: My Childhood at Salterns.* 1937. Boston: Beacon, 1988.

———. *The Death of Felicity Taverner.* London: Wishart and Co., 1932.

———. "Deosil." *Transatlantic Review* 1 (March 1924): 40–50.

———. *From Altar to Chimney Piece.* Kingston, N.Y.: McPherson and Co., 1992.

———. *Last Stories.* London: Brendin, 1938.

———. *The Macedonian.* London: William Heinemann, 1933.

———. "Pythian Ode." *Transatlantic Review* 2 (September 1924): 235–39.

———. *Scenes from the Life of Cleopatra.* London: Heinemann, 1935.

———. *Speed the Plough and Other Stories.* London: Chapman and Hall, 1923.

———. "A Story of Ancient Magic." Rev. of *The Corn King and the Spring Queen,* by Naomi Mitchison. *The Bookman* 80 (July 1931): 210.

————. *Traps for Unbelievers*. London: Desmond Harmsworth, 1932.

Campbell, Joseph. Introduction. *Myth, Religion, and Motherright: Selected Writings of J. J. Bachofen*. Trans. Ralph Manheim. Princeton: Princeton UP, 1967: xxv–lv.

Cantarella, Eva. *Pandora's Daughters*. Trans. Maureen B. Fant. Baltimore: Johns Hopkins UP, 1987.

Carpenter, Edward. *The Intermediate Sex*. New York: Mitchell Kennerley, 1912.

Carter, Angela. *The Sadeian Woman and the Ideology of Pornography*. New York: Pantheon, 1978.

Cather, Willa. *The Kingdom of Art*. Ed. Bernie Slote. Lincoln: U of Nebraska P, 1966.

Collecott, Diana. "H. D.'s Gift of Greek, Bryher's Eros of the Sea." *H.D. Newsletter*. 3 (1990): 11–14.

Cross, Amanda [Carolyn Heilbrun]. *No Word from Winifred*. New York: Ballantine, 1986.

Culler, A. Dwight. *The Victorian Mirror of History*. New Haven: Yale UP, 1985.

de Beauvoir, Simone. *The Second Sex*. 1949. Trans. H. M. Parshley. New York: Bantam, 1970.

DeJean, Joan. *Fictions of Sappho*. Chicago: U of Chicago P, 1989.

de Lauretis, Teresa. *The Practice of Love: Lesbian Sexuality and Perverse Desire*. Bloomington: Indiana UP, 1994.

Doane, Mary Anne. "Film and Masquerade; Theorising the Female Spectator." *Screen* 23 (Sept.–Oct. 1982): 74–87.

Dowling, Linda. *Hellenism and Homosexuality in Victorian Oxford*. Ithaca: Cornell UP, 1994.

————. "Nero and the Aesthetics of Torture." *Victorian Newsletter* 66 (Fall 1984): 1–5.

————. "Roman Decadence and Victorian Historiography." *Victorian Studies* 28 (1985): 579–607.

DuPlessis, Rachel Blau. *H. D.: The Career of that Struggle*. Bloomington: Indiana UP, 1986.

————. *Writing Beyond the Ending*. Bloomington: Indiana UP, 1985.

Dyhouse, Carol. *Girls Growing up in Late Victorian and Edwardian England*. London: Routledge and Kegan Paul, 1981.

Eisler, Riane. *The Chalice and the Blade: Our History, Our Future*. New York: Harper and Row, 1987.

Eliot, T. S. "Ulysses, Order, and Myth." *Selected Prose of T. S. Eliot*. Ed. Frank Kermode. New York: Harcourt Brace Jovanovich / Farrar Straus Giroux, 1975. 175–78.

————. "Euripides and Professor Murray." *Selected Essays*. New York: Harcourt, Brace and World, 1964.

Engels, Friedrich. *The Origin of the Family, Private Property, and the State*. (1884). New York: Penguin, 1985.

Evans, Arthur. *The God of Ecstasy: Sex Roles and the Madness of Dionysos*. New York: St. Martin's, 1988.

F.R.A.I. "The Eclipse of Woman." *New Freewoman* 15 June 1913: 11–12.

Farnell, Lewis R. *The Cults of the Greek States*. (1896) Vol. 1. New Rochelle: Caratzas Brothers, 1977.

———. *An Oxonian Looks Back*. London: Martin Hopkinson, 1934.

———. Rev. of *Themis*, by Jane Harrison. *Hibbert Journal* 11 (1912–13): 453–58.

Fetterley, Judith. *The Resisting Reader: A Feminist Approach to American Fiction*. Bloomington: Indiana UP, 1978.

Fitch, Noel Riley. *Sylvia Beach and the Lost Generation: A History of Literary Paris in the Twenties and Thirties*. New York: Norton, 1983.

Fleishman, Avrom. *The English Historical Novel*. Baltimore: Johns Hopkins UP, 1971.

Foley, Barbara. *Telling the Truth*. Ithaca: Cornell UP, 1986.

F.R.A.I. "The Eclipse of Woman." *New Freewoman*. 15 June 1913: 69.

Frazer, Robert, ed. *Sir James Frazer and the Literary Imagination: Essays in Affinity and Influence*. New York: St. Martin's, 1990.

Frazer, James George. *The Golden Bough: A Study in Magic and Religion*. 3rd ed. 12 vols. New York: Macmillan, 1935.

Freud, Sigmund. *The Standard Edition of the Complete Psychological Works of Sigmund Freud*. Trans. James Strachey. 24 vols. London: Hogarth, 1961.

Friedman, Susan Stanford. *Psyche Reborn: The Emergence of H. D.* Bloomington: Indiana UP, 1981.

Fussell, Paul. *Abroad: British Literary Traveling between the Wars*. New York: Oxford UP, 1980.

Garber, Marjorie. "Fetish Envy." *October* 53 (Fall 1990): 45–56.

———. *Vested Interests: Cross-dressing and Cultural Anxiety*. New York: Routledge, 1992.

Gardiner, Judith Kegan, "Mind Mother: Psychoanalysis and Feminism." *Making a Difference: Feminist Literary Criticism*. Ed. Gayle Greene and Coppelia Kahn. London: Methuen, 1985: 113–45.

Gardiner, Juliet. "Biography and Biology: The Historiography of Gender." *Encounter* 71 (Sept.–Oct. 1988): 49–50.

Gaskell, Elizabeth. *The Life of Charlotte Bronte*. Ed. Alan Shelston. Harmondsworth, England: Penguin, 1975.

Gay, Peter. *Freud: A Life for Our Time*. New York: Norton, 1988.

Gilbert, Sandra. "Potent Griselda: 'The Ladybird' and the Great Mother." *D. H. Lawrence: A Centenary Consideration*. Ed. Peter Balbert and Phillip L. Marcus. Ithaca: Cornell UP, 1985.

Gilbert, Sandra, and Susan Gubar. *No Man's Land: The Place of the Woman Writer in the Twentieth Century*. Vol 1, *The War of the Words*. Vol 2, *Sexchanges*. New Haven: Yale UP, 1988, 1989.

Goldring, Douglas. *South Lodge: Reminiscences of Violet Hunt, Ford Madox Ford, and the English Review Circle*. London: Constable, 1943.

Graves, Richard Percival. *Robert Graves: The Years with Laura 1926–1940*. New York: Viking, 1990.

Graves, Robert. *Oxford Addresses on Poetry*. New York: Greenwood, 1968.

———. *Poems (1914–1926)*. London: Heinemann, 1928.

———. *The White Goddess*. 1948. New York: Farrar, Straus and Giroux, 1972.

Greenblatt, Stephen. "Culture." *Critical Terms for Literary Study*. Ed. Frank Lentricchia and Thomas McLaughlin. Chicago: U of Chicago P, 1990. 225–32.

Gregory, Horace, and Marya Zaturenska. *A History of American Poetry 1900–1940*. New York: Harcourt Brace, 1942.

Grosz, Elizabeth. "Lesbian Fetishism?" *Differences: A Journal of Feminist Cultural Studies* 3 (1991): 39–54.

Guest, Barbara. *Herself Defined: The Poet H. D. and Her World*. Garden City: Doubleday, 1984.

Haldane, Charlotte. *Motherhood and its Enemies*. London: Chatto and Windus, 1927.

Haley, Bruce. *The Healthy Body and Victorian Culture*. Cambridge: Harvard UP, 1978.

Hall, Radclyffe. *The Well of Loneliness*. New York: Covici Friede, 1929.

Hanscombe, Gillian, and Virginia Smyers. *Writing for Their Lives: The Modernist Women 1910–1940*. London: Women's Press, 1987.

Harrison, Jane. "Primitive Hera-Worship. Illustrated by the Excavation at Argos." *Classical Review* 7 (1893): 74–78.

———. *Prolegomena to the Study of Greek Religion*. 1903. New York: Meridian, 1957.

———. *Reminiscences of a Student's Life*. London: Hogarth, 1925.

———. *Themis: A Study of the Social Origins of Greek Religion*. 2nd. rev. ed. Cambridge: Cambridge UP, 1927.

Hart, Francis Russell. *The Scottish Novel from Smollett to Spark*. Cambridge: Harvard UP, 1978.

H. D. [Hilda Doolittle]. *Bid Me to Live*. New York: Dial, 1960.

———. *Palimpsest*. Paris: Contact, 1926.

———. *Tribute to Freud*. Boston: David R. Godine, 1974.

Heilbrun, Carolyn. "Axiothea's Grief: The Disability of the Female Imagination." *From Parnassus: Essays in Honor of Jacques Barzun*. Ed. Dora B. Weiner and William R. Keylor. New York: Harper and Row, 1976: 227–36.

Henty, G. A. *Beric the Briton: A Story of the Roman Invasion*. London: Blackie and Co, n.d. [1892].

———. *The Young Carthagianian: A Story of the Times of Hannibal*. London: Blackie and Son, n.d.

Hogg, James. *Selected Poems*. Oxford: Clarendon P, 1970.

Homans, Margaret. *Bearing the Word*. Chicago: U Chicago P, 1986.

Howarth, Patrick. *Play Up and Play the Game: The Heroes of Popular Fiction*. London: Eyre Methuen, 1973.

Hughes-Hallett, Lucy. *Cleopatra: History, Dreams and Distortions*. New York: Harper and Row, 1990.

Huston, Nancy. "The Matrix of War: Mothers and Heroes." Suleiman, 119–36.

Irigaray, Luce. *This Sex Which Is Not One*. Trans. Catherine Porter with Carolyn Burke. Ithaca: Cornell UP, 1985.

Jackson, Laura (Riding). "The Bondage." *Chelsea* 30/31 (June 1972): 24–33.

———. *Collected Poems (by) Laura Riding: A New Edition of the 1938 Collection*. New York: Persea, 1980.

———. "Reply to Judith Thurman." *The Nation* 22 March 1975: 322.

———. *The Telling*. London: Athlone, 1972.

———— . *The Word Woman and Other Related Writings.* Ed. Elizabeth Fried-mann and Alan J. Clark. New York: Persea Books, 1993.

———— . "The Sex Factor in Social Progress." *Chelsea* 16 (March 1965): 114–22.

Jackson, Margaret. "Sexology and the Universalization of Male Sexuality." *The Sexuality Papers.* Ed. L. Covenay et al. London: Hutchinson, 1984. 69–84.

Jacobus, Mary. *Reading Woman: Essays in Feminist Criticism.* New York: Columbia UP, 1986.

Jarrell, Randall. "Graves and the White Goddess—Part II." *Yale Review* 45 (1956): 467–78.

Jay, Nancy. *Throughout Your Generations Forever.* Chicago: U of Chicago P, 1992.

Jeffreys, Sheila. *The Spinster and Her Enemies: Feminism and Sexuality 1880–1930.* London: Pandora, 1985.

Jenkyns, Richard. *The Victorians and Ancient Greece.* Oxford: Basil Blackwell, 1980.

Kabbani, Rana. *Europe's Myths of Orient.* Bloomington: Indiana UP, 1986.

Kaplan, Cora. "Speaking/Writing/Feminism." *On Gender and Writing.* Ed. Michelene Wandor. London: Pandora, 1983. 51–61.

Kelly-Gadol, Joan. "The Social Relations of the Sexes: Methodological Implica-tions of Women's History." *The Signs Reader: Women, Gender, and Schol-arship.* Ed. Elizabeth Abel and Emily K. Abel. Chicago: U of Chicago P, 1983. 11–26.

Kenner, Hugh. "Mary Renault." *New York Times Book Review.* 10 Feb. 1974: 15.

———— . *The Pound Era.* Berkeley: U of California P, 1971.

Kestner, Joseph A. *Mythology and Misogyny: The Social Discourse of Nine-teenth-Century British Classical Subject Pantings.* Madison: U of Wisconsin P, 1989.

Keuls, Eva. *The Reign of the Phallus: Sexual Politics in Ancient Athens.* New York: Harper and Row, 1985.

Kingsley, Charles. *Hypatia.* New York: Dutton, 1968.

———— . *The Roman and the Teuton.* Vol. 10 of *The Works of Charles Kingsley* (1884). Hildesheim, Germany: Georg Olins, 1969.

Kloepfer, Deborah Kelly. "Fishing the Murex Up: Sense and Resonance in H. D.'s *Palimpsest.*" *Contemporary Literature* 27 (1986): 553–73.

Kofman, Sarah. *The Enigma of Woman.* Trans. Catherine Porter. Ithaca: Cornell UP, 1985.

Kristeva, Julia. "Women's Time." *The Kristeva Reader.* Ed. Toril Moi. New York: Columbia UP, 1986.

LaCapra, Dominick. *History, Politics and the Novel.* Ithaca: Cornell UP, 1987.

———— . *Soundings in Critical Theory.* Ithaca: Cornell UP, 1989.

Lanchester, Elsa. *Elsa Lanchester Herself.* New York: St. Martin's, 1983.

Landow, George. "Victorianized Romans." *Browning Institute Studies* 12 (1984): 29–52.

Lawrence, D. H. *The Collected Letters of D. H. Lawrence.* Vol. 1. Ed. Harry T. Moore. New York: Viking, 1962.

———— . *The Escaped Cock.* Ed. Gerald Lacy. Los Angeles: Black Sparrow, 1973.

———— . *Etruscan Places.* (1932). London: Olive, 1986.

Leacock, Eleanor. "Women in Egalitarian Societies." *Becoming Visible*. Ed. Renate Bridenthal and Claudia Koonz. Boston: Houghton Mifflin, 1977. 11–35.

Leonardi, Susan. *Dangerous by Degrees: Women at Oxford and the Somerville College Novelists*. New Brunswick: Rutgers UP, 1989.

Lerner, Gerda. *The Creation of Patriarchy*. New York: Oxford UP, 1986.

Licht, Hans [Paul Brandt]. *Sexual Life in Ancient Greece*. 1932. Trans. J. H. Freese. Ed. Lawrence H. Dawson. London: Abbey Library, 1971.

Lloyd-Jones, Hugh. *Blood for the Ghosts: Classical Influences in the Nineteenth and Twentieth Centuries*. Baltimore: Johns Hopkins UP, 1983.

——— . *Classical Survivals: The Classics in the Modern World*. London: Duckworth, 1982.

Lukacs, Georg. *The Historical Novel*. Trans. Hannah and Stanley Mitchell. Lincoln: U of Nebraska P, 1983.

Macaulay, Thomas Babington. *History of England*. (1848). Vol. 1. Boston: Houghton Mifflin, 1900.

——— . "Lays of Ancient Rome." *Miscellanies*. Vol. 3 of *The Complete Works*. Boston: Houghton Mifflin, 1900. 167–280.

McGann, Jerome. "Laura (Riding) Jackson and the Literal Truth." *Critical Inquiry* 18 (Spring 1992): 454–73.

Maika, Patricia. *Virginia Woolf's* Between the Acts *and Jane Harrison's* Con/spiracy. Ann Arbor: UMI, 1987.

Manzoni, Alessandro. *On the Historical Novel*. Trans. Sandra Bermann. Lincoln: U of Nebraska P, 1984.

"Mary Renault." *World Authors 1950–1970*. Ed. John Wakeman. New York: H. W. Wilson, 1975.

"Mary Renault." *Dictionary of Literary Biography Yearbook*. Ed. Mary Bruccoli and Jean Ross. Detroit: Gale, 1983.

"Mary Renault." *New York Times* 14 Dec. 1983: B5.

Mitchison, Naomi. *All Change Here*. London: Bodley Head, 1975.

——— . *The Blood of the Martyrs*. 1939. New York: Whittlesey House, 1948.

——— . *Cleopatra's People*. London: Heinemann, 1972.

——— . *Cloud Cuckoo Land*. London: Jonathan Cape, 1925.

——— . *Comments on Birth Control*. London: Faber and Faber, 1930.

——— . *The Conquered*. New York: Harcourt Brace, 1923.

——— . *The Corn King and the Spring Queen*. London: Jonathan Cape, 1931.

——— . *The Delicate Fire*. London: Jonathan Cape, 1933.

——— . *The Home and a Changing Civilization*. London: John Lane, 1934.

——— . *The Hostages and Other Stories for Boys and Girls*. New York: Harcourt Brace and Co., 1931.

——— . *The Moral Basis of Politics*. 1938. Port Washington, N.Y.: Kennikat, 1971.

——— . "New Cloud-Cuckoo-Borough." *Modern Scot* June 1934: 30–38.

——— . "On Writing Historical Novels." *Cairo Studies in English*. Ed. Magdi Wahba. 1960: 113–18.

——— . *Return to the Fairy Hill*. New York: John Day, 1966.

——— . "Thinking of War." *Time and Tide* 10 Oct. 1936: 1386.

————. *We Have Been Warned.* 1935. New York: Vanguard, 1936.

————. *When the Bough Breaks and Other Stories.* London: Jonathan Cape, 1924.

————. "Writing Historical Novels." *Saturday Review of Literature* 27 (April 1935): 645–46.

————. *You May Well Ask: A Memoir 1920–1940.* London: Victor Gollancz, 1979.

Moi, Toril. *The Kristeva Reader.* New York: Columbia UP, 1986.

Mommsen, Theodor. *The History of Rome.* Vol. 5. Trans. William Purdie Dickson. New York: Scribner's, 1898.

Morris, Adelaide. "The Concept of Projection: H. D.'s Visionary Powers." *Contemporary Literature* 25 (1984): 411–36.

Munich, Adrienne. "Queen Victoria, Empire, and Excess." *Tulsa Studies in Women's Literature* 6 (Fall 1987): 265–82.

Murray, Gilbert. *Five Stages of Greek Religion.* (1925). 3rd ed. Garden City: Doubleday, 1955.

Murray, Margaret. *My First Hundred Years.* London: William Kimber, 1963.

————. *The Witch-Cult in Western Europe.* Oxford: Clarendon, 1921.

Nandy, Ashis. *The Intimate Enemy: Loss and Recovery of Self under Colonialism.* Delhi: Oxford UP, 1983.

Newton, Esther. "The Mythic Mannish Lesbian: Radclyffe Hall and the New Woman." *Signs* 9 (1984): 557–75.

O'Brien, Sharon. *Willa Cather: The Emerging Voice.* New York: Oxford UP, 1987.

Ong, Walter. *Fighting for Life: Contest, Sexuality, and Consciousness.* Ithaca: Cornell UP, 1981.

Ostriker, Alicia. "The Thieves of Language." Showalter, *New Feminist,* 314–38.

Pater, Walter. *The Renaissance.* London: Macmillan, 1904.

Payne, Harry C. "Modernizing the Ancients: The Reconstruction of Ritual Drama 1870–1920." *Proceedings of the American Philosophical Society* 122 (1978): 182–92.

Plato. *Phaedo.* Trans. G. M. A. Grube. Indianapolis: Hackett, 1977.

————. *Symposium.* Trans. Benjamin Jowett. Indianapolis: Bobbs-Merrill, 1979.

Plomer, William. *The Autobiography of William Plomer.* London: Jonathan Cape, 1975.

Plutarch. *The Lives of the Noble Grecians and Romans.* Trans. John Dryden, rev. Arthur Hugh Clough. New York: Modern Library, 1932.

————. *Makers of Rome: Nine Lives by Plutarch.* Trans. Ian Scott-Kilvert. New York: Penguin, 1987.

Power, Eileen. *Medieval People.* London: Methuen, 1924.

Randall-MacIver, David. *The Etruscans.* Oxford: Clarendon, 1927.

————. *Italy before the Romans.* New York: Cooper Square, 1972.

Rawson, Elizabeth. *The Spartan Tradition in European Thought.* Oxford: Clarendon, 1969.

Renault, Mary. *The Bull from the Sea.* New York: Pantheon, 1962.

————. *Fire from Heaven.* 1956. New York: Vintage, 1977.

————. *The Friendly Young Ladies.* 1944. London: Virago, 1984.

———. *Funeral Games*. 1981. New York: Pantheon, 1984.

———. *The King Must Die*. New York: Pantheon, 1958.

———. *The Last of the Wine*. New York: Pantheon, 1956.

———. *The Mask of Apollo*. New York: Pantheon, 1966.

———. "Notes on *The King Must Die*." *Afterwords*. Ed. Thomas McCormack. New York: St. Martin's, 1988. 80–87.

———. *The Persian Boy*. New York: Pantheon, 1972.

———. *Purposes of Love*. London: Longmans, Green, 1939.

Riding, Laura. *Four Unposted Letters to Catherine*. New York: Persea Books, 1993.

———. *The Poems of Laura Riding*. 1938. New York: Persea, 1980.

———. *Progress of Stories*. London: Constable, 1935.

———. *A Trojan Ending*. 1937. Manchester: Carcanet, 1984.

———. *The World and Ourselves*. London: Chatto and Windus, 1938.

Robinson, Sally. "The 'Anti-Logos Weapon': Multiplicity in Women's Texts." *Contemporary Literature* 29 (1988): 105–24.

Rohrlich-Leavitt, Ruby. "Women in Transition: Crete and Sumer." *Becoming Visible*. Ed. Renate Bridenthal and Claudia Koonz. Boston: Houghton Mifflin, 1977. 36–59.

Ruderman, Judith. *D. H. Lawrence and the Devouring Mother: The Search for a Patriarchal Idea of Leadership*. Durham: Duke UP, 1984.

Ruskin, John. *The Genius of John Ruskin: Selections from His Writings*. Ed. John D. Rosenberg. Boston: Routledge, 1980.

Scarry, Elaine. *The Body in Pain: The Making and Unmaking of the World*. New York: Oxford UP, 1985.

Schenck, Celeste M. "Songs (from) the Bride: Feminism, Psychoanalysis, Genre." *Literature and Psychology* 33 (1987): 109–19.

Schor, Naomi. "Female Fetishism: The Case of George Sand." Suleiman 363–72.

———. *Reading in Detail: Aesthetics and the Feminine*. New York: Methuen, 1987.

Schweickart, Patrocinio. "Reading Ourselves: Toward a Feminist Theory of Reading." *Speaking of Gender*. Ed. Elaine Showalter. New York: Routledge, 1989. 17–44.

Sedgwick, Eve Kosofsky. *Between Men: English Literature and Male Homosocial Desire*. New York: Columbia UP, 1985.

Segel, Elizabeth. "'As the Twig is Bent . . .': Gender and Childhood Reading." *Gender and Reading: Essays on Readers, Texts, and Contexts*. Ed. Elizabeth A. Flynn and Patrocinio D. Schweickart. Baltimore: Johns Hopkins UP, 1986. 165–86.

Shaw, Harry. *The Forms of Historical Fiction*. Ithaca: Cornell UP, 1983.

Sheridan, Dorothy, ed. *Among You Taking Notes . . . The Wartime Diary of Naomi Mitchison 1939–1945*. London: Victor Gollancz, 1985.

Showalter, Elaine. *A Literature of Their Own*. Princeton: Princeton UP, 1977.

———, ed. *The New Feminist Criticism: Essays on Women, Literature, and Theory*. New York: Pantheon, 1985.

Smoller, Sanford J. *Adrift among Geniuses*. University Park: Penn State UP, 1975.

Smyers, Virginia. "'Classical' Books in the Bryher Library." *H. D. Newsletter* 3 (1990): 15–25.

Sokolova, Lydia. *Dancing for Diaghilev: The Memoirs of Lydia Sokolova*. Ed. Richard Buckle. San Francisco: Mercury House, 1989.

Spacks, Patricia. *Gossip*. Chicago: U of Chicago P, 1986.

Spender, Dale. *Time and Tide Wait for No Man*. London: Pandora, 1984.

Squier, Susan Merrill. *Babies in Bottles: Twentieth-Century Visions of Reproductive Technology*. New Brunswick: Rutgers UP, 1994.

Squier, Susan M., and Louise A. DeSalvo, eds. "Virgina Woolf's *The Journal of Mistress Joan Martyn*." *Twentieth Century Literature* 25 (1979): 237–69.

Stewart, Jessie. *Jane Ellen Harrison: A Portrait from Letters*. London: Merlin, 1959.

Stopes, Marie. *Married Love*. London: Putnam's, 1928.

Suleiman, Susan Rubin, ed. *The Female Body in Western Culture*. Cambridge: Harvard UP, 1985.

Swanson, Vern G. *Alma-Tadema: The Painter of the Victorian Vision of the Ancient World*. New York: Scribner's, 1977.

Sweetman, David. *Mary Renault: A Biography*. New York: Harcourt Brace, 1993.

Swiney, Frances. *The Awakening of Woman or Women's Part in Evolution*. London: William Reeves, 1908.

——— . *The Bar of Isis or The Law of the Mother*. London: C. W. Daniel, 1909.

Tompkins, Jane. *Sensational Designs: The Cultural Work of American Fiction 1790–1860*. New York: Oxford UP, 1985.

Torgovnick, Marianna. *Gone Primitive: Savage Intellects, Modern Lives*. Chicago: U of Chicago P, 1990.

Turner, Frank M. *The Greek Heritage in Victorian Britain*. New Haven: Yale UP, 1981.

Vicinus, Martha. *Independent Women: Work and Community for Single Women 1850–1920*. Chicago: U of Chicago P, 1985.

Vickery, John B. *The Literary Impact of the Golden Bough*. Princeton: Princeton UP, 1973.

Wagstaff, Barbara. Afterword. *The Crystal Cabinet*. By Mary Butts. Boston: Beacon, 1988. 275–82.

Wagstaff, Christopher, ed. *A Sacred Quest: The Life and Writings of Mary Butts*. Kingston, N.Y.: McPherson, 1995.

Watt, Ian. *Conrad in the Nineteenth Century*. Berkeley: U of California P, 1979.

Weeks, Jeffrey. *Sex, Politics, and Society: The Regulation of Sexuality since 1800*. London: Longman, 1981.

Weigall, Arthur. *The Life and Times of Cleopatra, Queen of Egypt*. New York: Putnam's Sons, 1924.

Weston, Jessie. *From Ritual to Romance*. Garden City: Doubleday, 1957.

White, Hayden. *The Content of the Form: Narrative Discourse and Historical Representation*. Baltimore: Johns Hopkins UP, 1987.

——— . *Metahistory: The Historical Imagination in Nineteenth Century Europe*. Baltimore: Johns Hopkins UP, 1973.

Whyte-Melville, G. J. *The Gladiators*. Ed. Herbert Maxwell. Vol. 22 of *The Works of G. J. Whyte-Melville*. London: W. Thacker, 1901.

Wolf, Christa. *Cassandra: A Novel and Four Essays*. Trans. Jan van Heurck. New York: Farrar Straus Giroux, 1984.

Woolf, Virginia. *Between the Acts*. New York: Harcourt, Brace, and World, 1941.

——— . *The Pargiters*. Ed.. Mitchell Leaska. New York: Harcourt Brace Jovanovich, 1978.

——— . *Orlando: A Biography*. London: Hogarth, 1990.

——— . *A Room of One's Own*. New York: Harcourt Brace and World, 1929.

——— . *The Voyage Out*. New York: Harcourt, Brace, Jovanovitch, 1948.

Yourcenar, Marguerite. *Memoirs of Hadrian*. Trans. Grace Frick in collaboration with the author. 1954. New York: Farrar, Straus, and Giroux, 1977.

——— . *With Open Eyes: Conversations with Matthieu Galey*. Trans. Arthur Goldhammer. Boston: Beacon, 1984.

Zimmern, Alfred E. *The Greek Commonwealth: Politics and Economics in Fifth Century Athens*. Oxford: Clarendon, 1914.

INDEX

landscape: in Bentley, 161; in Bryher, 96, 99–100; in Butts, 50, 56n; as "geographical emotion," 170

Lawrence, D. H.: on Etruria, 114, 144; on fascism, 116; and Frazer, 35–37; and Magna Mater, 19, 57; and Mitchison, 33; works: *The Escaped Cock*, 37; *Etruscan Places*, 144

Lerner, Gerda, 6, 94; on matriarchy, 24n

lesbianism, 11; and Bryher, 89–90; and desire 79–80, 99–100; and fetishism, 76, 170, 173; Freud on, 20; and the "mannish lesbian," 11, 78–79, 90; and *Regiment of Women*, 44; and Renault, 73–74, 83; and Sappho, 23

Life and Letters To-day, 91

Lukacs, Georg, 4, 12, 100; on historical novel as a genre, 12–13n

Macaulay, Thomas, 46, 104, 106, 111, 157–58; and Butts, 112; and Mitchison, 119

magic, 179; in Butts, 46, 54; in Mitchison, 37–38, 128

Magna Mater. *See* goddesses: earth goddess

mana: Butts's depiction of, 47, 51–52, 54, 179; in Butts's *Cleopatra*, 137, 140–42, 144; in Butts's *The Macedonian*, 141; Harrison's description of, 47;

masquerade: and Renault, 75

maternity: in Bentley, 158–60; in Mitchison, 28, 40; Riding's response to, 58–59

matriarchy, ancient, 18–19; Bachofen on, 18; Cantarella on, 24n; Frazer on, 36; Graves on, 60, 81–82; Lerner on, 24n

Matthews, Tom, 63

McAlmon, Robert, 7, 91, 165

McGann, Jerome, 64, 68

metonymy, 8–9, 96, 166, 170–71

Mitchison, Naomi, 25–41; 119–36; and Butts, 7; childhood and education of, 25–26; and Henty, 122; on historical fiction and sex, 13n; as "honorary boy," 2, 25; impact of Frazer's *Golden Bough* on, 21, 25, 37–40, 133; on Isis, 115, 140; and Lawrence, 35–36, 39, 41n; and Macaulay, 119; marriage of, 26; motives for writing historical fiction of, 27; and Plato, 1–2, 23, 25; and Riding, 7, 71; sibling relationships in, 126; and Whyte-Melville, 112, 122, 129–30; and Woolf, 7; works: *The Blood of the Martyrs*, 116, 120, 130–36; *Cloud Cuckoo Land*, 26, 27–33; *Comments on Birth Control*, 35, 39; *The Conquered*, 120, 121–30; 135n; *The Corn King and the Spring Queen*, 26, 33–40, 179; "Cottia Went to Bibracte," 135n; *The Delicate Fire*, 41n; *The Home and a Changing Civilization*, 31; *The Hostages*, 120–21; *The Moral Basis of Politics*, 27, 119; "Quintus Getting Well," 130, 135n; "Romantic Event," 122–24; *We Have Been Warned*, 29–30

Mithraism, 26

modernism: and *The Golden Bough*, 22, 35; and myth, 21; and women, 21–22

Mommsen, Theodor: on Cicero, 147; on Etruria, 114; on Isis, 140; as source for Bentley's *Freedom, Farewell!*, 115, 162n

Mullard, Julie, 73

Munich, Adrienne, 139

Murray, Gilbert: and Cambridge Ritualists, 17; on Hellenistic Greece, 51, 56n; influence of, 56n

Murray, Margaret, 7, 90

myth, 178–79; and Butts, 46–51, 56n; and history, 178–79; and Mitchison, 34, 132, 134–35; and modernism, 21; and women, 21–22